With interviews
inspiration fro

Abbe Luersman

Adam Grant

Anneke Brouwer

Barbara Doeleman-van Veldhoven

Brodie Riordan

Caroline Goyder

H.R.H. Princess Annemarie de Bourbon de Parme

Ingrid Nieuwenhuis

Ingrid van den Maegdenbergh

Jacqueline A-Tjak

Jan J. Wever

Jan Zijderveld

Joanna Barsh

Josette Dijkhuizen

Koen Schruers

Leena Nair

Lex Meijdam

Lynda Gratton

Paul-Peter Feld

Pieter Waasdorp

Rick Goings

Robert Kegan

Sebastiaan Besems

Srini Pillay

Sven Smit

Tex Gunning

Veronica Azua

Wilmar Schaufeli

With a general foreword by **H.R.H. Princess Annemarie de Bourbon de Parme LLM-MA,** a business-oriented foreword by **Jan Zijderveld,** former Chief Executive Officer Avon Inc. and President of Unilever Europe, and an academic foreword by **Prof. Koen R.J. Schruers**, MD PhD, psychiatrist, professor of Affective Neuroscience at Maastricht University and Director of Research & Innovation at the Mondriaan Mental Health Center Maastricht/Heerlen, Netherlands

"In this powerful book, the authors transform confidence from a feeling one must wait for into a psychological skill that one can produce. Authentic confidence is a stance of awareness, openness and trust in one's purpose, values and true capabilities. Instead of running from fear or insecurity or hiding from one's own weaknesses, it teaches the reader to face them head-on with peaceful self-awareness and a commitment to growth. Filled with insights and tools to help you face challenging situations more effectively and mindfully, this book teaches the small set of skills that research shows account for the lion's share of positive life trajectories in your career and beyond. Highly recommended."

Steven C. Hayes, Psychology professor at the University of Nevada, Reno. Originator and co-developer of Acceptance and Commitment Therapy and one of the most cited scholars worldwide on acceptance, mindfulness and values

"This is a book about the Science, Art and Practice of Authentic Confidence. Brassey, Van Dam and Van Witteloostuijn carefully and cleverly build bridges between the fields of Neuroscience & Psychology and translate this into pragmatic, action-oriented insights enriched with true stories from senior leaders across multiple sectors."

Susan David, PhD, Psychologist Harvard Medical School, Author of *Emotional Agility*

"Solid values and principles are the foundation of what guides our behaviours. This includes acting with purpose, authenticity and humility, which are the hallmarks of ethical and lasting conduct. This book simply helps you to become better."

Paul Polman, CEO of Unilever 2009-2019, business leader, campaigner, author of *Net Positive: How Courageous Companies Thrive by Giving More Than They Take*

ADVANCING AUTHENTIC CONFIDENCE THROUGH EMOTIONAL FLEXIBILITY

AN EVIDENCE-BASED PLAYBOOK OF INSIGHTS, PRACTICES AND TOOLS TO SHAPE YOUR FUTURE

JACQUELINE BRASSEY | NICK VAN DAM | ARJEN VAN WITTELOOSTUIJN

AUTHENTIC CONFIDENCE

Authors and publishers are fully aware of their duty to ensure the most reliable publication possible. Nevertheless, they cannot accept any liability for (the consequences of) imperfections that may appear in this publication.

VMN media
Utrechtseweg 44
3704 HD Zeist
Publisher: Sandra Britsemmer
ISBN: 978-94-6215-826-9
NUR: 807

Design: COLORSCAN BV (www.colorscan.nl)
Illustrations: Original design by Vorm in Functie (www.vorminfunctie.nl) together with Bingo! Graphic design (www.bingo-graphicdesign.com)
Printed by: Drukkerij Wilco, Amersfoort

For everyone who believed in me and truly sees me for who I am...
and also, for the critics who challenged me...
...you all have helped me to become authentically confident...
...which to me - apart from family and friends – is the greatest gift in my life!

For my precious Nicholas, Josephine and Samuel, my dad†, mum and sisters, who accept and love me fully for who I am -XXX-
Jacqueline Brassey

For my students, colleagues, friends and loved ones
Nick van Dam

For everyone who may benefit from this
Arjen van Witteloostuijn

REACTIONS

Praise for Authentic Confidence

"Too often leaders dismiss words like 'self-esteem' as a passing self-help fad, with few if any practical applications at work. But with penetrating analysis and drawing insights from the leading edge of research, Brassey, van Dam and van Witteloostuijn provide a compelling argument that not only is authentic confidence important for individual development, but they also help leaders understand that authentic confidence is crucial for success in the workplace. Leaders around the world will benefit from taking these insights and applying them in companies, government and non-profit organizations in order to help their employees thrive at work."

Tim Welsh, Vice Chairman, Consumer and Business Banking, U.S. Bank

"Courage (or authentic confidence) does not come easy and it certainly does not come at a low price. It requires effort and continuously connecting with what is important to you. This book provides you with the tools you need to clarify your purpose, to prioritize your values and to effectively manage ambiguity that potentially challenges your courage. I highly recommend it."

Her Excellency Madam Thenjiwe Mtintso, The South African Ambassador to Spain

"I might be only thirteen years old, but I do have an experience that kind of changed my life. Something happened, and it made me sad and insecure. So my mom told me to take a risk and tell everybody who was involved how I felt about the situation, it worked out very well. My mom inspired me and not only me but other people too. Anybody can be insecure, but we all are confident and strong people if we just dig a little deeper. This book that my mom wrote is about Authentic Confidence. It's a beautiful book about how to encourage people to be more themselves and to be okay and confident about it."

Josephine Brassey, At the time of this reconfirmed reflection, a 13-year-old student of life and at the European School in Luxembourg. I love learning, fashion, cooking, music and dancing

"For any professional committed to Lifelong Learning, Authentic Confidence provides essential ingredients for success. Not only is this book evidence-based and practically oriented, it also offers a toolkit which has been successfully implemented in the workplace and academically validated. This is a rather unique combination providing a rich opportunity for personal development and growth. I highly recommend it!"

Kevin Sneader, Co-President of Asia-Pacific (ex Japan) Goldman Sachs

"A powerful combination of deep scientific analysis, practical recommendations for action, and stories from real leaders that bring the concepts to life. Every leader can benefit from the evidence-based practices described in this book. I certainly have."

Matt Smith, Executive Coach and former Partner and Chief Learning Officer at McKinsey & Company

"One of the many things that my father taught me is that you always have to challenge yourself in the things you may find hard in life. By doing this you'll become an expert in areas you once thought were your weaknesses."

Yannick van Dam, Student at IE Business School in Spain

"Being a leader in a world with no certainties can be very scary. Daring to lead in an Authentic Confident way requires a thorough understanding of what truly matters to your organization, your teams and to you. Living up to this purpose on a daily basis requires an active mindfulness muscle and awareness radar to help you focus and skilfully deal with any distracting and difficult emotions. This book offers you an excellent evidence-based toolkit to contribute to the journey ahead of you. Make the most of it!"

Rasmus Hougaard, Managing Director of Potential Project International. Author of *Compassionate Leadership – how to do hard things in a human way*

"If I reflect on the many conversations that I have had with leaders all around the world, I am convinced that the most successful leaders have authentic confidence. They are authentic, they dare to admit

the mistakes they make, and they dare to venture outside their comfort zone. Because they have the courage to do so, they also dare to face difficulty. That combination makes them successful. This is a book that teaches you how to do this. It explains how it all works in theory and it also offers an extensive toolkit with practical exercises and tips - which I find particularly interesting - on how to hit the ground running and develop authentic confidence. I truly enjoyed the book and recommend it to everyone who is interested in reaching their maximum potential!"

Peter de Wit, Senior Partner and Managing Partner North Europe, McKinsey & Company

"This is an important book about confidence because it is based on sound empirical research and presents some eminently actionable steps to build this most crucial of personal and business qualities. This book really is a must read for everyone in business."

Ian H Robertson, Co-Director of the Global Brain Health Institute, Trinity College Dublin and author of *How Confidence Works: the new science of self-belief*

"Authentic Confidence through Emotional Flexibility teaches you how emotions can get in the way of moving towards what truly matters to you and how you can effectively manage these emotions. An insightful piece of work that offers many practical tools to support you in leading your life as opposed to life leading you."

Vikram Malhotra, Senior Partner at McKinsey & Company and co-author of *CEO Excellence: The Six Mindsets That Distinguish the Best Leaders from the Rest*

"Our energy is the most important driver of our performance. Workplaces today are very demanding, and it is critical that we find ways to maintain the most important driver of our performance, namely our energy. We can enhance our energy by looking after our well-being at all levels, namely physical, emotional mental and purpose. This book provides some excellent practical insights on how we can be our best and thrive in a demanding workplace - bringing energy and joy to all we work with - and in so doing make work a life

enhancing experience. A must read for all who want to be at their best and get the best out of their fellow human beings."

Geoff McDonald, former Global VP HR Unilever; now Global Advocate, Campaigner and Consultant for Mental Health at Work

"We all have our insecurities both in our daily lives and in the work environment. This book offers great suggestions and tools to embrace these insecurities, be yourself and get the most out of life. Jacq, I'm proud of you and your ongoing journey that has led to this book."

Anjo de Rooij, Finance professional and Jacqui's best friend since high school

"Simply to survive in today's competitive, unrelenting business environment, many of us feel a need, consciously or not, to control our fears and anxieties by adopting undermining numbing behaviors. The problem is that we cannot selectively numb our emotions - we numb them all, even the positive ones like joy and love. We are doing this at a time when our businesses and our communities need more caring and human connection than ever. This prophetic book offers profound yet practical tools and strategies to manage our emotions with greater precision and awareness. With focused application, these lessons can enable us to let go of old patterns and to bring our very best selves to our work, whatever challenges we may confront."

Henry Ritchie, former Partner, McKinsey & Company

"In a world of dynamic change there can be nothing more important than the acquisition of skills to support resilience and sustainable high performance. We are faced with the daily reality of VUCA ... where volatility, uncertainty, change and ambiguity are the norm. Turning this to our advantage, sustainably, requires us to dig deep and unlock our unique capability and talent... in short to discover our authentic, purpose-inspired confidence. No doubt this practical playbook will be useful in supporting your journey in this regard... building insights and skills, reducing stigmas and unhelpful dogmas, allowing you to thrive rather than just survive in the turbulence of today and tomorrow. Enjoy!"

Nicholas Brassey, Global HR Executive

DISCLAIMER

Get the right medical and mental health support
'If you suffer from anxiety, please be aware that this is also common for people with ADHD or other mental health conditions. Please talk to your medical doctor or mental health professional if you need help or want to find out more.

Recognition - standing on the shoulders of giants
This book is a light mix of academic and practical input, flavoured with original research. For that reason, we have included many references in the text but tried to avoid an overly academic focus on writing and referencing. It is our intention to recognise and appreciate all the great work that has previously been done on this book's subject. With our work, we bring not only insights from our own extensive research through surveys and interviews but are also standing on the shoulders of giants: research conducted by many others and insights from highly experienced practitioners. We were inspired by the work in a wide variety of fields, including organisational behaviour, (organisational) psychology and sociology, neuroscience, learning and development, relational frame theory and acceptance and commitment therapy (ACT). The toolkit that we present in this book is primarily based on ACT but we have adapted it to fit the context of the workplace using insights accumulated through our practical experience in leadership development and professional learning. Where relevant, we have enriched our argument with tools and insights that perhaps fall slightly outside the boundaries of the pure ACT method but that we have found to be very valuable in the workplace.

Perfect in imperfection
This work and research is always dynamic and never perfect in content nor formatting. We always wish to improve our work. Therefore in case you find inconsistencies, mistakes however big or small, please do let us know so we can make it better for a next edition. If you find particular parts of this book, or perhaps even the whole book, helpful and inspiring, we would appreciate hearing from you as well. It gives us the inspiration and energy to continue with our work!

CONTENTS

OVERVIEW OF THE TOOLS INCLUDED IN THIS BOOK

PREFACE

GENERAL PREFACE

BY H.R.H. PRINCESS ANNEMARIE DE BOURBON DE PARME

Characteristic of our era is that changes take place at a furious pace. Scarcely has one innovation taken place than another two are on the way. A few decades ago, for example, it was unthinkable that we would communicate with mobile phones that would also function as debit cards, calendars, email servers and websites. Social media such as Facebook, LinkedIn, Instagram, Snapchat and Twitter have changed and accelerated our communication enormously.

Related to this, the attacks in the United States on September 11 in 2001 and political upheavals, such as the Arab Spring and the annexation of Crimea by Russia, have led to major transformations in the world. Obviously, they are not over, either. Since the Russian invasion of Ukraine on 24 February 2022, geopolitical instability is on the rise, which greatly affects our political, social and economic orders. Problems we all face today include high energy prices, inflation and resource scarcity. We have also been dealing for some time with the risks of cyber attacks aimed at disrupting societies. National borders are fading. The world's population has exploded. In 1900, the Earth was inhabited by less than two billion people; since then, the number has grown to almost eight billion and it continues to swell. As the numbers grow, so too do the ideas and more ideas lead to even more changes. The process is accelerated in an environment in which half of the world's population is connected via the aforementioned social media.

Change, however good it may sometimes be, can also cause upheaval and people sometimes struggle to keep up. Changes in the global and national economy, as well as the challenges in industry and business, are so rapid that people, forced out of their comfort zones, increasingly feel that they are no longer in control of their lives and that their day-to-day concerns are controlling them.

Concerns about a rapidly changing world order, international conflicts, pandemics and climate change affect people's minds worldwide. So too do migration flows and the ever-increasing diversity of people in society. A workforce which consists of people with different ethnic backgrounds, educational levels, physical capabilities and gender identities does not automatically create an inclusive corporate culture. On the contrary, a new position in a heterogeneous group often gives an individual the initial conviction of not being treated equally. Especially if the majority group has been dominant for a long period of time and has entrenched their norms and behavioural patterns.

Owing to these social developments, characterised as they are by the loss of social cohesion, people often surrender their self-confidence and self-esteem. Fear and stress are the result as people experience a feeling of being outside a safe zone that has clear levels of certainty and predictability.

Innovative developments and great unpredictability require firm decisions and resilient leaders. In recent leadership literature, it is generally accepted that in fast changing times it is not only the cognitive intelligence (IQ) of the manager or director that is decisive in keeping an organisation efficient and effective. Especially in times of rapid transformation, other factors are equally or maybe even more necessary. To be effective and inspiring, today's and tomorrow's leaders would be wise to focus on developing multiple intelligences simultaneously. In addition to logical and verbal intelligence, emotional intelligence (EQ) and spiritual intelligence (SQ) are indispensable. These forms of intelligence are understood to mean the ability to let one's behaviour be determined by a wisdom generated in the space of reflection that is both inward and outward looking. Through compassion and through inner serenity and outer imperturbability in whatever situation one finds oneself. This implies managing ourselves and our relationships well.

Empathy, the ability to share and understand the feelings of another, is maybe the most important of all leadership skills and is taking on a new level of meaning and priority. A study by non-profit organisation Catalyst among almost 900 employees revealed that 50% of people with empathic leaders reported their workplace as being inclusive, compared with only 17% of those with less empathic leadership. When people reported that their leaders were empathetic, they were much more likely to be innovative and engaged and to have a better work-life balance.

That the empathy of the leader is so decisive for the success of a company, in rapidly evolving times, is actually a far-reaching insight. After all, anyone who can put themselves in the shoes of others can understand what their needs are and profit from their knowledge, talents and skills. This process encompasses more than simply knowledge obtained through cognitive intelligence. It extends to insights gained through emotional and spiritual intelligence that leaders can deploy to provide their staff with a firmer foundation in their company and in society. The result, which is plain to see, is decision-making that, operating within a much broader frame of reference, is qualitatively better.

This book contains clear theoretical findings about the interaction between emotions and concrete behaviour, including practical exercises designed to develop personal wisdom and resilience. I highly recommended this book, as it is unique in the benefits it offers.

H.R.H. Princess Annemarie de Bourbon de Parme (LLM-MA)

The Hague, May 2022

BUSINESS PREFACE

BY JAN ZIJDERVELD

Authentic Confidence: how to lead a purpose-driven career
From a young age I was inspired by a book that my father had on his bookshelf and gave me to read in the sixties, *Success Through a Positive Mental Attitude*, written by Napoleon Hill and Clement Stone (1959).[1] This book signified for me the power of mind over matter. In other words, whatever challenge you face, if you put your mind to it, you can get it. You are what you think you are. This made me think about the role and power of the inner voice, positive or negative, and how a negative inner voice is at the core of insecurity at work.

Everyone has an inner critic, we are hardwired to have one. However, some of us are more influenced by it on a day-to-day basis. Some are really bothered by this inner critic, to the degree that it hinders them in reaching their full potential at work. Success in life is not about avoiding falling or getting hurt. It is more about having the right positive 'can do' mindset to deal with or reframe issues and challenges. A set of skills to help in this is key.

As I look back on a long career in multinational organisations - from my time as a management trainee at Unilever to roles as an Executive Board Member and President of Unilever Europe and later as CEO at Avon Cosmetics - I have always seen one thing that distinguished great talent from the average. This is a common theme and holds true all over the world. Those colleagues who had the courage to continue leaning in at work, even after they had failed, those who were able to face their fears and get out of their comfort zone and those who followed their true purpose even when scared or facing big obstacles - they were the ones who were the most successful and engaged at work. After getting bruised they would take time to recover and then get back in the saddle, always facing forward in the direction that truly mattered to them. Having a clear end in mind serves as a magnet that draws you towards your goal.

1 Original date of publication is 1959; see the list of references for a later edition that was published in 1997.

It is about 3H's: **H**umility to learn and reflect, **H**unger to win and get things done and **H**eart to give you courage and determination when things get rough and tough.

Of course, at times they were insecure as well, but they would not allow themselves to be distracted by it. They would never become arrogant or think they could do it all and knew it all - actually those with this attitude were the ones who did not make it! Rather, the successful ones would remain humble and yet driven by a clear inner purpose that would keep pushing them forward towards what mattered most. The distinguishing factor between those who were reaching their full potential versus those who did not was 'mind over matter'! They would continuously (sometimes unconsciously) advance their true confidence by developing a set of skills that are summarised in this book as emotional flexibility skills.

We do not learn these skills at school or university, although I think they should be part of every core curriculum. If we are lucky, we learn them partly from experience, stepping out of our comfort zones, taking some risk, making mistakes and having the right mentors and sponsors to guide us through our careers. A lot of great talent gets lost because these skills are not learned much earlier. At the same time, we are facing more mental and emotional challenges than ever before so there is a new imperative to integrate these skills into core leadership programmes.

The current world is in constant flux. In 21st century careers there is no reliable comfort zone. There are no certainties anymore for anyone. Because of this, all of us need to maintain a lifelong learning mindset. This is what turns fear and uncertainty into an exciting experience. If we are interested in providing for our families and in continuing to grow and develop, we have to face the unknown. We need the skills to build the right mindset and the emotional flexibility that can help us face these challenges. Also, it is important to put things into perspective. The more experiences we have, the better we can do that for our challenges and setbacks.

What is central to it all is that you have to be extremely clear about what is truly important for you. What are the values and the principles you want to live by and, more importantly, what purpose are they serving in your life? What do you want to leave behind? What is your leaving speech and what is your legacy?

You want to be sure that you are living your life so that you can give it your best. That you are strongly purpose-driven and inspired by one guiding principle, that you will never look back on life and regret the things that you did not do because you lacked confidence. Ask yourself: 'What would I do if I were not scared?'

The skills you will find in this book will help you to leverage your talent. Unlocking your potential by giving your career the best you can, not avoiding challenges and opportunities because you are afraid, but leaning in to those opportunities that serve what is important to you. And have fun while enjoying the ride! This book offers you evidence-based techniques. Some may seem a bit strange because you are not used to them. Others may be more familiar because you have experienced them before in leadership development programmes. Taken together, they form a powerful mix for developing the mental strength and emotional flexibility that will support your future career success. Most senior leaders who take their roles seriously spend time developing not only their physical fitness but also their emotional and mental bounce-back power. That is what this book offers you and I strongly encourage you to give it a good try!

Finally, in addition to the self-empowerment opportunity offered by this book, I want to make another important point. As senior leaders, we have a responsibility to create environments in which everyone can thrive. We sometimes forget the influence we have, either positive or negative, on our organisations and our colleagues. Do we give energy to or take energy from others through the way we talk, the way we engage with our colleagues on a daily basis, through the behaviours we tolerate and the rewards we allow?

Staying close to our authentic selves and reflecting on this on a daily basis play a role in inspiring mental strength and emotional flexibility in others in our organisations. If we create environments that offer psychological safety for our people to be who they are and to see mistakes as an opportunity learn, we can unlock the potential in everyone.

I truly enjoyed being part of the journey of this book and I trust you will learn and benefit a lot from it. Enjoy the read!

Jan Zijderveld, former Chief Executive Officer, Avon Inc. and President of Unilever Europe

ACADEMIC PREFACE

BY PROF. KOEN SCHRUERS

My field of study is a mix of neurobiology, psychiatry and experimental psychology, and I specialise in anxiety, obsessive compulsive disorders and psychotrauma. As a research scientist, however, I find it very important to keep my feet firmly planted in clinical reality as well and it is for this reason that I spend a lot of time treating patients. This gives me a better understanding of why exactly we carry out research and it is also why I subject myself wherever possible to my own treatments and research methods.

This book about authentic confidence lies at the opposite end of the spectrum with regard to the kind of work that usually occupies my time. It is aimed at the professional in a working environment, whereas I tend to focus on the patient. This does not make the subject matter any less relevant, of course. The flip side of confidence is uncertainty and even anxiety. An anxiety disorder that is left untreated can cause a 'healthy professional' to turn to doctors and scientists like myself for help when they don't know what else to do. Fortunately, there are many ways to prevent anxiety and uncertainty from becoming so overwhelming that the only solution is to resort to psychiatric help.

The field of prevention is a very wide-ranging one and many gains can still be made in the areas of education (e.g., in our schools) and training (the corporate sector) that will help people to take better care of themselves, both physically and emotionally, and so be able to cope with stress and anxiety in an effective manner. The field of affective neuroscience and the related field of cognitive psychology are constantly in motion. Each day we learn a little bit more and these insights can help to provide those who suffer from anxiety with the right kinds of tools. And that is precisely the aim of the authors of this book, too. They have one foot firmly rooted in professional reality and the other in science, but their focus is on the working professional.

From my own experience I know just how important it is to be able to find help when you are struggling with uncertainty and anxiety. Over the past few years I have found myself becoming increasingly occupied with patients and even professional carers who suffer from anxiety, fatigue and burnout. The coronavirus crisis has led to an explosive rise in stress-related complaints, but thankfully also to more attention for the problem.

The society of today and tomorrow is going to need all of the skills outlined in this book. It is an evidence-based volume and a pioneer in its field. It brings scientific insights from cognitive psychology and the affective neurosciences together in a practical manner for its readers in the world of business. Scientific research carried out recently by the authors has shown that the techniques in this book can facilitate greater emotional flexibility and increased self-confidence among knowledge workers. Their studies have also shown that this can even help to boost physical health (for example, by improving heart rate variability). The authors base their findings on the latest scientific insights, but do not get bogged down in the details so that the book remains highly readable for the practitioner. It is a wonderful book full of practical tips and exercises that can help to tackle uncertainty and anxiety. Indeed, knowing that you can do something about anxiety and uncertainty is a great way of generating more self-confidence, and becoming more comfortable with these problems by developing greater emotional flexibility is a key factor. I recommend this book to anyone who wants to boost their own self-confidence and levels of resilience, but also to business leaders, Health and Well-being leaders and Learning & Development professionals who wish to promote a culture of resilience, adaptability, sustainable development, performance and employability among their employees.

Prof. Koen R.J. Schruers, MD PhD, Psychiatrist, Professor of Affective Neuroscience at Maastricht University and Director of Research & Innovation at Mondriaan Mental Health Center Maastricht/Heerlen, The Netherlands

REFLECTIONS FROM THE AUTHORS

Personal reflections – Jacqui Brassey

The first edition of this book was published in 2019 and was the result of an amazing learning journey from an intense 'confidence crisis' to a process of healing fuelled by a renewed sense of meaning and purpose. I have told my personal story to the world in my TEDxINSEAD talk,[2] which was later posted on Arianna Huffington's global site.[3] Since then, we have published an updated Dutch edition of the book, which spent 32 days in the management book top 100 and received many great reviews from independent reviewers.[4] We also published our first scientific paper based on this book in the academic journal PLOS One.[5] Research continues to evolve and so much has happened in the meantime. I am very grateful now that we can present an updated second edition in English at a time when the subject matter of the book seems more relevant than ever!

Our work is all about building on a dream and a purpose. Together with amazing colleagues and friends, I have worked to roll out skill building and awareness on authentic confidence and emotional flexibility in my own organisation (McKinsey & Company) and in other organisations and we are now also slowly entering the world of education. IE University is offering training on authentic confidence and HAN University of Applied Sciences in The Netherlands has integrated our content into their learning and development programmes for students. We hope that many more institutions will follow suit, as that would really help to change the profile and resilience of young leaders entering the world of work. Additionally, this work will contribute to driving sustainable human development and performance and supporting mental health, resilience and well-being at work.

---

2 https://www.ted.com/talks/jacqueline_brassey_authentic_confidence_through_emotional_flexibility

3 https://thriveglobal.com/stories/advancing-authentic-confidence-through-emotional-flexibility-let-s-build-skills-not-stigmas/

4 https://www.managementboek.nl/boek/9789462156869/authentiek-zelfvertrouwen-jacqueline-brassey

5 https://journals.plos.org/plosone/article?id=10.1371/journal.pone.0237821

I have become authentically confident about my own insecurities, which has enabled me to lead my life with purpose and meaning, and I am continuing to move *towards* what matters most to me. For that I will be forever grateful. In the course of our research, we found that at least one out of two people feel they *would be able to perform better at work if they were less worried about making mistakes*. We have also learned that this book is highly appreciated by readers with different kinds of motivations. People may read it for themselves or to help others. So, whatever your motivation may be, I hope the book will empower and help many!

Personal reflections - Nick van Dam

The pandemic has accelerated existing organisational trends. Many leaders around the world were surprised by the level of their workforce's resilience—the ability of people to change their way of working and build new digital skills—virtually overnight. Indeed, today we are already living in the future of work, a future most of us imagined would take another decade to reach. It is expected that many of these changes to business are here to stay and may even be taken to the next level. Organisations are reflecting on the key learnings of the pandemic, the new realities of the future of work and the opportunities in the post-pandemic era. A number of trends will define work in the new era including:

- Digitisation transformation
- Automation and shifting work arrangements
- Hybrid and remote work
- Empowerment of teams
- Focus on talent
- Human leadership
- An emphasis on well-being and vitality

Consequently, people will have to double down on developing and advancing new competencies, take ownership of their careers and learn and grow at the speed of business. Of course, all of this comes with some challenges. Professionals are being pushed frequently out of their 'comfort zone' because of their being empowered to make many individual decisions that drive business performance and impact. As a result, the number of (in particular, young) people with burn-out has been on the rise.

It is my personal passion to help individuals to become the best version of themselves. Our research indicates that there are a number of 'unlockers of potential'. One of them is building personal authentic confidence, the theme of this book, and we provide a number of research-based insights and field-tested tools and methods that are aimed at achieving just that.

Even though we have learned that a lack of authentic confidence is still a developmental topic that many people don't want to acknowledge publicly as a personal barrier to their ability to realise their full potential, we have learned that every single person - independent of age, role, education level or experience - faces moments at work where their confidence is not at its peak level. Having a clear understanding of your internal compass, based on your values and purpose, plus the emotional flexibility to master the many stressful moments in life, together form the foundation blocks for building the kind of authentic confidence needed to be successful at work, in your career and in life.

I am very optimistic that the insights in this book will contribute positively to the advancement of people's potential. Enhancing self-confidence requires a mindset shift that we also facilitate when people experience the workshops that we offer. Finally, in the years to come, I anticipate that we will gain many new and fresh insights based on ongoing research in the neurosciences and positive and development psychology. Thank you for joining us on this journey and I hope that this book will contribute to your personal well-being and success.

Personal reflections - Arjen van Witteloostuijn

Funnily enough, or ironically, I am not exactly the 'personal reflections' type. Actually, I cannot recall ever having done anything that comes close to the exercises and tools revealed in this book. Do not ask me why. Perhaps I am too much of a non-reflector or non-thinker. But maybe I have simply been lucky, having had a smooth ride so far in my career. Also, fate has dictated that I am old enough to have missed the tiring and widespread move to agility and flexibility in modern life. Burnout only became prevalent by the time I had hit my ceiling. But certainly, I might have benefited a lot from being wiser. Who knows where I would have ended up if I had known what I could have done to further develop my own authentic confidence earlier in my career. In my working life, I see many colleagues struggling to find a healthy modus operandi in the jungle of modern employment, an environment with many more uncertainties than I ever encountered. And from my academic research I have learned that emotional agility is critical to surviving, progressing and staying healthy in many modern organisations. And this goes far beyond modern organisations, too, and can be applied in many spheres of life. So I hope this book will contribute a little to improving the quality of life of - hopefully - quite a few people.

> **"A few years ago I found myself at a crossroads in life and unable to make a firm decision as to which path I should choose, primarily because of a crippling lack of self-confidence. Thanks to the help of others and a healthy dose of perseverance on my part, I eventually found the courage to accept my situation for what it was and to move on without feeling guilty about errors made in the past. In short, this song came out of a new-found appreciation for our most valuable asset: time. Time for the living of it all."**
>
> **Danny Guinan,** songwriter

The Greatest Gift

Now is the time to start out again
The waiting is done, the tale can begin
No pushing everything back to the floor

Now is the time to start out anew
The track has been found, the track it is true
No telling where we've been ever before

So I will arise and hold out my hands
And carry the torch all throughout the lands
And gather the greatest gift that can be given to anyone
Time for the living of it all

Now is the time for telling the truth
The trickery's done, the folly of youth
No turning everyone back at the door

Now is the time to play out the game
The stage it has changed, the story's the same
No telling where it might take us this time

So I will arise and hold out my hands
And carry the torch all throughout the lands
And gather the greatest gift that can be given to anyone
Time for the living of it all

From the album 'Now Is The Time' by Danny Guinan

PART I
INTRODUCTION

THE WHY AND WHAT

CHAPTER 1

1. WHY WRITE A BOOK ON AUTHENTIC CONFIDENCE AND EMOTIONAL FLEXIBILITY?

In the last couple of years we have experienced at least three paradigm horizons in the world. First, the horizon regarding the awareness that the world of work was going to change tremendously because of automation and digitalisation. Secondly, we experienced a global pandemic on top of that, which changed our outlook but also opened us up to topics like mental health and well-being. Thirdly, we continue to experience more moments of volatility that are both new and impactful. We have become increasingly aware that we are vulnerable. In this context the workplace has changed forever, and it is continuing to change fast. It is changing because the whole ecosystem of the world is changing. The most recent development we have noticed is the reshuffling of employees in the marketplace and the increasingly ferocious competition for talent, also referred to as the 'great resignation'.[6] This is not the first time that such rapid change has happened, of course. But many argue that this time the nature and speed of change feels as if we have arrived in a world beyond VUCA: Volatile, Uncertain, Complex and Ambiguous, an acronym introduced by the US Army to describe the new global context after the Cold War ended. Since the 1990s, this term has also been widely used in strategic leadership literature.

Due to modern digital technologies, we now have full transparency about everything that is happening everywhere in the world. We have the news at our fingertips. Both good and bad. Both real and fake. What seems to be true today can be a different reality tomorrow. Facts compete with alternative facts and real news vies with its fake counterpart. Hackers and bots invade our digital world, impacting us and our communities, unbeknownst to most. Many live their lives in bubbles with like-minded 'alikes', together disliking all the 'unalikes'. Our devices discourage face-to-face communication. So

6 See, e.g., https://www.mckinsey.com/business-functions/people-and-organisational-performance/our-insights/great-attrition-or-great-attraction-the-choice-is-yours

not only is the change fast, but it is also accelerating exponentially, producing a new way of (not) living together along the way.

An interesting metaphor for the times we live in today was used by one of the keynote speakers at a major HR conference in 2016. It prompted the audience to reflect on the fast-changing world due to digitalisation. Little did we know then what else was coming beyond digitalisation. The speaker compared our current world with the experience of the Indian Ocean tsunami in 2004. In some areas in the rupture zone, the sea receded temporarily from the beach for many metres, revealing about 2.5 kilometres of beach. It was surely difficult to believe your eyes if you were there at the beach and curious adults and children came to check out what was happening, walking toward the receding water and trying to figure out what was going on. It was an unknown phenomenon. The atmosphere at the beach was very calm and quiet, peaceful even. The speaker compared that calm before the rupture to where we were that day (in 2016). Although we were a bit anxious about what was going to happen in the world, we were looking forward to seeing what would come, perhaps thinking that it could not be 'that bad' or that 'we will be able to deal with it', whatever that 'it' might turn out to be. If only we knew back then what we know today!

No one can predict exactly what the digital revolution will bring to the world and in a way we are already in the middle of it. However, many believe that all the fuss and anxiety surrounding the expected change is unnecessary. It might all take a while and require some readjustment on our part, but when the dust settles we will find ourselves in a much better world. New technologies may even help us to tackle our biggest challenges, such as climate change and energy transition, and take over physically demanding tasks from humans. Who knows? When compared with the previous (industrial) revolution, there are very significant differences, particularly in terms of speed and volume. These features are essential attributes of all our new digital technologies. Data, information and news – fake or not – travel so much faster today and in much larger volumes that it implies a structural break with the past. The next novelty might arrive even faster still, and what it will be and what it will do are both extremely unpredictable. The many moving parts of this revolution make it much more difficult to control and predict, whether that be by individuals, organisations, states or international bodies.

When the tsunami finally hit the beach none of the people standing there was prepared, and we all know the tragic results of that event.

Today we are experiencing a similar situation and we don't really know what's around the corner.

All these changes are affecting the world of organisations, too. Take the typical example of a large multinational enterprise. It was not so long ago (relatively speaking) that business processes and planning cycles were organised on an annual or multi-year basis. Strategic plans were made for the next five years in a neat, structured manner. Subsequently, the strategy was executed on an annual basis and the changes tracked per quarter. This is what we learned at business school and how we executed our strategies in the real world; it was considered good practice. This thinking was further complemented by measurement excellence. What gets measured is what gets done. At first it was a challenge to make this happen in large corporations, but we arrived at a happy set of organisational routines and processes that allowed us to measure the gap between our plans and the end result. A few years ago, however, some companies started to move away from this rational and structured approach. Instead, quick learning cycles full of experimentation and immediate feedback were introduced. This came with new hypes and terminology like agile working, effectuation and lean entrepreneurship.

> **"I think increasingly around me people are unable to cope. Not because they don't have the skills, intellect or track record. They are unable to cope because they don't have the inner game. They don't have the moral compass that allows them to stay anchored, and to stay flexible and unlearn the past and become relevant for a changing world. And these (changes) feel increasingly out of our control. There was a time when we could plan – in business, in life – that is now completely gone, life changes so quickly."**
>
> **Leena Nair,** former Chief Human Resources Officer (CHRO), Unilever; current CEO of Chanel

Moreover, modern technologies are impacting the nature of the work of many employees and machines are set to replace workers in a wide variety of tasks. Robots can carry out more and more jobs that used to be the exclusive domain of humans. Modern warehouses are largely bereft of humans and many administrative tasks are now performed by algorithms. Advertising is also fast becoming fully automated. To further increase the organisation's agility and flexibility, full-time employees are being replaced by freelancers.

The impact of these changes on workers, employees and freelancers is significant. It demands constant upskilling to stay abreast of all the new skills required to perform adequately. Aligning the intelligence quotient (IQ) side of upskilling with the constantly changing skills that organisations are looking for is a big challenge. Additionally, life expectancy has increased and people are now expected to work longer.[7] To address this, people must master lifelong learning. However, many are not exactly happy about the effort involved in lifelong learning. Yet, at the same time, most people want to enjoy lifelong employment. With the arrival of the digital era, in order to earn an income over a whole lifetime you need to constantly upskill and reskill yourself. It is expected that if you want to remain relevant in the workplace, you need to build an M-shaped profile of various deep specialisations combined with a generalist skillset.[8] Whereas not so long ago a degree in one specialty was the foundation for a lifetime livelihood, in the future multiple degrees might be required to build a successful career (Van Dam and Brassey, 2017).

Lynda Gratton, Professor of Management Practice at London Business School explains:

> **"I have a rather positive view on the future of work. One of the things that is apparent: if you live a long time, for example, if you are going to live a hundred years (our most recent book was called A 100 Year Life), you have a lot more opportunity to be yourself. I remember a quote that we used in this book: *"When life is long, you can build a cathedral rather than a shopping mall."* As life gets longer, you have more years to explore and you are not under so much pressure. Technology is changing work. It is giving us an opportunity to do different things. There is real opportunity for people to learn about themselves, to understand what's important to them and to experiment. One of the most important human traits is curiosity, and with a long life you get a lot of opportunities to be curious. Traditional societies can be very restrictive, giving you very few options. However, in these societies you did not have to really think a great deal about who you were and what you wanted to become. If you look at the future of work, most of the changes mean that you must now take more decisions yourself, you have to be more reflective, you have to consider things more,**

7 See, e.g., https://www.mckinsey.com/industries/public-and-social-sector/our-insights/planning-for-an-aging-population

8 See Figure 49 on page 303 for a visualization of this.

> **you have more options; and those are all sources of anxiety. So, I look at it through a positive lens and say: 'Isn't it marvellous that you can build your own life?' Of course, the downside is that there are a lot of choices for you to make and some of them are big choices with consequences that you may not fully understand when you are taking them."**
>
> **Lynda Gratton,** Professor of Management Practice, London Business School

And we are already seeing the results of these developments in society, with the changes also being accelerated by the coronavirus pandemic and ongoing disruption in the world. A less positive side of all these developments is the fact that mental health challenges have never been as prominent as they are today. The number of employees reporting burnout symptoms is on the rise and it is a topic that is keeping organisations increasingly occupied.[9] According to the World Health Organisation (WHO)[10] mental health issues cost the global economy an estimated 1 trillion US dollars in lost productivity each year. The impact of the global pandemic was large and unevenly distributed and it hit minorities, young people and working parents particularly hard.[11] Many people worry about all kinds of competing demands: at work, at home, in their careers, their family, and so on. The outlook is not positive either, with the WHO predicting that depression will be the leading cause of disease globally by 2030.[12]

It may be no surprise that employee engagement worldwide is simultaneously decreasing after a slow but steady rise over the last ten years. A report by the Gallup organisation found that 20% of the

9 See, e.g., the McKinsey Health Institute report on Employee Mental Health and Wellbeing (May 2022): https://www.mckinsey.com/MHI/Our-Insights/Addressing-employee-burnout-Are-you-solving-the-right-problem (www.mckinsey.com/Employee Burnout); and https://www.mckinsey.com/mhi/overview but also others including: https://www.mhanational.org/mind-workplace

10 http://www.who.int/mental_health/in_the_workplace/en/

11 See, e.g., https://www.healthdata.org/infographic/covid-19-pandemic-has-had-large-and-uneven-impact-global-mental-health; https://www.thelancet.com/journals/lancet/article/PIIS0140-6736(21)02143-7/fulltext and https://www.mckinsey.com/industries/healthcare-systems-and-services/our-insights/covid-19-and-burnout-are-straining-the-mental-health-of-employed-parents?cid=soc-web

12 http://apps.who.int/gb/ebwha/pdf_files/EB130/B130_9-en.pdf

workforce worldwide was engaged in 2020,[13] a 2 per cent drop compared with the year before. The same report indicated an increase in the incidence of daily stress, (rising from 38% in 2019 to 43% in 2020).[14]

Another recent and related trend in the workplace is what is known as the 'great attrition'.[15] The extent to which companies can help their workforce with the above-mentioned challenges will dictate much of their ability to attract and retain people in the months and years to come. McKinsey & Company found that employees who had recently voluntarily left a job indicated that experiences with uncaring leaders, unsustainable expectations of work performance and lack of career advancement were key factors in their decision-making.[16] Organisations that have integrated mental health and well-being into their employer value proposition (and are therefore walking the talk) will be able to attract talent more easily than others. The World Economic Forum predicts that Gen Z will make up close to 30% of the global workforce by 2025.[17] A consumer healthcare insights study found that that 59% of the Gen Z think that mental health resources are important when selecting an employer (compared to 36% of Baby Boomers), and 57% say these resources are important for them to stay at their employer (compared to 31% of Baby Boomers).[18]

The concept of burnout includes exhaustion, cynicism and negative feelings about work (Schaufeli and Salanova, 2007). Schaufeli and de

---

13 According to Gallup (2021:5): "Employee engagement reflects the involvement and enthusiasm of employees in their work and workplace." https://www.gallup.com/workplace/349484/state-of-the-global-workplace.aspx

14 https://www.gallup.com/workplace/349484/state-of-the-global-workplace.aspx

15 https://www.mckinsey.com/business-functions/people-and-organizational-performance/our-insights/great-attrition-or-great-attraction-the-choice-is-yours

16 https://www.mckinsey.com/business-functions/people-and-organizational-performance/our-insights/gone-for-now-or-gone-for-good-how-to-play-the-new-talent-game-and-win-back-workers?cid=eml-web

17 "How Gen Z employment levels compare in OECD countries", World Economic Forum, 2021

18 https://www.mckinsey.com/industries/healthcare-systems-and-services/our-insights/helping-us-healthcare-stakeholders-understand-the-human-side-of-the-covid-19-crisis; October 2020, n=1,305 respondents.

Witte (2017) concluded that work engagement is indeed negatively related to burnout and that it is uniquely related to job demands, job resources and various outcomes, for example. So if someone is not engaged at work, it does not necessarily mean that they are burned out but may instead be suffering from other negativities (See Schaufeli and de Witte, 2017 and 2017; Laurentiu et al., 2017; and Goering et al., 2017). A report by the McKinsey Health Institute on Employee Mental Health and Wellbeing put a further spotlight on new insights regarding burnout in the workplace.[19] Their research found that, on average, 1 in 4 of all employees (in 15 countries, representing approximately 70% of the global population) experience burnout symptoms. While it is important to emphasise that burnout in the workplace is a multifaceted problem and that the solution needs to be systemic, there is certainly an important role for authentic confidence and emotional flexibility. The study identified both the amplifying (increasing engagement) and buffering effects (less impact of work stressors on engagement) of affective adaptability, a concept related to emotional flexibility.[20] Furthermore, employees with greater affective adaptability reported a higher intent to leave in the case of toxic workplace environments – their increased sense of agency may have given them more confidence to make courageous choices!

The above findings are also confirmed by practical and scientific research. Professional self-efficacy, or self-confidence as defined in this book, is a positive driver of work engagement. It has been negatively associated with job burnout[21] and positively linked with work-related performance.[22] Positive self-confidence allows people to pro-actively build a positive social context at work. Negative self-confidence, on the other hand, can create a negative spiral of reduced energy and demotivation and a subsequent loss of engagement (Schaufeli and Salanova, 2007). The role of exhaustion is quite important. Two studies by Rogala and colleagues (2016)[23] found that exhaustion negatively influenced self-confidence, which in turn fed into decreased engagement over a six-month period. Many studies have shown the positive effects of self-efficacy at work on job satisfaction, learning, decision-making, focus, attention and physical

---

19 https://www.mckinsey.com/MHI/Our-Insights/Addressing-employee-burnout-Are-you-solving-the-right-problem (www.mckinsey.com/EmployeeBurnout); and https://www.mckinsey.com/mhi/overview

20 See, e.g., https://psycnet.apa.org/record/2020-44121-001

21 https://www.tandfonline.com/doi/abs/10.1080/10615806.2015.1058369

22 https://psycnet.apa.org/doiLanding?doi=10.1037%2F0033-2909.124.2.240

23 https://www.frontiersin.org/articles/10.3389/fpsyg.2015.02032/full

and mental well-being (Graham, 2009). In an applied study it was found that, as a result of an adaptability development programme, multi-rater surveys showed that participants who were highly engaged in the learning journey displayed 3x higher rates of improvement in several leadership dimensions and behaviours compared with those who were not engaged in the learning journey. Additionally, self-reported levels of well-being improved 7x more versus the 'control' group that did not actively engage.[24]

Wilmar Schaufeli, Professor and Expert in Burnout and Work Engagement, comments:

> **"Self-confidence, the way it is described in this book, is related to burnout such that reduced belief in competence can be both a possible cause and consequence of burnout. You can look at it as a risk factor. If you feel you are not competent enough in your role at work, this might emotionally drain you and you will start feeling exhausted, which may lead or contribute to a burnout. The other way around may also be true - feeling tired and exhausted can contribute to the fact that you feel less competent, thus developing self-confidence and belief in your competence may be an important factor in preventing and bouncing back from a burnout process."**
>
> **Prof. Wilmar Schaufeli,** Burnout and Work Engagement Expert, Utrecht University

The global facts stated above are quite alarming, considering the current and predicted increase in mental health problems. In the UK, it is estimated that roughly one in four people experience a mental health issue each year; in the USA, this is estimated to be one in five.[25] In Australia, 20 per cent of people aged 16 to 85 are likely to

24 Source: McKinsey & Company People and Organization Performance - Adaptability Learning Program; multi-rater surveys showed improvements in adaptability outcomes including: performance in role, sustainment of well-being, successfully adapting to unplanned circumstances and change, optimism, development of new knowledge and skills; well-being results were based on self-reported progress as a result of the programme. Also mentioned in: www.mckinsey.com/EmployeeBurnout

25 https://www.mind.org.uk/information-support/types-of-mental-health-problems/statistics-and-facts-about-mental-health/how-common-are-mental-health-problems/#.Wp2zC-jwY2w and https://www.nami.org/learn-more/mental-health-by-the-numbers

experience a mental health condition in any given year.[26] Mental health issues can have many causes and we are aware that by studying the confidence and anxiety aspects we are only looking at a small part of the broader topic.[27] However, we have found it to be very relevant to the business context, hence our eagerness to understand the extent of the problem in the day-to-day lives of professionals. In our research, we endeavoured to ascertain how many people actually struggle with worries at work, primarily as an indicator of lost mental energy and a potential cause of burnout or related mental health issues. When we first began to investigate this issue a few years back, we found there was very little research that clarified the statistics around 'worry' and 'confidence' in relation to the workplace. Gallup reports that the number of employees who experienced significant daily worry increased slowly over the past ten years and then showed a sudden and steep increase from 35% of all employees in 2019 to 41% in 2020.[28]

A study carried out in 2011 by the Institute of Leadership & Management involving 2,960 participants found that 31% of men admit to suffering from feelings of self-doubt, compared with 50% of women.[29] In our own exploratory study, we asked people a number of questions regarding worry, including whether it prevents them from achieving their best performance and how much time they spent worrying during their working week. Figure 1 provides an overview of the responses. The results are striking: more than 40% said they spend between 20% and 40% of their time at work worrying.

26 https://www.abs.gov.au/statistics/health/mental-health/national-survey-mental-health-and-wellbeing-summary-results/latest-release

27 For a further reflection of mental health and related topics see, e.g., https://www.nimh.nih.gov/health; https://medlineplus.gov/anxiety.html and https://www.who.int/teams/mental-health-and-substance-use/promotion-prevention/mental-health-in-the-workplace

28 https://www.gallup.com/workplace/349484/state-of-the-global-workplace.aspx

29 https://www.institutelm.com/resourceLibrary/ambition-and-gender-at-work.html

FIGURE 1: PERCENTAGE OF TIME SPENT WORRYING ABOUT PERFORMANCE AT WORK

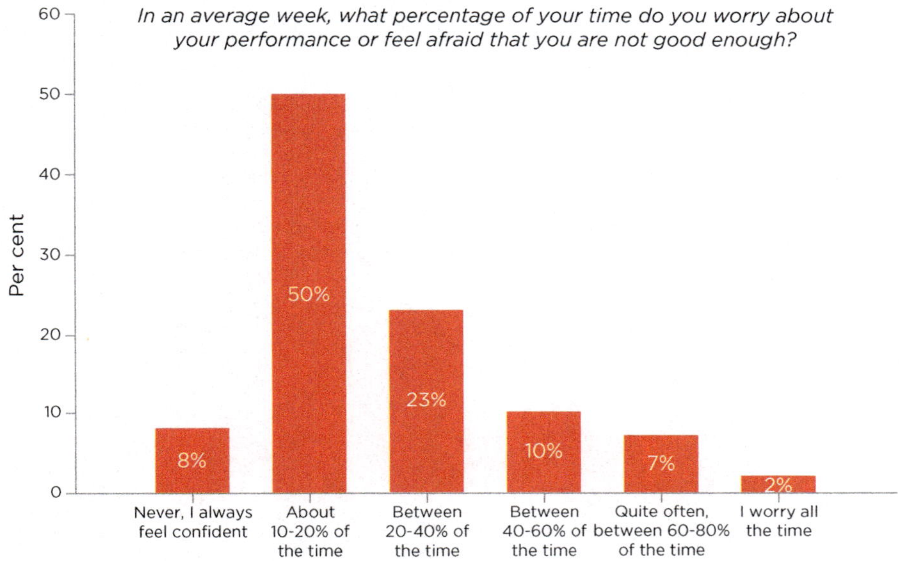

Source: Online Authentic Confidence Survey, Brassey, van Dam and Van Witteloostuijn; global version results snapshot from January 2019; *N* = 864.

We also studied the differences between men and women.[30] Nearly 46% of women indicated that they worry 20-40% of their time, whereas the figure for men was 33%. When we compare the different sub-groups, we see that the percentages are very high for young, highly-educated professionals. About 54% of young professionals employed by professional services firms spend 20-40% of their time worrying and almost a quarter of them do so at least 40% or more of their time. For young medical professionals,[31] these percentages are even higher: nearly 60% of this group indicated that they worry about their performance at least 20-40% or more of their time, with 35% of the group stating that they spend over 40% of their time worrying. Results (post-pandemic, 2022) from a new stu-

30 Total N of this survey is 864; Female N=574; Male N=290.

31 We are working with small sub-sample sizes here, which can of course impact the results: 80 young professionals from professional services firms and 17 young medical professionals.

dy among business students[32] showed that 49% worry at least 20-40% of their time or more, while 28% indicated that they worry at least 40% of their time.

When we asked if people could perform better if they were less worried about making mistakes, 47% of the participants agreed strongly or very strongly (Figure 2: scores 4 and up combined).

FIGURE 2: PERFORM BETTER IF LESS WORRIED

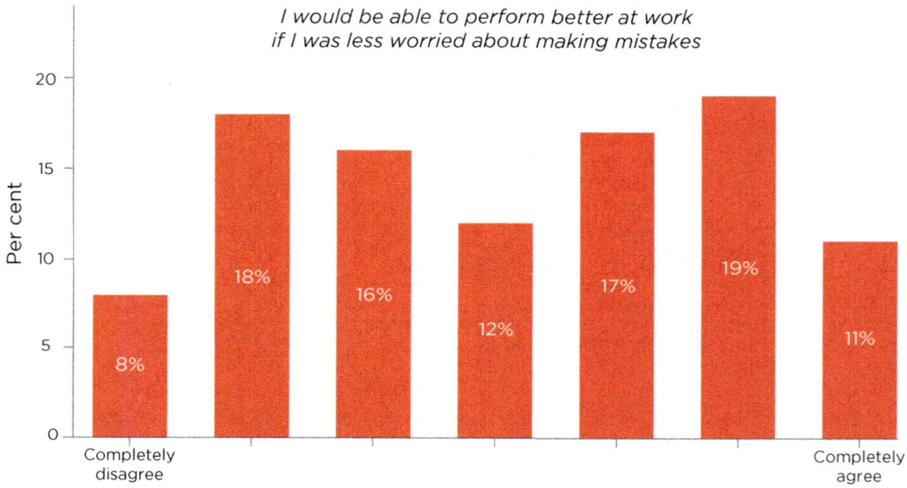

Source: Online Authentic Confidence Survey, Brassey, van Dam, and Van Witteloostuijn, global version results snapshot from January 2019; *N* = 864.

For men, this percentage was 46%, while for women it was 47%. So, in this sample, a lack of confidence and the effects of worry are not only prominent among women. As with the previous question, we also found higher percentages who 'agreed' with this statement among young service professionals (64%) and young medical professionals (70%). We also looked at this question in the post-pandemic study of business students and found that 52% of them agreed with the statement. More research is needed to understand what goes on - and why - within specific sub-groups, ideally in the context of a longitudinal design, but the numbers were already alarming enough in 2019 (before the pandemic) and were also alarming in our recent study of students, which supports the case that we are making in this book for developing emotional flexibility and authentic confidence skills.

32 A study in Q1 2022 at the VU Amsterdam amongst first-year Bachelor students of the International Business Studies (n=124).

Skills that can certainly be developed, as confirmed by our own evolving scientific research.[33]

We also asked which specific behaviours people avoid because they lack confidence. It was an open question, triggering many different responses that we clustered into several themes. Figure 3 shows the outcome of this exercise. The top three involve avoiding (1) leaning in, (2) speaking up and (3) presenting, closely followed by giving feedback (in particular to more senior leaders). Examples of work-related opportunities or challenges that people avoid under the category of leaning in include assuming responsibility for a new project or difficult analyses and accepting a new role or promotion.

FIGURE 3: WHAT ARE YOU NOT DOING WHEN YOU LACK CONFIDENCE

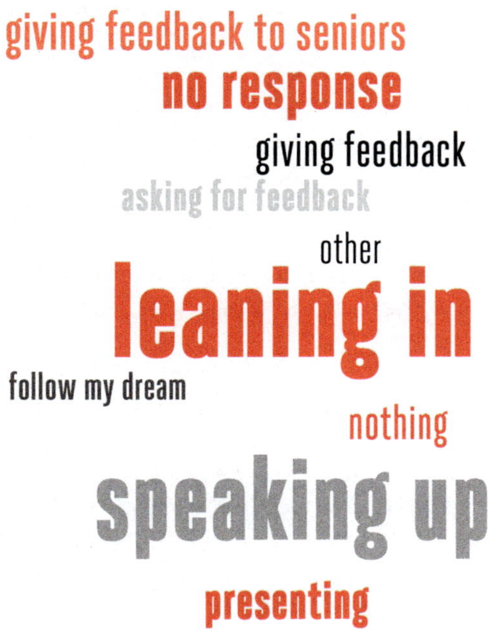

Source: Online Authentic Confidence Survey, Brassey, van Dam and Van Witteloostuijn, global survey results snapshot from January 2019; N = 864.

33 See, e.g., https://journals.plos.org/plosone/article?id=10.1371/journal.pone.0237821; Brassey, J., Witteloostuijn, A. V., Huszka, C., Silberzahn, T., & Dam, N. V. (2020). Emotional flexibility and general self-efficacy: A pilot training intervention study with knowledge workers. PloS one, 15(10), e0237821.

The above qualities are precisely what organisations need from their employees, especially in today's new world. In conversations with several groups of professionals during workshops, we learned that the fear of leaning in, speaking up and giving feedback (to seniors) was driven by emotional anxiety related to, for example, the fear of failure or repercussions from making mistakes. Additionally, workshop participants frequently referred to a perceived lack of skill. Knowing how to lean in, how to learn, how to speak up and how to give feedback involves a series of key skills. Accumulating the required experience with these qualities, and doing so skilfully, can help to build confidence as well. In the study that we carried out post-pandemic among business students, we found a slightly different pattern, given that they do not have similar interactions yet as business professionals have with seniors. Most of their answers related to speaking up, presenting or leaning in, while some responses were more related to the social challenges that young students have to face.

As part of our ongoing research, we also interviewed an interesting mix of almost 40 senior professionals and experts, collecting candid stories about insecurity and courage and how they learned to cope with these challenges. Two important overarching insights emerged from these interviews: (1) we all experience challenges, in some form or other, during our career; and (2) no one can be successful in their professional career without being challenged, making mistakes and worrying.

In recent years we have learned (even more so than before) how important it is in the professional context to be healthy and fit – to eat well, to sleep well and to make sure we have the right skills to foster emotional as well as physical health. Over the past two decades, a focus on emotional intelligence (EQ) related skills has been added to the curriculum in leadership development programmes as well. We now see a need for an additional form of fitness in organisations, one that is becoming more and more urgent: emotional and mental fitness (including adaptability and deliberate calm).[34] This involves skills that go beyond our existing EQ focus and that refer to the emotional ability to deal with fears in a new and uncertain world. In

34 https://www.mckinsey.com/business-functions/people-and-organizational-performance/our-insights/future-proof-solving-the-adaptability-paradox-for-the-long-term; and https://www.harpercollins.com/products/deliberate-calm-jacqueline-brasseyaaron-de-smetmichiel-kruyt?variant=40244138344482

our conversations during interviews and workshops we also discovered that there is a huge stigma surrounding the topic of insecurity, lack of confidence, anxiety and being worried. We are taught that it is important to exude success and so we pretend we are doing fantastic all of the time. "Never let them see you sweat" or so the saying goes. The moment we dare to reveal that things are not going well, we experience a form of disengagement from our colleagues and leaders (the rather rare exceptions excluded, of course). This is all part of the problem and it is our hope that by telling the stories of the professionals and experts we interviewed, we may start to shift that tough paradigm.

The observations above may not make for comfortable reading but they reflect a reality that must be acknowledged. Thankfully, many terrific initiatives have been undertaken in recent years aimed at increasing our awareness of these issues, creating a different employee experience and promoting the development of the emotional skills required to deal adequately with the challenges of modern life.

Apart from being a potential buffer for stress and an amplifier for engagement, research has shown that confidence is also associated with performance.[35] A study published in 2017 by Georgetown University in collaboration with Tupperware[36] has shown that there is a convincing business case for investing in building confidence in an organisational context, particularly for women. Workers who were told that failure is part of the road to success reported higher levels of confidence and an increased ability to overcome challenges. Confident workers are more successful at work and are more optimistic about future success than workers with less confidence.

To be more specific, greater confidence turned out to be associated with an increase in recruiter effectiveness (an average of 27% more recruits) and those with more confidence achieved an average of 22% more sales. More confident workers were 16% more likely to come up with better ways of getting things done, 17% more likely to be innovative at work and 24% more likely to overcome work-related

35 See, e.g., https://psycnet.apa.org/doiLanding?doi=10.1037%2F0033-2909.124.2.240

36 Tupperware is primarily known for its kitchen and home storage products. You can read more about the study here: https://www.businesswire.com/news/home/20170306005328/en and related published paper here: https://meridian.allenpress.com/accounting-review/article-abstract/96/2/205/436091/How-Controlling-Failure-Perceptions-Affects

challenges. This is very promising and it provides additional encouragement for organisations to start taking the development of skills to support confidence more seriously.

Tupperware's former CEO, Rick Goings:

> **"I think the topic of developing confidence amongst employees and colleagues is very important for the companies of today and tomorrow. All a company is, is a collection of people. For a company to sustain itself, it needs to continue to have competitive advantage and the ideas generated by their people lead to strategies to achieve this. Companies that can attract, develop, empower, and retain the best people have lasting success. When you create an open landscape of individuals who are working to become the best version of themselves, leveraging individual strengths and the areas where they have confidence, you heavily influence their chances for success."**
>
> **Rick Going,** Tupperware's former CEO

However, despite the evidence that developing these skills can make a difference in many ways, both for employees and organisations, and even though demand is increasing and the topics are being more widely discussed, we have not yet seen enough convincing proof that these skills are being embraced and integrated as an *essential* and *core* part of the learning and development curricula in the majority of organisations and universities. Which brings us to the key message of this book: by developing high-quality emotional skills that support the development of authentic confidence, people will be more able to handle the challenges of the digital age (or any age, actually).

Lynda Gratton, Professor of Management Practice, London Business School has this to say:

> **"I think that the world is changing faster than many companies are able to comprehend, and so I think they are in catch-up mode. For 10 years, we have run the Future of Work Conference which brings companies together to talk about the future world of work. It is obvious that technology and demographics, social changes, are happening at an exponential pace. Most companies are built as bureaucracies, which is good. This is a great way of getting stuff done but they are not really built around the needs of the individual worker. You see all sorts**

> **of areas where people would love to see things happening: people would love to have flexible work schedules; they would love to have time off to relearn; they would like to do more experimentation but companies at the moment often struggle with that. There is a bit of an anomaly at the moment in terms of what people want and what companies are able to provide."**
>
> **Lynda Gratton,** Professor of Management Practice, London Business School

So what will you find in this book? Well, we want to take you on a journey where we will explore the 'what' and 'how' of authentic confidence in a professional context and explain why we use the word 'authentic' and not just 'confidence' alone. We will introduce an evidence-based approach towards developing authentic confidence, putting emotional flexibility centre stage. In doing so we are building on the work done by Steven Hayes and many colleagues who developed the concept of Acceptance and Commitment Therapy (ACT), also known as Acceptance and Commitment Training or Emotional Flexibility. In 2016, it was Susan David who brought this concept very successfully to a larger audience in her book *Emotional Agility*. Up until then, the concept had been primarily used - and very effectively - in clinical psychology tailored to fit therapeutic settings. The approach has proven its effectiveness in the clinical world. Over a thousand studies have been published, along with hundreds of randomised control studies (RCTs).[37] As of March 2011, the approach has been officially acknowledged as 'evidence-based' in the United States.[38] And while it has been successfully used to treat anxiety, depression and psychological burnout, for example,[39] we also know that it can be used to develop self-efficacy[40] and facilitate being more positioned in the 'prevention' space on the continuum of mental health and well-being.[41]

37 https://contextualscience.org/act_randomized_controlled_trials_1986_to_present

38 For more information: https://contextualscience.org/.

39 https://www.psychologytoday.com/us/blog/the-mindful-path-self-acceptance/202203/psychological-burnout-and-acceptance-and-commitment?eml

40 https://journals.plos.org/plosone/article?id=10.1371/journal.pone.0237821

41 For a visualization of the mental health continuum we refer to this article (Exhibit 1) https://www.mckinsey.com/industries/life-sciences/our-insights/using-digital-tech-to-support-employees-mental-health-and-resilience

We bring the 'what' and the 'how' alive with the personal stories of the senior professionals and experts we interviewed and the insights we gained through our survey and workshops. In the first part of this book there will be more emphasis on the 'what' of authentic confidence and how emotional flexibility can support the development of such confidence. The second part will be a deep dive into a practical toolkit tailored to suit working professionals. Our aim is to provide insights into and an understanding of what it really takes to build mental and emotional muscle, the kind that can help you to reach your maximum talent potential and boost your health and well-being.

CHAPTER 2

2. AUTHENTIC CONFIDENCE: WHAT IS IT AND WHY IS IT IMPORTANT?

> **"William James (1890-1983) first introduced the topic of self-esteem to psychology over a century ago, making this area one of the oldest in the entire discipline."**
>
> **Mruk,** 2013b: 157

> **"Leaders need humility to know what they don't know, but have the confidence to make a decision amid the ambiguity."**
>
> **Adam Bryant**[42]

2.1 What is authentic confidence?

Taking the above quotes into account, we can be quite sure we are facing an audacious task: defining a term that comes from the large scientific family of self-esteem concepts (and is one of the oldest in the discipline of psychology) and subsequently applying it to the future of the digital age. Staying close to our intention with this book, which is focused on the practical application of concepts, we will first define what we mean by authentic confidence before elaborating on the roots of this term.

The Oxford English Dictionary defines confidence as "the feeling or belief that one can have faith in or rely on someone or something" and "the feeling of self-assurance arising from an appreciation of one's own abilities or qualities." It is interesting that the word 'feeling' is included in both definitions. When defined like this, confidence refers to a feeling and does not imply an objective truth but rather a personal state or experience. Whenever the word confidence is used or discussed, the question is often raised as to whether it is actually a good or bad state of being.

42 https://www.nytimes.com/2017/10/27/business/how-to-be-a-ceo.html

In their book *The Confidence Code* (2014) Kay and Shipman explain very colourfully the assumption that 'confidence equals competence'. Something that a confident person claims to be the truth is often believed without their opinion being challenged. As a result, confidence is frequently considered to be a sign of competence. In this situation, where the confident person is believed but not challenged, one can imagine the potential damage to an organisation if this person turns out to be not so competent after all. To clarify the definition of confidence we therefore decided to include the word 'authentic' and focus subsequently on what we refer to as authentic confidence. In doing so we seek to differentiate between the kind of confidence that is correctly associated with competence and that which is not.

However, this opens another can of worms, as the concept of authenticity is also associated with other definitional and philosophical challenges. Authentic is defined as 'of undisputed origin and not a copy', 'genuine', 'based on facts' and 'accurate or reliable'. Our aim with this book is to be precise, accurate and also practical. Because of the difficulties involved in using the word 'confidence' without an adjective, we decided to add the word 'authentic' and to define authentic confidence - the central concept in this book - as follows:

> **Authentic confidence is the internal and secure awareness of your true capabilities, values and purpose. You acknowledge and are okay with your insecurities regarding your competencies and you deal with those insecurities in an action-oriented and skilful manner. You trust that you can and will succeed in the tasks you accept and that you will have the courage to decline or seek help for the challenges that are beyond your capabilities or are not in line with your values and purpose.**

In this definition, the word 'authentic' represents the ability to accept your insecurities - instead of sweeping them under the carpet you handle them with confidence. Authentic confidence implies inner peace and courage and the ability to tackle challenges at work in a realistic manner. Authentic confidence means being aware of both your competencies and your weaknesses.

How does this definition hold up when compared with the academic literature? Most of the time, the literal term 'confidence' is not used in science to refer to the concept that we are talking about in this book.[43]

43 Often, other terms are used. The one that comes closest is self-efficacy; more on that later in this chapter.

In scientific literature there is much debate as to whether confidence is a personality or ability trait.[44] Some authors define it as a 'subjective estimate of decision quality'.[45] The original and most fundamental term for confidence is probably 'self-esteem', along with its many relatives, including self-efficacy. Ever since the term was first coined by William James, the research has evolved in various directions, which has resulted in a host of contradictory definitions (Mruk, 2013b). In the context of this book, we find that the two-factor explanation of self-esteem offered by Mruk (2013 and 2019) covers our intentions more than adequately. Mruk argues and clarifies that the two-factor approach to self-esteem represents 'authentic self-esteem', which comes close to what we are focusing on in this book.

Self-esteem in the two-factor approach is defined as: "... the lived status of one's competence at dealing with the challenges of living in a worthy way over time" (Mruk, 2013a: 27). In this definition, competence (level of competence at a task, skill or activity) and worthiness (level of feeling accepted, virtuous or worthy) are two sides of the same coin and balanced self-esteem would be the result of high levels of worthiness and competence. To quote Mruk, "the worthiness component of self-esteem balances the tendency to overvalue success or to pursue it in negative ways, such as those associated with contingent self-esteem. In this sense, being good at bad things, such as taking advantage or harming others, would not have a positive impact on self-esteem. Similarly, the dangers associated with simply feeling good about one's self without earning that effect are also avoided by the two-factor approach" (Mruk, 2013b: 162).

Authentic self-esteem is paraphrased by Mruk (2013a: 158) as "genuinely high self-esteem that is secure enough to allow the individual to perceive and admit personal faults or limitations; consistent, across conscious (explicit) and nonconscious (implicit) levels; true, in that it does not require continual validation of worthiness from others or endless success to sustain itself; and stable, which is to say that it is largely balanced over time." This definition is very much in line with our pragmatic description of authentic confidence earlier

44 Burns, K. M.; Burns, N. R.; Ward, L. Confidence—More a Personality or Ability Trait? It Depends on How It Is Measured: A Comparison of Young and Older Adults. Front. Psychol. 2016, 7, 518. https://doi.org/10.3389/fpsyg.2016.00518

45 Brus, J.; Aebersold, H.; Grueschow, M.; Polania, R. Sources of Confidence in Value-Based Choice. Nat. Commun. 2021, 12 (1), 7337. https://doi.org/10.1038/s41467-021-27618-5

in this chapter. High self-esteem, according to Mruk (2013 a:160), includes having higher degrees of self-awareness and openness to experience, which offers an important bridge to the concept of emotional flexibility that we will explain in the next chapter.

In the two-factor model of self-esteem, anxiety can be an important factor driving non-authentic self-esteem. In the next section, we will explore a few different perspectives on how to look at anxiety, where it comes from and how it impacts our behaviour and performance at work, including the psychoanalytical and neuroscientific explanation, as well as the role of language. For the purposes of this book, we will use the term 'self-confidence' as opposed to 'self-esteem' or 'self-efficacy', since the former is more accepted and often used within the professional work context.

2.2 What drives a lack of authentic confidence?

The drivers of low confidence can be understood when we view them through different lenses. In this chapter we will briefly explore three different paradigms. We will first examine the topic from a psychoanalytical point of view. This will help to clarify where our unhelpful thoughts and inner critics come from. The second perspective is the neuroscience behind fear and anxiety. In other words, what happens in the brain and body when we experience the negative effects of our worries and fears? The third perspective explains the role of language in dealing with anxiety and fears, and how lasting the impact is once we have learned to feel anxious or fearful. At the end of this chapter we will bring all these perspectives together and apply the resulting conclusion to the context of work.

2.2.1 The origins of self-doubt and its impact in the workplace

Lead author of this section is Dr Veronica Azua, organisational psychologist and executive coach

> **"They f**k you up, your mum and dad.**
> **They may not mean to, but they do.**
> **They fill you with the faults they had**
> **And add some extra, just for you."**
>
> **Philip Larkin,** "This Be the Verse", from Collected Poems, 1988:142

Self-doubt

The term 'self-doubt' produced 19,400,000 results in a Google search in February 2018, while a more recent search produced 581,000,000 (!) results (December 2021). The term was also referred to in more than 25,000 academic journal articles (Discovery, February 2018). Along with other closely related concepts, such as inner critic and impostor syndrome, the term 'self-doubt' seems to be well-known by the public and is used widely in the media, non-fiction publications and many other resources (such as *Harvard Business Review*, blogs, BBC, websites, books, etc.) Fictional literature is also full of examples and traces of the inner critic. Actors, writers, first ladies, vloggers, authors of self-help books, spiritual gurus, yogis and so on openly discuss their self-doubts, critical self-talk and other people's self-doubts, as well as offering advice on how to tame our critical inner voices. We can probably all relate to the effects of negative self-talk at some point or other in our lives and careers.

For instance, 70% of people are affected by the 'impostor syndrome' at some point in their lives (Gravois, 2007). The imposter syndrome is defined as follows: Impostor syndrome (also known as impostor phenomenon, fraud syndrome or the impostor experience) is a concept describing individuals who are marked by an inability to internalise their accomplishments and have a persistent fear of being exposed as a 'fraud'.[46]

This definition came as no surprise to us. In our work on leadership development and leadership roles over the past ten years, we have noticed a number of key characteristics in senior leaders: they are plagued by self-doubt and self-criticism and tend to demand too much of themselves. In other words, they lack (authentic) confidence. This is not a rare phenomenon higher up in hierarchies, although many mask it by building a façade of self-promotion.

Many of these leaders seem to believe deep down, consciously or unconsciously, that they have progressed in their careers primarily by accident and good fortune. A typical phrase is: "I somehow slipped through the net." Their self-doubt manifests itself in uncertainty about the value of their contributions at work, concerns about being judged for saying something wrong or overlooking potential errors, feeling out of place in meetings, doubts about their own ability to deliver on projects and an all-round sense of inadequacy. Most discussions with these kinds of leaders revolve around their perception

46 https://en.wikipedia.org/wiki/Impostor_syndrome

of the demands and expectations of their clients, colleagues and superiors. They refer to the external demands that put pressure on modern workers, but also to the internal demands that the leaders place upon themselves and their employees. It is these internal demands in particular that are worth examining. There is a sharp contrast between how these senior leaders are seen by others as capable and successful professionals and their own high levels of self-doubt. This is all familiar to us from our own personal histories. All of this self-doubt, self-criticism and high self-demand resonates so clearly with us that it inspired us to carry out our own scientific research on the topic.

Self-doubt and self-criticism can be linked to (or can be seen as evidence of) what is known in psychoanalytical circles as the 'superego' (Freud, 1927). The superego is defined as a part of the organisational psyche that houses the internalisation of authority figures and manifests itself in the form of a disciplinary and critical internal voice (Freud, 1927; Kramer, 1958; Meyer 1998; Frank 1999). From a psychoanalytical point of view, the key to understanding self-doubt and self-criticism can be found in the early years of our upbringing. It is the quality of an infant's interactions with their main authority figures, such as parents, older siblings, teachers, close relatives and main care givers, that defines and shapes the individual's inner life, with the subsequent impact being felt throughout adulthood. It is during these early years, when the child introjects the authority figures' voices, that the superego precursors appear and set the stage for the type of personality that will be carried into the future, depending on what the child makes of these voices in their own mind (Meyers, 1998; Frank 1999).

The term 'superego' has been discussed for decades in the psychoanalytical field. Additionally, the contemporary concept of 'inner critic' (Gendlin, 1981) is closely related to the notion of the superego. The inner critic has received a lot of attention in psychotherapy and in the coaching arena. Many regard it as much 'trendier' than the old Freudian superego. From a patient-centred/experiential psychotherapy perspective, the inner critic is defined as the impersonal inner voice that "nags and repeats him- or herself relentlessly ... with which some people block themselves" (Stinckens et al., 2002: 41). The inner critic is a voice that attacks the individual and grinds him/her down. It uses words such as 'must', 'ought' and 'should'. If too dominant, this negative and discouraging inner voice results in the individual feeling anxious and restrained (Stinckens et al., 2002: 41). Similar to what psychoanalysis also proposes, a past history of rejection, restriction and neglect is closely linked to the quality of the critical inner voice. The inner critic develops as a replica of the parents' criticism of or lack of sensitivity towards the infant. Consequently, the infant grows up lacking a sense of self-worth and feeling unloved or unlovable (Stinckens et al., 2002).

Arguably, the imposter phenomenon is the consequence of a very active superego or inner critic. The term 'impostor phenomenon' was originally coined by the psychologists Clance and Imes (1978) and is defined as an internal experience of intellectual phoniness, which appears to be particularly prevalent in high-achieving individuals. For a more contemporary psychoanalytical outlook on the effects of the superego in leadership development in the work context we can turn to the work of Kets de Vries, a Dutch management scholar, psychoanalyst and professor of leadership at INSEAD, who has developed an influential clinical-psychoanalytical approach to coaching and leadership development. He (1990, 2005, 2012) refers to imposter phenomenon as 'neurotic imposture', which he recognises as being common among highly educated professionals. These individuals are perfectionist overachievers who have the tendency to self-sabotage their careers by letting self-doubt get in the way of progressing successfully.

Again, it is suggested that the origins of the impostor phenomenon or a neurotic disposition are linked to one's early upbringing. Drawing on his experience in coaching executives and psychoanalytical thinking, Kets de Vries suggests that family dynamics influence the quality of the inner critical voice and consequently the kind of person an individual becomes in adulthood.

Examples of specific family dynamics that contribute to the impostor phenomenon include parents who overinvest in their children's achievements or, paradoxically, parents who do not expect their children to succeed (Kets de Vries, 2005). Also, a lack of parental human warmth contributes to the development of the impostor phenomenon. Kets de Vries argues that these family dynamics can result in individuals being driven to excel, so as to be noticed by their parents or to meet their high expectations. Later on in life, these individuals may turn into insecure overachievers. Their sense of inadequacy and guilt can be linked to growing up in a socially disadvantaged environment. Those children who manage to advance and do well in their careers, outperforming their parents, siblings and childhood friends in the process, often end up feeling guilty and inadequate about their achievements and are unable to internalise their success and fail to capitalise on career opportunities (Kets de Vries, 2005). There are other factors beyond the parent-child relationship, including the broader make-up of the family, that can result in impostor phenomenon feelings and self-doubt. The family's social status, the child's birth order and the perception of traditional gender roles, for example, also play a part (Kets de Vries, 2006).

> **"There is one major source of illness ... and that is childhood trauma. This is true whether I talk about anxiety, depression, ADHD, addiction, etc. ... just about everything that we call illness is rooted in compensations and adaptations that have to do with childhood trauma..."**
>
> **Dr Gabor Maté,** in *When the Body Says No in Psychotherapy*[47]

At work

Many earlier studies have linked self-criticism with depression because a sense of feeling worthless can be a precursor of depression (Warren et al., 2016). Self-doubt and self-criticism seem to generate such high levels of anxiety and aggression towards oneself that, when sustained over a long period of time, they can cause depression. Of course, depression is not an unavoidable outcome, but self-doubt and self-criticism definitely have an impact on the way we see ourselves, the way we see the world around us and how we relate to others. This is particularly evident in the workplace. To what extent do self-doubt and self-criticism negatively or positively impact performance at work? Based on our own experiences with leaders and extant research, we have identified two main effects: firstly, that leaders may end up overworking to compensate for a low sense of self-worth and, secondly, that leaders may risk developing unbalanced working relationships as a result of feeling not good enough. Both can eventually be harmful to the leader him- or herself, as well as to the organisation or unit they are leading.

When considering the impact of self-criticism, the findings of clinical case studies carried out within the patient-oriented field of psychotherapy are certainly fascinating (Stinckens et al., 2002). The evidence suggests that, due to the quality of their early upbringing, individuals with a strong inner critic develop dysfunctional or maladaptive ways of perceiving themselves that are linked to worthiness. These maladaptive self-perceptions affect the individual's ability to process and filter information and develop and maintain his or

47 https://www.youtube.com/watch?v=7V5qn9dkzlU&t=98s

her interpersonal relationships. For example, these individuals may only pay attention to the information around them that confirms their low sense of worthiness. Indeed, extensive research carried out by Prof. Empson (2018) with leaders of professional services firms suggests that white-collar employees are chronically overworked, putting in extraordinarily long hours under increased pressure, resulting in negative effects on their mental and physical health. At the heart of all this, Empson points out, is insecurity and she refers to this group of individuals as 'insecure overachievers'. These leaders are extraordinarily capable and highly determined to progress in their careers, yet this is driven by a deep sense of their own inadequacies (Empson, 2018). This sense of inadequacy mixed with self-doubt and self-criticism can make them even more conscientious and ultimately result in counterproductive perfectionism.

The disconcerting aspect here, Empson (2018) argues, is that many organisations try to capitalise on their leaders' insecurities and strong work ethic. The above studies support the proposition that leaders affected by self-doubt and self-criticism tend to work harder in order to compensate for their lack or low sense of worthiness. When self-doubt and self-criticism start creeping in, these individuals tend to work longer hours, agree to take on extra projects and are over-accommodating to other people's requests as a way of compensating for their feeling of not being good enough. Needless to say, the result of this in many cases is negative stress. This is more than likely linked to the impoverishment of life outside work and the risk of burnout. In many cases, these leaders don't even feel entitled to ask for a pay rise, negotiate better terms when offered a new job or feel genuinely confident about accepting a promotion. This is true as well for other (often young) professionals who do not (yet) hold leadership positions.

Unsurprisingly, research on self-criticism has also revealed that it can have a negative effect on interpersonal relationships (Warren et al., 2016). Individuals who are highly self-critical have a tendency to seek constant confirmation from others and often feel inferior in their interpersonal relationships. This can result in asymmetric and unbalanced relationships and leave them vulnerable not only to their own self-criticism but to the criticism of others, too (Stinckens et al., 2002). In our experience, leaders (or professionals in general) often feel as if they are constantly being placed under the microscope. This feeling arguably has its roots in their own self-criticism and can result in a tendency to seek approval from their bosses. In many cases, leaders are already on the back foot when starting a new job or working with a new client and feel they are not good enough before they even get going.

The consequences include undercharging for the work they do for their clients and offering something 'extra' as a way of compensating for their own feelings of inferiority. They enter into working relationships blind not only to their I-am-less-worthy-than-others mindset but also to the consequences of that mindset. Given that self-doubt and self-criticism can have a serious impact on performance at work, it is vital to be able to explore, digest and develop self-awareness of our default mechanisms and tendencies in this context and to acknowledge when they are no longer serving us well. Becoming aware of our own patterns of thought and emotion is the first step on the road to consciously changing those patterns and neutralising their negative impact. These patterns and experiences are part of our frames of reference and what we will refer to as 'concepts' later on in this chapter. Many of the tools presented in the second part of this book can help you to become more aware of your self-doubt and self-criticism mechanisms and to behave in a balanced manner so that you can reach your full potential at work. In the next sub-section we will explore the neuroscience of the stress and anxiety that you experience when you feel insecure on the work floor, almost as if you are some kind of impostor.

2.2.2 Insights from neuroscience

In order to effectively apply the tools and solutions to develop authentic confidence that we offer later on in this book, it is important to first understand how our brain and body work in relation to this topic. This will also be instrumental in understanding why certain tools and solutions can be more effective in particular situations than others. Being insecure or lacking confidence is perfectly normal in many situations, especially when you are learning something new. The skills you need in such situations are not 'soft' skills; they are based instead on hard (neuro-)science. We like to refer to them as 'essential' skills. Some of the solutions and instruments in the toolkit may seem strange at first, but they will make more sense when you understand what actually happens in your brain and body when you experience a lack of confidence or stress related to insecurity. In this sub-section we will summarise the relevant information about our brain and confidence-related issues. Of course, we will only be scratching the surface here, but it will be sufficient to explain why the tools and exercise in the second part of this book can be very effective.

How does stress manifest itself in our brain and body?
Stress manifests itself in our brain and body in different ways (in this book we focus mainly on the role of thoughts, perceptions and emotions in relation to stress). Stress can be experienced as a positive or a negative thing and it can either help or harm us. It is regulated by the autonomic nervous system, which consists of the parasympathetic nervous system and the sympathetic nervous system. Both are active when we are in our 'normal' state of being, but the parasympathetic nervous system is more dominant when we are deeply relaxed, while the sympathetic nervous system becomes more dominant when we are under stress. In his 'polyvagal theory', Steven Porges[48] explains very clearly how the brain and body react to positive and negative stress. The theory describes how an important nerve - the vagus or wandering nerve - is crucial to how we regulate stress in our body. This nerve, which is part of the parasympathetic nervous system, plays a crucial role in regulating internal organ functions, for example the digestive system and our heartbeat. The vagus nerve runs from the brainstem to the stomach and has many side branches. One of these is called the ventral vagus, which is connected to the muscles in our face and middle ear. The development of this nerve plays an important role in how we connect with others and it is stimulated from an early age by the bond between mother and child. This branch of the vagus nerve is myelinated, meaning that it facilitates a rapid response. Another side branch is the dorsal vagus (dorsal means 'behind'), which runs down the back of our body to the lower back (see Figure 4). This nerve plays an important role when the body switches to survival mode as a result of extreme stress or trauma, for example. So what role do both nervous systems and this nerve play during stress? We will explain this by means of a number of practical scenarios.[49]

48 Porges, S.W. (2011). The polyvagal theory: neurophysiological foundations of emotions, attachment, communication, and self-regulation. Norton Series on Interpersonal Neurobiology. WW Norton & Company.

49 A 'spoken' version of the explanation in this section can also be listened at via the TedX Wassenaar talk of Jacqueline Brassey: https://www.ted.com/talks/jacqui_brassey_zoning_in_and_out_of_stress - please note that for practical reasons this is a liberal interpretation of Porges' Polyvagal theory.

FIGURE 4: THE VAGUS NERVE

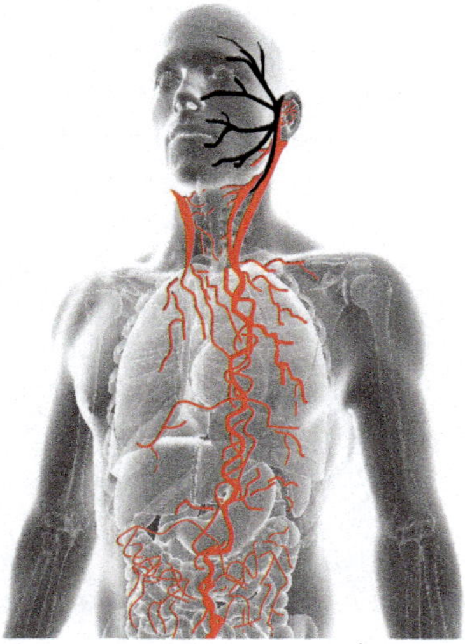

Imagine you are enjoying yourself at work and fully in the flow. You are enjoying what you are doing, feel a deep sense of satisfaction and forget all about time. At that moment you are in a positive state of calm and security and your body is optimally balanced. Your heart rate is normal, you are not experiencing any negative emotions, you feel safe and relaxed and you can concentrate fully. In this state you are able to optimally apply what you know to what you are working on. According to the polyvagal theory, when you feel safe the ventral vagus is activated. You are in your calm, secure zone.

Now imagine you decide to check your email. After all, you've been concentrating on your work for a few hours and you want to see if there is anything in your mailbox that requires your attention. You open your email and immediately see a message from one of the senior executives you work with. The subject line doesn't bode well. It reads: *URGENT - please reply immediately*. You read it, and even though there is nothing in the sentence that indicates a problem you immediately interpret it as a potentially major issue.[50] You are startled, you feel a knot in your stomach and your heart is pounding. You have done your very best on the project but your relationship with this particular executive isn't great, there's no click, and you're really

50 Actually, prediction plays an important role, but more on that later! Porges uses the term 'neuroception' but we have used a 'pragmatic' way of explaining a possible situation here. More about neuroception in the work of Porges (2011)

worried that there might be a major problem. The moment you notice that you are startled and feeling stressed, your stress system is activated (in other words, you have pressed your 'stress button'). This is a result of feeling unsafe (or predicting a potentially unsafe situation). Your sympathetic nervous system is activated (we will explain what happens in your brain later on in the section on the emotional system). In this kind of situation you are likely to experience tunnel vision, see reality more in a negative light and find it more difficult to remain focused, which affects your performance. Not only are you less able to think analytically, but your brain also sends a signal to your body; your heart starts pounding and you get a knot in your stomach. You are now in the stress zone. In the polyvagal theory this is referred to as a state of 'mobilisation'.

Next, imagine having to appear before the project steering committee because there was, in fact, a problem with your work. You have to report to senior leadership and discuss how the problem can be solved. You feel very tense in advance and when the meeting starts the knot in your stomach just gets bigger and bigger. You have prepared well but in the run-up to this meeting you did not take care of yourself, slept badly, did not eat well and ignored your need for recovery. You feel a bit shaky. You start your presentation with your heart thumping in your chest and suddenly you don't remember what it was you wanted to say. Everything goes black before your eyes and you pass out. Fortunately, this is an extreme example and this kind of thing doesn't occur very often, but what happened here is that the stress you experienced (over a longer period of time) was so great that your body decided to take over. According to the polyvagal theory, the reaction from your body is not a response from the sympathetic nervous system but is linked instead to the dorsal vagus in the parasympathetic nervous system. If the stress becomes too great and your body thinks you may be in mortal danger (even if you're not), it can trigger a response that puts your body into survival mode. You either pass out or withdraw completely from the here and now. This is a state of burnout and one that is often linked to traumatic experiences. Quite simply, it is your body's way of protecting you by pressing the 'off' button.

These three situations: 1) calmness and safety, 2) stress, mobilisation and (3) 'off' or immobilisation are explained independently of each other but can also occur in two positive combinations. A key concept here is the experience of safety. When we feel safe we remain in a positive state and in that state stress can also be positive. For example, the combination of 1) calmness and security with 2) mobilisation is a positive state. For the sake of convenience we can also refer to this as 1a) a state of 'play'. We are in this state when, for example, we are playing sports or doing something outside our comfort zone but in a safe manner. This state of play is one in which we are challenged (outside our comfort zone) but still retain a sense of security. It's a state where we can learn new things because we have a growth mindset and a place where new things can be tried because there is room to learn from mistakes. At work we would call this a 'psychological safety zone'. We can create this safety for ourselves by applying the skills explained in this book, but we can also create the same kind of safety for our teams. Safety ensures that the ventral vagus remains active even when our stress system is active as well. You can use the exercises in this book to create a sense of security in the knowledge that the exercises help to calm us down and make us feel safe. The other possible combination is 1) calmness and security with 3) immobilisation. This is a positive state where we feel safe but also find ourselves in a deep mode of relaxation. Like when we are sleeping or in a deep meditative state. Polyvagal theory refers to this as a state of 1b) recovery. Figure 4A summarises the five states described above.

FIGURE 4A: VAGUS NERVE AND 5 STATES

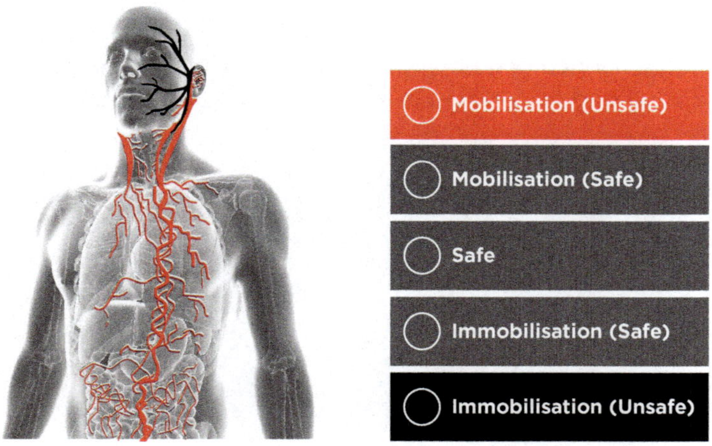

During the 24-hour cycle of day and night, we are usually in the 1b) safe immobilisation state when we are asleep. During the day we tend to move between calmness (safety) and stress (mobilisation). It is important that we are aware of this process because it can affect our health, reactions and performance, as well as our self-confidence. Our self-confidence is challenged when we are in the stress mode. This is not a bad thing when it only happens every now and then. In fact, it's a normal reaction when we challenge ourselves (or when we are challenged). However, if we are in this mode too often and for too long it can be bad for our health and we can even end up suffering a burnout (immobilisation, unsafe). If we learn to recognise this state, we can take preventative action, for example by using the tools in this book. Later on we will explain how to recognise the signals in your brain, body and behaviour (Figure 15 in Chapter 4). First, however, we will explore what actually happens in our brain when we experience stress (the emotional system) and also what happens when we have positive experiences that can help us build habits that will support our self-confidence (the reward system and the habit system).

In the above section we summarised how stress manifests itself in the body. In the next section we will explore what happens in the brain by examining three cognitive processes: 1) the emotional system, 2) the reward system, and 3) the habit system. These systems do not work on their own but in combination with each other. Nevertheless, it helps to understand the individual functional circuits first. We will therefore discuss the three processes one by one. In addition, we will also explore the topic of neuroplasticity. Neuroplasticity explains how you continue to learn and grow even as you get older and how you can 'rewire' your brain to support the development of authentic self-confidence. Along the way, we will also explain how neuroscience can be applied practically and how specific processes are related to certain types of tools in Part II of the book.[51]

51 We are aware that when we describe the various 'systems' here, we are providing a highly simplified account. We have tried to keep the content as close as possible to extant knowledge but also relevant and interesting for the reader - not always an easy balance to strike. For more technical information on neuroscience, we include references at the end of each sub-section.

The Emotional System – zooming in on the amygdala and prefrontal cortex and how 'predictions' determine our response and emotions[52]

Special contributions from Dr Srini Pillay, Harvard-trained psychiatrist and brain researcher; Chief Medical Officer and Co-Founder of Reulay and CEO of NeuroBusiness Group; and Dr Ingrid Nieuwenhuis, Neuroscientist

> **"Many people believe that certain situations are the cause of their anxiety, but anxiety always begins in the brain, not with the situation."**
>
> **Pittman and Karle,** 2015: 68

> **"An emotion is your brain's creation of what your bodily sensations mean, in relation to what is going on around you in the world."**
>
> **Feldman Barrett,** 2018:66

Anxiety is an important term when it comes to authentic confidence. The Oxford English Dictionary defines anxiety as "a feeling of worry, nervousness or unease about something with an uncertain outcome." In the scientific literature anxiety is widely regarded as a state of heightened distress, arousal and vigilance that can be elicited by potential harm.[53] This is a normal human emotional response that impedes our capacity to reach our maximum potential when we assign it more significance than we need to. When we become too attached to certain outcomes, such as wanting to be liked by our colleagues, earning an excellent performance review or winning a major contract, they can cause worry or nervousness. We worry that if the outcome

---

52 We want to clarify that in this chapter we will focus on a few core concepts in support of the evidence-based exercise toolkit that we present in Part II of the book. We will provide a 'simplified' overview of the latest and greatest in research on this topic. Therefore, it will be impossible to be fully complete and we are also aware that the research is always evolving. As a matter of fact, today we still don't have all the answers in this complex field of study. For that reason, we have included links for those who want to explore the research.

53 Shackman, A. J.; Fox, A. S. Two Decades of Anxiety Neuroimaging Research: New Insights and a Look to the Future. Am. J. Psychiatry 2021, 178 (2), 106–109. https://doi.org/10.1176/appi.ajp.2020.20121733

is not in line with what we expect or want we will disappoint ourselves or others, which subsequently may result in rejection or a lost career opportunity. Sometimes we fail to make the required adjustments or corrections along the way. The worrying involved can impact us lightly or severely, depending on how strong our perception of the possible danger is. We may fail to recognise what is important to us and inadvertently allow our worries to get in the way on our journey towards achieving a sense of purpose. Anxiety can be either helpful or harmful. If you are in danger, it can be a helpful warning sign, making you ready to respond. Often, however, when we feel anxiety (and thus worry) we 'have a sense of dread or discomfort but aren't, at that moment, in danger' (Pittman and Karle, 2015:2). Even though we are not in danger, consciously or unconsciously, the feeling of anxiety can influence what we do (or what we avoid doing). It can affect our performance and our overall feeling of well-being.

How is anxiety related to authentic confidence? The definition of authentic confidence we gave above refers to being okay with your insecurities. On the one hand, when you allow anxiety to adversely impact your performance it erodes authentic confidence. On the other hand, if you have low anxiety, stress can make you overconfident.[54] Once you are able to deliver and perform in line with your true purpose and goal, irrespective of the anxiety that you experience, you will feel that you are authentically confident. This helps you to stay in the beneficial state of 'flow'.[55] The reason we include the word 'authentic' is to remind ourselves that anxiety is part of who we are and not to ignore it by trying to artificially boost our sense of self-confidence. This is in line with the logic spelled out in Acceptance and Commitment Therapy (ACT), which we acknowledge as offering key insights into how to develop the kind of response needed to deal with anxiety (we will explore this in more detail later on).

We embrace the philosophy that suffering and anxiety are part of the life and learning and development journey of every professional. Achieving pure confidence, without feelings of worry or anxiety, is a rare exception rather than the rule. It may not even be desirable to reach that state, as moderate anxiety can be a key driver of learning and performance. So when we build our self-confidence and are honest about our experiences, admitting a certain level of anxiety is never an issue. Even when we feel confident and lean in to what is important to us, it is natural to have some worries and anxiety along

54 https://www.ncbi.nlm.nih.gov/pubmed/25705012

55 https://www.ncbi.nlm.nih.gov/pubmed/24050472

the way. If we never feel anxious, it means we are not spending time outside of our comfort zone and hence are less likely to be learning anything new. In other words, not all stress is bad.

The concept of stress was developed from Selye's 'general adaptation syndrome' but it has since expanded and evolved significantly. Stress is now defined as arising when your state of homeostasis is challenged (including both system stress and local stress).[56] A specific stressor may potentially bring about specific local stress, while the intensity of stress beyond a threshold may activate the hypothalamic-pituitary-adrenal axis[57] and result in a systematic stress response. There are three types of stress that many researchers refer to: sustress (inadequate stress), eustress (good stress) and distress (bad stress). Both sustress and distress can disrupt normal physiological functions and even lead to pathological conditions, while eustress can benefit health through hormesis-induced optimisation of homeostasis. Therefore, an optimal stress level is essential for building biological shields to guarantee normal life processes. However, not all researchers agree with this classification and some believe that the adaptation of an organism to stress is neither good nor bad but dependent on a host of other factors that make the result good or bad.[58]

Learning how to be okay with our anxiety is not easy and neither is there one simple, straightforward way to learn how to deal with stress. Anxiety is complex and can be sparked in various ways. Learning how to be okay with anxiety involves multiple perspectives and different tools that can be effective for different people and/or in different situations. In order to make this easier to understand and accept, we will explain what actually happens in the brain when we experience anxiety and what the source of that anxiety might be. We will do this with the help of a few key concepts in neuroscience. To make it all digestible we will keep it simple, so the information may be somewhat incomplete. If you are interested in a more detai-

56 Lu, S.; Wei, F.; Li, G. The Evolution of the Concept of Stress and the Framework of the Stress System. Cell Stress 2021, 5 (6), 76–85. https://doi.org/10.15698/cst2021.06.250

57 Explained simply here: https://www.simplypsychology.org/hypothalamic%E2%80%93pituitary%E2%80%93adrenal-axis.html and in this video: https://www.youtube.com/watch?v=QAeBKRaNriO

58 Bienertova-Vasku, J.; Lenart, P.; Scheringer, M. Eustress and Distress: Neither Good Nor Bad, but Rather the Same? BioEssays News Rev. Mol. Cell. Dev. Biol. 2020, 42 (7), e1900238. https://doi.org/10.1002/bies.201900238.

led explanation of these theories and concepts, we recommend that you explore the references sprinkled throughout this chapter.

Recently, a lot of attention has been paid to Lisa Feldman Barret's work on the theory of constructed emotions. She claims (along with others) that our emotions are made by us or, in other words, that we 'construct' them.[59] Under optimal circumstances, the primary focus of our brain is to keep us alive and well so that we can survive and thrive.[60] It does that by constantly predicting what is going to happen next so that it can respond quickly. We are always in learning mode, basically. Social context plays an important role in this theory. There are three ingredients that combine to make this process of prediction happen, according to Feldman Barrett: our body budget,[61] our concepts based on past experience and the context or situation in which we find ourselves. What we will explain next in a deep dive into the brain systems should be read with the theory of constructed emotion in mind. In the knowledge that we are always learning, predicting and constructing our own emotions, we can feel more and more empowered to change ourselves by broadening our frames of reference (a process that can be enabled by the toolkit in Part II of this book).

> **"...your brain issues predictions and checks them against the sense data coming from the world and your body. What happens next still astounds me, even as a neuroscientist. If your brain has predicted well, then your neurons are already firing in a pattern that matches the incoming sense data. That means that this sense data itself has no further use beyond confirming your brain's predictions. What you see, hear, smell and taste in the world and feel in your body in that moment are completely constructed in your head. By prediction, your brain has efficiently prepared you to act."**
>
> **Feldman Barrett,** 2020:81

59 See https://blog.dropbox.com/topics/work-culture/the-mind-at-work--lisa-feldman-barrett-on-the-metabolism-of-emot and https://neurohacker.com/explaining-neurochemistry-emotions-an-interview-with-lisa-feldman-barrett-ph-d and https://lisafeldmanbarrett.com/

60 And in that context the brain focuses on efficient use of energy.

61 Feldman Barrett also explains that our body budget can impact how we construct emotions; see, e.g., https://www.frontiersin.org/articles/10.3389/fpsyg.2019.01946/full and her book *How Emotions are Made* (see reference list).

In light of the ever-evolving scientific insights and dialogues, when writing this book we found ourselves at the crossroads of a transitioning period in science, one that may take many years. In the next sections we will explore a number of individual brain functions and areas that have been extensively researched and discussed in relation to emotion, anxiety and fear and that are relevant to the topic of authentic confidence. First, however, we want to refer to some critical notes from the emerging research. The first one (which we emphasise throughout this book) is that when practice meets science we need to be conscious of the fact that there is much that we still don't know. Nevertheless, we chose to address a number of key views from the field of neuroscience because we want to stress that authentic confidence and/or a lack thereof can be explained by science. It is not a 'soft' topic and has nothing to do with being 'weak' or 'strong'. It can be explained by means of various scientific paradigms. Adding these insights to this book also required a certain level of humility and a continued openness to new research along the way.[62]

> **"The theory of constructed emotion predicts and matches the latest scientific evidence about emotion, the mind, and the brain, and yet so much about the brain is still a mystery."**
>
> **Feldman Barrett,** 2018:524

Feldman Barret's (FB) view of emotion is not uncontested among emotion experts. For example, Caltech psychology professor Ralph Adolphs (RA) made a comparison between his research-based conclusions, the conclusions of esteemed professor Jaak Panksepp (JP) and Feldmann-Barret's conclusions.[63] It revealed some salient differences. Whereas FB regards emotions as non-modular and distributed throughout the brain, RA and JP think of emotions as modular and localised. And while FB thinks of emotions as being mostly cortical, RA and JP tend to see them as mainly subcortical, with some cortical component. Also, while FB regards emotions as not being

62 See also this dialogue between scientists on 'fear' and related topics: https://www.scientificamerican.com/article/on-the-nature-of-fear/

63 Adolphs, R. How Should Neuroscience Study Emotions? By Distinguishing Emotion States, Concepts, and Experiences. Soc. Cogn. Affect. Neurosci. 2017, 12 (1), 24–31. https://doi.org/10.1093/scan/nsw153

innate, RA and JP do. And the latter also see emotions as being domain-specific, whereas FB does not.[64]

These differences suggest that well-informed researchers interpret the available data differently and that FB thinks of emotions as cortical and constructed brain states that are acquired, while the other two researchers view emotions as having a strong subcortical component and as innate. In the workplace, this translates into the fact that different researchers would say you have different ways of controlling your emotions. Pillay believes that "while emotions are imminently controllable in certain instances,[65] there are many factors that reduce one's ability to control them."[66] For instance, reappraisal is relatively ineffective for bottom-up emotion, and mindfulness is helpful for bottom-up emotion in long-term meditators, and top-down emotion in recent meditators. He believes that the reason we have this degree of variability in findings is that group data cannot translate accurately for any given individual, and individuals differ widely. The more we understand through personalisation, the more accurate we can be. Also, emotions are what we observe. They are

---

64 *"Unlike a locationist approach, which hypothesizes that a single brain region will be consistently and specifically activated across instances of a single emotion category, a psychological constructionist approach hypothesizes that the same brain areas will be consistently activated across the instances from a range of emotion categories (and, although it is beyond the scope of this article, even in non-emotional states), meaning that that brain region is not specific to any emotion category (or even to emotion per se)"*, from: https://www.ncbi.nlm.nih.gov/pmc/articles/PMC4329228/

65 See, e.g., Schweizer, S.; Grahn, J.; Hampshire, A.; Mobbs, D.; Dalgleish, T. Training the Emotional Brain: Improving Affective Control through Emotional Working Memory Training. J. Neurosci. 2013, 33 (12), 5301–5311. https://doi.org/10.1523/JNEUROSCI.2593-12.2013. & Côté, S.; Gyurak, A.; Levenson, R. W. The Ability to Regulate Emotion Is Associated with Greater Well-Being, Income, and Socioeconomic Status. Emot. Wash. DC 2010, 10 (6), 923–933. https://doi.org/10.1037/a0021156

66 See, e.g., Comte, M.; Schön, D.; Coull, J. T.; Reynaud, E.; Khalfa, S.; Belzeaux, R.; Ibrahim, E. C.; Guedj, E.; Blin, O.; Weinberger, D. R.; Fakra, E. Dissociating Bottom-Up and Top-Down Mechanisms in the Cortico-Limbic System during Emotion Processing. Cereb. Cortex N. Y. N 1991 2016, 26 (1), 144–155. https://doi.org/10.1093/cercor/bhu185 & McRae, K.; Misra, S.; Prasad, A. K.; Pereira, S. C.; Gross, J. J. Bottom-up and Top-down Emotion Generation: Implications for Emotion Regulation. Soc. Cogn. Affect. Neurosci. 2012, 7 (3), 253–262. https://doi.org/10.1093/scan/nsq103

not brain states. Brain states correlate with the emotions we observe. Also, the emotions we observe may have heterogeneous correlations in the brain. To date, there are no ubiquitous biomarkers of emotional states. For example, imagine that you see two people trembling. One may be paralysed, while the other may only be acting. In both cases, however, it is quite likely that the amygdala will be activated,[67] as many studies have demonstrated that it plays a crucial role in emotional processing. It is also true that the amygdala is connected to the prefrontal cortex, though more recent research has elucidated that this connection is dynamic.[68] Hence, cognitive strategies that tap into the prefrontal cortex are still likely to be effective, though the success of the reappraisal depends on the inten-

67 Helmuth, L. Cognitive Neuroscience. Fear and Trembling in the Amygdala. Science 2003, 300 (5619), 568–569. https://doi.org/10.1126/science.300.5619.568. & Puccetti, N. A.; Schaefer, S. M.; Reekum, C. M. van; Ong, A. D.; Almeida, D. M.; Ryff, C. D.; Davidson, R. J.; Heller, A. S. Linking Amygdala Persistence to Real-World Emotional Experience and Psychological Well-Being. J. Neurosci. 2021, 41 (16), 3721–3730. https://doi.org/10.1523/JNEUROSCI.1637-20.2021. & Šimić, G.; Tkalčić, M.; Vukić, V.; Mulc, D.; Španić, E.; Šagud, M.; Olucha-Bordonau, F. E.; Vukšić, M.; R. Hof, P. Understanding Emotions: Origins and Roles of the Amygdala. Biomolecules 2021, 11 (6), 823. https://doi.org/10.3390/biom11060823. & Kim, J. E.; Dager, S. R.; Lyoo, I. K. The Role of the Amygdala in the Pathophysiology of Panic Disorder: Evidence from Neuroimaging Studies. Biol. Mood Anxiety Disord. 2012, 2, 20. https://doi.org/10.1186/2045-5380-2-20. & He, Y.; Xu, T.; Zhang, W.; Zuo, X. Lifespan Anxiety Is Reflected in Human Amygdala Cortical Connectivity. Hum. Brain Mapp. 2015, 37 (3), 1178–1193. https://doi.org/10.1002/hbm.23094

68 Berboth, S.; Morawetz, C. Amygdala-Prefrontal Connectivity during Emotion Regulation: A Meta-Analysis of Psychophysiological Interactions. Neuropsychologia 2021, 153, 107767. https://doi.org/10.1016/j.neuropsychologia.2021.107767. & Alexandra Kredlow, M.; Fenster, R. J.; Laurent, E. S.; Ressler, K. J.; Phelps, E. A. Prefrontal Cortex, Amygdala, and Threat Processing: Implications for PTSD. Neuropsychopharmacology 2022, 47 (1), 247–259. https://doi.org/10.1038/s41386-021-01155-7. & Sladky, R.; Hahn, A.; Karl, I.-L.; Geissberger, N.; Kranz, G. S.; Tik, M.; Kraus, C.; Pfabigan, D. M.; Gartus, A.; Lanzenberger, R.; Lamm, C.; Windischberger, C. Dynamic Causal Modeling of the Prefrontal/Amygdala Network During Processing of Emotional Faces. Brain Connect. 2021. https://doi.org/10.1089/brain.2021.0073

sity of the threat as well as the goal of the cognitive intervention.[69] For authentic confidence, this implies that threat reappraisal that undermines your confidence should be addressed by first reducing the magnitude of the perceived threat and then applying the cognitive intervention with deep engagement.

It has long been known that this works less effectively when the anxiety is sudden and apparently uncontrollable[70] or if a person would rather avoid their fear.[71] In fact, trying to reframe what you would rather avoid is likely to elevate amygdala activation.

The second critical note concerns how this transitioning can be translated into practical solutions. How can we keep insights and learnings that are valuable from the past and link these insights to helpful thinking in the future?

> **"In the coming years, I hope we'll all see fewer and fewer news stories about brain blobs for emotion in people or rats or fruit flies, and more about how brains and bodies construct emotion"**
>
> **Feldman Barrett,** 2018:525

69 Sokołowski, A.; Morawetz, C.; Folkierska-Żukowska, M.; Dragan, W. Brain Activation During Cognitive Reappraisal Depending on Regulation Goals and Stimulus Valence. Soc. Cogn. Affect. Neurosci. 2021, nsab117. https://doi.org/10.1093/scan/nsab117. & Ng, S. K.; Urquhart, D. M.; Fitzgerald, P. B.; Kirkovski, M.; Cicuttini, F. M.; Maller, J. J.; Enticott, P. G.; Rossell, S. L.; Fitzgibbon, B. M. Neural Activity during Cognitive Reappraisal in Chronic Low Back Pain: A Preliminary Study. Scand. J. Pain 2021, 21 (3), 586–596. https://doi.org/10.1515/sjpain-2020-0146. & Wang, H.-Y.; Xu, G.-Q.; Ni, M.-F.; Zhang, C.-H.; Li, X.-L.; Chang, Y.; Sun, X.-P.; Zhang, B.-W. Neural Basis of Implicit Cognitive Reappraisal in Panic Disorder: An Event-Related FMRI Study. J. Transl. Med. 2021, 19, 304. https://doi.org/10.1186/s12967-021-02968-2

70 McRae, K.; Misra, S.; Prasad, A. K.; Pereira, S. C.; Gross, J. J. Bottom-up and Top-down Emotion Generation: Implications for Emotion Regulation. Soc. Cogn. Affect. Neurosci. 2012, 7 (3), 253–262. https://doi.org/10.1093/scan/nsq103.

71 Denny, B. T.; Fan, J.; Liu, X.; Ochsner, K. N.; Guerreri, S.; Mayson, S. J.; Rimsky, L.; McMaster, A.; New, A. S.; Goodman, M.; Siever, L. J.; Koenigsberg, H. W. Elevated Amygdala Activity during Reappraisal Anticipation Predicts Anxiety in Avoidant Personality Disorder. J. Affect. Disord. 2015, 172, 1–7

We decided to walk the talk in this book and, armed with a burning curiosity and an open mind, to retain these different (perhaps even opposing) paradigms, while at the same time exploring the insights that we can use to develop authentic confidence. The book is primarily focused on practice and tools and on the 'how' in developing authentic confidence. The tools in this playbook and the underlying theory, which we will explain in the next chapters, have been proven repeatedly in research.[72] In this first part of the book we explore what we know today about the science behind these concepts, while accepting, in true ACT fashion, that neuroscience and related fields of research are still evolving, as is our story. In the following section we will explore research that has examined specific brain areas in relation to emotion processing, fear, worry and anxiety, and we will weave in what we have learned so far from the theory of constructed emotions.[73]

In this context, and knowing that it is not a 'simple' matter and that the entire brain and body are involved, we intend to examine what existing research has to say about the role of various brain elements, including the cortex, thalamus and amygdala. Some scientists say that the amygdala is a very old structure in evolutionary terms and that it processes all our emotions, including fear, while others contradict this.[74] The amygdala is important for survival and responds

72 By now Acceptance and Commitment Training and Therapy has hundreds of Randomized Control Trial studies published, more about this can be found here: https://contextualscience.org/act_randomized_controlled_trials_1986_to_present

73 We accept that this won't be perfect but until we know more through research, we will work with what we have; additionally, in this book we won't be able to cover all that is known in science and are making a conscious choice to zoom in on a few relevant areas, but we know there is much more out there. We will focus on what serves the purpose of this book: providing a practical playbook that is inspired by and based on science, as opposed to offering a complete science review resulting in a few practical tools.

74 See, e.g., https://nautil.us/issue/98/mind/that-is-not-how-your-brain-works

very fast when the brain predicts potential danger.[75] It can react to a facial expression before you have even consciously seen the face in question, a mechanism known as 'subliminal processing of faces'. Most of the processing in the amygdala happens unconsciously, as is explained in the theory of constructed emotions: the brain is always actively predicting and scanning. The prefrontal cortex, the part of our brain that is often referred to as the epicentre of our executive thinking, is closely connected to the amygdala and it can regulate amygdala processing (up or down).[76]

> **"It's become clearer that the amygdala plays a role in signalling the rest of the brain to information that is important to learn because it is relevant to allostasis – the brain's process of anticipating the needs of the body and attempting to meet those needs before they arise. Whether threatening, rewarding or novel, this to-be-learned information will help the brain better predict future occasions."**
>
> **Feldman Barrett**[77]

75 We want to emphasise that the amygdala increases activity on many occasions, including thinking, remembering the past or imagining the future, etc.; the amygdala is explored in this section but should not be seen as the brain centre that is only involved with fear, which is how it is often portrayed in popular literature. More about the Amygdala, Real-World Emotional Experience and Psychological Well-being here: https://www.jneurosci.org/content/jneuro/41/16/3721.full.pdf

76 https://www.ncbi.nlm.nih.gov/pubmed/20331363

77 https://www.sciencedaily.com/releases/2018/08/180821145223.htm and https://www.ncbi.nlm.nih.gov/pmc/articles/PMC6469707/pdf/nihms-1525978.pdf

FIGURE 5: KEY ELEMENTS OF THE FEAR SYSTEM IN OUR BRAIN

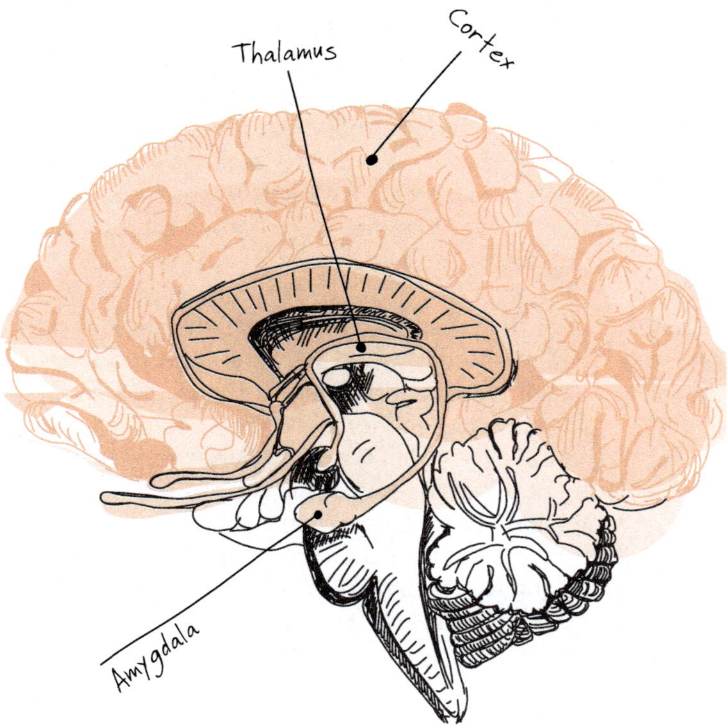

Source: based on 3D Brain app; www.dnalc.org

Keeping in mind that the amygdala plays a broader role, let's examine what the research tells us about the role it plays with regard to fear, emotions and stress response. There are many routes we can take to construct an emotion and a response using the amygdala (Pittman & Karle, 2015).[78] These can range from a low-grade feeling of discomfort and nervousness to a high state of alertness in which we essentially suffer a nervous breakdown and are unable to continue performing. Where anxiety originates exactly will be explained in the following sections.

One of the brain structures central to the fear system is the thalamus. The thalamus is a structure in the middle of the brain. It is located between the cortex[79] and the midbrain. In the brain, the tha-

78 https://www.ncbi.nlm.nih.gov/pubmed/26311778
https://www.ncbi.nlm.nih.gov/pubmed/15862214
https://www.ncbi.nlm.nih.gov/pmc/articles/PMC3025529/

79 Technically: 'Cerebral Cortex'

lamus serves as a kind of air traffic control system that is critical for relaying sensory information to the brain. It transfers the data it receives to many parts of the brain, including the amygdala (where emotions are regulated) and the prefrontal cortex (where rational thinking occurs). When we feel, hear, see or taste something the incoming sensory data goes to the thalamus, which then helps to process it by integrating it with prediction signals it has generated, prior to sending it to the cortex.[80] All of the senses, except smell, have a relay station in the thalamus. Smell goes directly to its final destination in the brain.

Research has shown that there are two roads that fear can travel in the brain: the low and the high road.[81] By the high road we mean a route or pathway that is more indirect or a longer process from the moment the thalamus registers something to when it is translated into anxiety. In this case the brain is able to 'learn' more before it responds. When you spot someone who might pose a threat to you the brain does a 'quick and dirty' assessment using the low road and a more detailed assessment using the high road. As a result, you can respond in an adequate manner and take a course of action (e.g., withdraw) that you may or may not correct once the high road comes back with an assessment. Upon seeing this person, the cortex is bypassed and there is an immediate response. The image goes from the eye directly to the thalamus and then to the amygdala, which responds accordingly. This is referred to as the low road. It is faster, though probably more inaccurate.

While this is happening, the image that is registered by the eye travels through the thalamus and numerous parts of the cortex before the amygdala processes the information and you respond with anxiety if, along the way, more information has been added to indicate that the person is dangerous. You may also change your response if the high road corrects your initial impression. The two routes are visualized below in Figure 6.

80 Sieveritz, B.; Raghavan, R. T. The Central Thalamus: Gatekeeper or Processing Hub? J. Neurosci. 2021, 41 (23), 4954–4956. https://doi.org/10.1523/JNEUROSCI.0573-21.2021

81 https://www.ncbi.nlm.nih.gov/pmc/articles/PMC4624861/

FIGURE 6: THE LOW ROAD AND THE HIGH ROAD

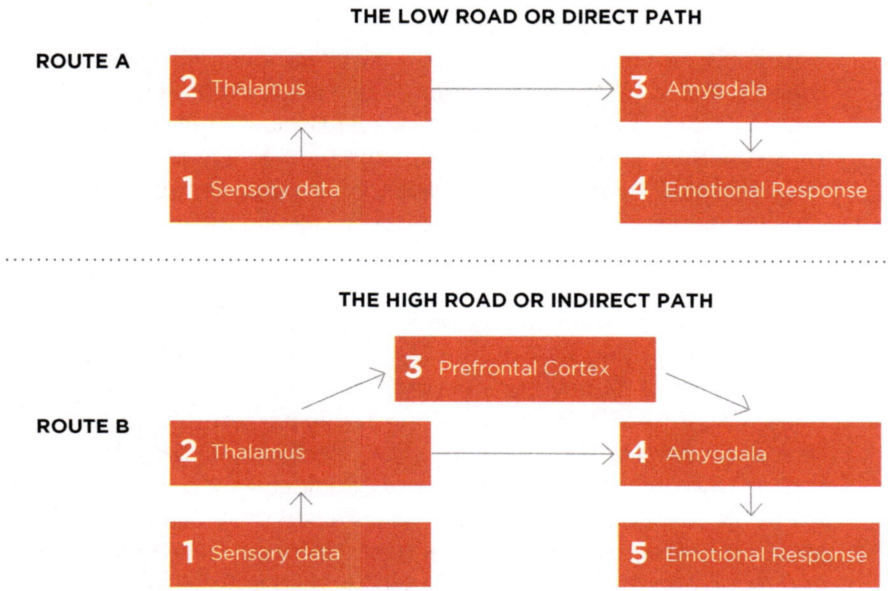

Source: Adapted from Pillay, S.S., *Life Unlocked* (2010)

Route A: the amygdala – a key to learning and prediction

If our amygdala predicts immediate danger, this may lead to the release of cortisol and adrenaline after travelling down the 'low road' or the 'direct path', as visualized in the figure above. Cortisol raises our blood sugar levels and helps us to use our muscles in an emergency, while adrenaline gives us energy, acts as a painkiller and increases our heart rate. All other related information will eventually reach the cortex, but by that time you will have already executed an initial response. In such situations, the response we see is usually fight, flight or freeze.[82]

Let's look at an example involving an employee called Jack. He is about to give a presentation to the executive board on the progress of a large-scale transformation that is happening at his company. He has worked for many long nights to create a series of slides and has put together a folder with coloured sticky notes arranged according to question and topic. When he enters the boardroom his stomach is churning and his heart is racing. When he is standing in front of the board he drops his pen and accidentally knocks over a glass of water. He feels nervous and his hands are shaking, but he thinks to

82 http://gruberpeplab.com/3131/LeDoux_2000_Emotioncircuitbrain.pdf

himself: "I prepared well, so what can go wrong?" But a few minutes in, the CFO asks him how much money the transformation will save the company. Jack panics because he was not able to calculate this figure, nor does he have a quick answer at hand. He is afraid to just make something up—he has already had a few difficult conversations with this CFO before—and he freezes. He just stands there before them unable to respond, and it doesn't help even when they ask him if he is feeling OK. After a few seconds he snaps out of it and, feeling very embarrassed, asks a colleague to finish the presentation for him.

There are several neural models that could explain this fear response.[83] According to Adolphs, fear can only be defined based on observation of behaviour in a natural environment, not neuroscience. And different kinds of fear probably correspond with different neural circuits. According to Fanslow, fear is a neural-behaviour system that evolved to protect animals against environmental threats. In Jack's case, his fear response was based on 'possible threats', likely from recalling events in the past. Unfortunately, when he is asked a question that exposes a gap in his thinking the threat becomes real. The people in the room are signified as predators in his brain and this activates a cascade of fear circuits. According to Lisa Feldman Barret, his fear is the result of a brain plan for how Jack might react. Jack's brain has prepared for the presentation based on past events. The situation itself may not be the fearful stimulus. The actual fear might reside in a past situation (or neural circuit) that resembles the current one. This process is not fixed but dynamic and it changes as the current situation changes. According to LeDoux, the fear that Jack is feeling is constructed by cortical circuits. His brain is telling him that he is in harm's way. And this becomes more apparent when the gap in his thinking is exposed. His subcortical structures (e.g., the amygdala) are continuously providing inputs, too, but they do not act independently of other circuits that carry memories. As such, the present is a reflection of the past. According to Pillay, if we integrate all of the above models, the experts are suggesting that Jack's present fear responses are a combination of his memories, predictions and the actual situation. This is useful because you may become more successful at extinguishing your fear if you

83 Neuroscience, D. M., Ralph Adolphs, Michael S. Fanselow, Lisa Feldman Barrett, Joseph E. LeDoux, Kerry Ressler, Kay M. Tye, Nature. On the Nature of Fear https://www.scientificamerican.com/article/on-the-nature-of-fear/ (accessed 16-01-2022).

can reframe the past, present and future and not just the situation you are facing.[84]

Other examples are when people suddenly become very angry and react extremely emotionally (fight) or decide to withdraw from a situation altogether (flight). The reaction is almost always regretted afterwards because the integration of past experiences, together with what is actually happening and the predictions of what could happen, are either not aligned or inaccurately represent what is actually happening.

Route B: the cortex – a thinking, analytical centre in the brain
A prediction and response is not always triggered by an external event. Sometimes an external event may not be interpreted by the brain as immediately dangerous, so the data reaches the cortex via the high road or 'indirect path'. But if the cortex, which takes past experiences and context into consideration, processes the data in a way that creates worry, eventually the amygdala may be signalled, setting off the stress response after all. For example, if someone takes on a new project at work, this information may not trigger immediate concern in the amygdala. But as the cortex assimilates and feeds more information to the rest of the connected 'fear' circuitry, they may start anticipating (predicting) many possible outcomes of the project, including potentially negative ones (based on past experiences, context changes and so on). These thoughts can create or cause worry,[85] which can trigger the amygdala, thereby prompting a response and activating the stress system.[86]

84 For readers interested in additional perspectives related to this, we recommend Dr Andrew Huberman's podcast: https://hubermanlab.com/erasing-fears-and-traumas-based-on-the-modern-neuroscience-of-fear/

85 https://www.ncbi.nlm.nih.gov/pmc/articles/PMC5472113

86 Of course, there is a process of prediction and response to that prediction. It is an ongoing cycle where more information is assessed along the way in an ever-continuous cycle of prediction. As already mentioned, this is very complicated and its is beyond the scope of this book to explain it in detail. We hope this high-level explanation is sufficient to understand the value of the tools in Part II.

It is important to note that these brain connections may operate differently in different people.[87] There are also several other routes to anxiety via the cortex. For example, in some cases an external trigger may not cause a stress reaction. Instead, people create the anxiety themselves. In this case the anxiety is the result of an interpretation of internal 'anxiety' signals. These interpretations can then evolve into full narratives that influence our thinking when we start ruminating about something. This often starts in the areas in our brain where our logical and rational thinking is based. Our thoughts can be very powerful and when these kinds of worry-laden thoughts escalate they can lead to anxiety. Ultimately, this process can become so severe that it triggers a variety of anxiety 'nodes' like the amygdala and produces a subsequent emotional response. For example, you might begin to worry about something you said in a meeting and start weighing up the reactions of others and how they might have interpreted your words, as well as the effect those words may have on how your work is perceived. This is the result not of something that was caused by an external event, but rather of something that started inside your own mind.

Anxiety can also be the result of our imagination. We can create anxiety based on images or visualizations of what might happen (which are also predictions). This is more likely to originate in the part of our brain where we visualize things and where our imagination and intuition come alive. To give an example: you might be sitting behind your desk and suddenly imagine yourself failing during a presentation you are scheduled to give. This visualization might make you so anxious and nervous that you will consider opting out, simply because you start believing you will not be able to perform well enough.

87 LeDoux, J. E.; Lau, H. A New Vista in Psychiatric Treatment: Using Individualized Functional Connectivity to Track Symptoms. Proc. Natl. Acad. Sci. U. S. A. 2020, 117 (9), 4450–4452. https://doi.org/10.1073/pnas.2000934117. & Sylvester, C. M.; Yu, Q.; Srivastava, A. B.; Marek, S.; Zheng, A.; Alexopoulos, D.; Smyser, C. D.; Shimony, J. S.; Ortega, M.; Dierker, D. L.; Patel, G. H.; Nelson, S. M.; Gilmore, A. W.; McDermott, K. B.; Berg, J. J.; Drysdale, A. T.; Perino, M. T.; Snyder, A. Z.; Raut, R. V.; Laumann, T. O.; Gordon, E. M.; Barch, D. M.; Rogers, C. E.; Greene, D. J.; Raichle, M. E.; Dosenbach, N. U. F. Individual-Specific Functional Connectivity of the Amygdala: A Substrate for Precision Psychiatry. Proc. Natl. Acad. Sci. 2020, 117 (7), 3808–3818. https://doi.org/10.1073/pnas.1910842117

Our hypothesis is that experiencing a stress response when we feel unsafe (unsafe mobilisation according to the polyvagal theory)[88] may cause an increased or stronger SNS activation and stress hormone release, resulting in our having to spend more energy on getting ourselves to a safe space. In that case, it is much harder for us to learn. However, if we experience a stress response in a safe way (safe mobilisation according to the polyvagal theory), the response will still be activated but less strongly (this process can be seen as a continuum). As a result, it is still possible to engage the prefrontal cortex, manage the stress response, learn and perform, even when you are outside your comfort zone. As far as we are aware, brain research has still not found a definitive answer, but we will explain the toolkit in Part II of this book based on the latest insights and this hypothesis.

How you respond to stress depends on a number of interrelated brain circuits that represent emotion, motivation, arousal, memory and reinforcement. According to LeDoux, 'survival' circuits may have nothing to do with emotion at all, and there may be more than one survival circuit, too.[89] Without getting into these arguments, we can instead learn that our self-questioning, when we want to change the ways in which we respond to apparent threats, may take the form of questions or reappraisals that represent each of these categories. For instance, Jack could say: What I feel (emotion) is probably a combination of my past (memory), present (incoming data) and the future (my brain's predictions). I'll breathe in deeply to stop the avalanche of arousal (arousal and stopping reinforcement). I'm here to do my best job now (motivation) and I'll welcome any reminders of my gaps (moving out of a defensive stance). However, if Jack is overwhelmed by negative memories, predictions of disaster, hyperarousal and blindness to his own motivations, panic is likely to set in as he constructs the experience of being in the presence of a predator. This activates a new system in his brain that correlates with this kind of extreme fear, of which the periaqueductal gray

88 We are aware that we may be using very different theories simultaneously that in academia would not usually be lumped together. Our approach in this book is focused on insights that can be leveraged for practical application represented by different paradigms.

89 LeDoux, J., Rethinking The Emotional Brain. Neuron 2012, 73 (4), 653-676. https://doi.org/10.1016/j.neuron.2012.02.004

(PAG) is a critical part.[90] In this state, cortical interruption may be insufficient in the moment and Jack may need more time to reset.

Keeping in mind the newly evolving insights on the theory of constructed emotions, we have summarised the key routes through which confidence-eroding anxiety can originate in Figure 7.

FIGURE 7: THE NEUROSCIENCE OF ANXIETY — THE MAIN SOURCES

SIMPLIFIED OVERVIEW OF SOURCES IN OUR BRAIN WHERE CONFIDENCE-RELATED ANXIETY ORIGINATES - PREDICTIONS THAT CAN EVENTUALLY LEAD TO VARIOUS 'EMOTIONAL' RESPONSES				
KEY BRAIN SYSTEM INVOLVED:	**A. THE AMYGDALA** • The emotional centre (predictor) in our brain	**B. THE CORTEX** • Executive functioning, anticipating, planning, decision-making, analytical center in our brain		
PREDICTIONS FOCUSED ON:	**External Event**	**External Event**	**Internal Event**	
BASED ON:	Interpretation (conscious, unconscious)	Interpretation	Thoughts	Imagery
EXAMPLE(S):	• Experience a complete brain freeze when in an important client meeting; • Extreme sweating, not being able to think clearly when performing a difficult task	Seeing two colleagues talking at coffee machine and interpreting this conversation differently	Ruminating about the meeting you ran last week, thinking you were a failure	Thinking about your child cycling home from school, visualizing potential accident
PRACTICAL SOLUTIONS SOMETIMES DIFFER PER (SUB-)SOURCE; AND IT IS HELPFUL TO UNDERSTAND THIS SO THAT YOU CAN FOCUS ON THE SOLUTIONS SPACE				

Source: the authors, based on Pitman and Karle (2015)

The good news is that we can broaden our experiences and repertoire of possibilities, thereby ensuring a broader spectrum of predictions, which makes us more adaptive in our amygdala response. We can apply 'top-down' (emotion regulation) or 'bottom-up' (by acti-

90 Franklin, T. B. Recent Advancements Surrounding the Role of the Periaqueductal Gray in Predators and Prey. Front. Behav. Neurosci. 2019, 13. & Mobbs, D.; Petrovic, P.; Marchant, J. L.; Hassabis, D.; Weiskopf, N.; Seymour, B.; Dolan, R. J.; Frith, C. D. When Fear Is near: Threat Imminence Elicits Prefrontal-Periaqueductal Gray Shifts in Humans. Science 2007, 317 (5841), 1079–1083. https://doi.org/10.1126/science.1144298

vating our parasympathetic nervous system) techniques to manage challenges that arise from a lack of confidence. For example, we can improve our adaptability or flexibility in our responses by practicing meditation. We can also manage the overall sensitivity of the amygdala to stress by ensuring we get enough sleep and exercise and by listening to music. We will discuss more of the evidence for this in later chapters. When we are in an immediate stress situation, and we are fully conscious of it, we can apply deep belly breathing to calm down our system. This and other tools are discussed in the chapter about mindfulness. For anxiety that is influenced by your interpretation of events (originating in the cortex), the tools that help you to look differently at the situation (reframing or the iceberg technique) can be very helpful. For other cortex-based anxiety, the best tools include those that help you to explore your thoughts and emotions (known as acceptance and defusion tools). To counter an overall feeling of lack of direction and focus on what is important to you (in your work, for example), basic reflection tools for your goals and values can be helpful. You will find a complete overview of the various tools and situations in Chapter 4 (see Figure 16).

For more detailed and specific explorations of cortex and amygdala-originated anxiety, please refer to the work of Srini Pillay (2010), *Life Unlocked* and Pittman and Karle (2015), *Rewire your Anxious Brain*. For more scientific introductions to the link with resilience training and neuroplasticity,[91] please refer to Tabibnia and Radecki (2018), *Resilience training that can change the brain*[92] and other sources in the footnotes for this chapter. Finally, for more about the theory of constructed emotions and critical notes on existing neuroscience research we recommend exploring the work of Lisa Feldman Barrett.

91 Neuroplasticity refers to the brain's capacity to continue to develop new connections and reorganise itself over a lifetime, meaning that we still can develop our brain in old age.

92 http://psycnet.apa.org/buy/2018-09962-005 & https://www.ncbi.nlm.nih.gov/pmc/articles/PMC8341642/

The reward system

> **"The reward of a thing well done is having done it."**
>
> **Ralph Waldo Emerson**

The next cognitive process is the reward system. When something great is predicted in our brain it sends a reward signal.[93] This system has evolved to support our basic drives, including addiction but also motivation. We all remember situations where we felt instantly good about ourselves after we achieved something great, for example when we passed our exams, won a sports game, had a paper accepted by a top journal or enjoyed a lovely dinner. We remember these events because our brain helps us to remember. Specifically, when we experience something pleasurable a neurotransmitter called dopamine is released. This activates four other areas in the brain: the places where we (1) experience emotion (amygdala), (2) remember things (hippocampus), (3) focus (prefrontal cortex) and (4) feel motivated (nucleus accumbens).[94] The brain tells our body: 'This was good, let's do it again.' We feel happy, we store the experience and important cues in our memory and we learn that we want more of that experience. This is visualized in Figure 8.[95]

93 See, e.g., also: https://www.neuroscientificallychallenged.com/blog/know-your-brain-reward-system and Carole Yue's explanation via YouTube: https://youtu.be/YzCYuKX6zp8

94 This is a highly simplified explanation but used for the sake of readability.

95 For more related readings see:
http://www.jneurosci.org/content/jneuro/37/3/673.full.pdf
and https://academic.oup.com/scan/article/2/1/62/2362763
and https://www.ncbi.nlm.nih.gov/pmc/articles/PMC3840169/

FIGURE 8: REWARD SYSTEM IN THE BRAIN

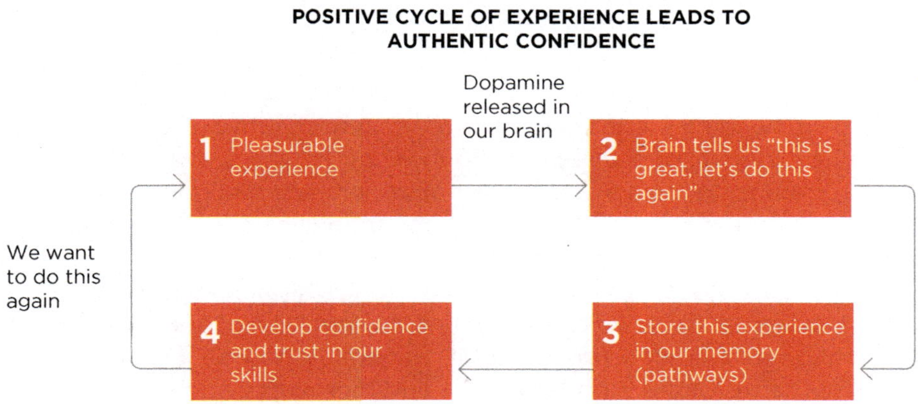

Source: authors and input from:
https://www.physiology.org/doi/full/10.1152/physrev.00023.2014

Why is it important to know about the reward system in the context of developing authentic confidence? The reward system is focused on a positive cycle of experience. Small wins and moments of pleasure help us to develop a positive cycle of experience and this insight can support the development of authentic confidence in various ways. Although fear can sometimes override reward, experiencing reward can also be a stronger learning cue than fear. For example, research has shown that you can teach monkeys a task faster by rewarding them with juice for a good answer instead of administering an electric shock for a wrong answer.[96]

Learning to be aware of and grateful for small successes will support the positive feeling of reward and satisfaction. This will help you to establish a positive cycle of confidence and trust. Breaking our tasks up into smaller, bite-sized chunks can enhance the feeling of being rewarded along the way. When we complete each piece we experience a reward (dopamine), which motivates us to continue. When we have too large a task we have few reward moments, which increases the likelihood of us becoming discouraged.

Many of the tools in the second part of this book are related to the experience of reward and the associated positive cycle of development and delivery. Focusing on positive goals, or what we

96 See, e.g., also: https://hbr.org/2017/09/what-motivates-employees-more-rewards-or-punishments

value, is more effective than focusing on what we want to avoid (negative goals). The brain has the capability to ignore negative thoughts (called 'thought suppression') but it is unable to do so when under stress.[97] Therefore, exploring what excites us in life and our careers helps us to focus on how we want to lead our lives. As we become more aware of how we want to move along these paths, we begin to develop confidence in the steps we need to take, enhancing our sense of accomplishment and feeling of reward. Also, leaning in to new challenges, moving out of our comfort zone and creating small wins along the way will generate positive emotions about those small steps forward (using acceptance tools, for example, such as the habit of saying 'yes!'). The discussion of committed action in Chapter 10 will explain how deliberately thinking in terms of creating small wins and moments of achievement when you are building new skills and taking steps forward helps to trigger a positive cycle of authentic confidence development.

There is a drawback to all of this that is clearly explained in a highly insightful podcast with Dr Andrew Huberman and Dr Anna Lembke, the author of *Dopamine Nation: Finding Balance in the Age of Indulgence*.[98] A key takeout is that too much dopamine release can cause a disbalance and that recovery is essential to stay balanced after positive achievements.

The habit system

Learning new skills can also boost the development of authentic confidence. The four stages of learning or growth that are often referred to in a business and coaching context support that process: when we learn something new we move from 'unconsciously incompetent' to 'unconsciously competent'. These four stages are summarised in Figure 9.

97 Some further readings for those interested in the scientific background: https://www.ncbi.nlm.nih.gov/pmc/articles/PMC2822038/; https://www.ncbi.nlm.nih.gov/pmc/articles/PMC3354918/; https://www.ncbi.nlm.nih.gov/pubmed/14596713; and https://www.ncbi.nlm.nih.gov/pmc/articles/PMC3779532/

98 The podcast can be found here: https://hubermanlab.com/dr-anna-lembke-understanding-and-treating-addiction/ and we highly recommend other related podcasts by Dr Andrew Huberman which can be found here: https://hubermanlab.com/

FIGURE 9: THE FOUR STAGES OF COMPETENCE

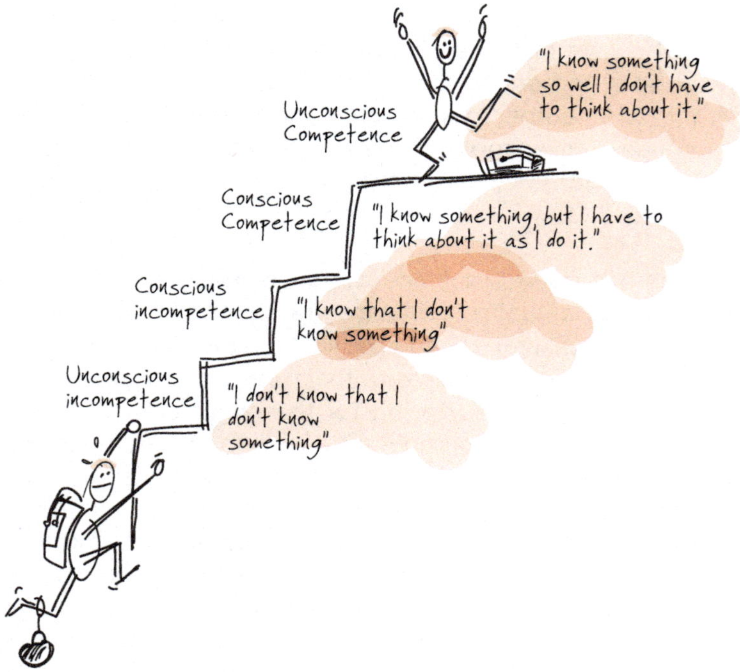

Based on: Howell, W.S. (1982)[99]

We often become aware of our need to learn something when we find ourselves in a personal crisis situation (an upset is a set-up for growth). If we really want to learn and grow, we need to be open to challenges and adopt a learning mindset so that we can move from the unconscious incompetence stage to the conscious incompetence stage and beyond.

The basal ganglia are a cluster of structures in the brain that play an important role in reward and reinforcement, but also in habit formation.[100] What happens in the basal ganglia when you are learning something new and forming a new habit? There is a well-known saying in neuroscience that goes: 'neurons that fire together, wire together' (Donald Hebb, 1949). And that is exactly what happens. When we learn something new our brain cells communicate with each other by sending and receiving neurotransmitters. When this

99 https://www.fka.com/four-stages-learning-retention-factors

100 3D brain app available for android and IOS; developed by the Cold Spring Harbor Laboratory DNA Learning Center, www.dnalc.org.

happens repeatedly, a neural network is eventually formed that helps us to learn, store and recall information. And if these processes happen repeatedly, they become automatic and that is the moment when we become unconsciously competent. The process is fundamental to both positive and negative habits and it is very important to remember this when we talk about developing authentic confidence. For example, if you find yourself in a negative thought loop, the longer you stay in it the more difficult it becomes to stop it.

Research has shown that one way of learning something new and turning it into a habit is constant practice and repetition (and also by making mistakes!)[101] Going back to the moment when we learned how to ride a bike can illustrate this process. It probably took most of us days if not weeks to master the art of cycling, starting with being unconsciously incompetent and then quickly becoming consciously incompetent when we became aware of our lack of skill. After a few days of practice we were able to keep ourselves moving forward and became consciously competent, but still with a high sense of vigilance. Eventually, we got to the stage where we no longer even had to think about what we were doing - we just got up on our bike and cycled. At that stage you have become unconsciously competent and once you have learned how to cycle you will never unlearn it. So even when you do not cycle for many years you will never forget the basics. The moment you get on a bike again you will be able to cycle like a pro. This shows just how enormous the power of learning can be. But it is also the reason why it is so hard to unlearn a habit once you have formed it. There is always a risk that you will become less open to new insights and consequently less willing to undergo (behavioural) change.

When we start learning a new skill, like riding a bike, it demands a lot of effort from our brain. But as we continue to learn (and the more neural networks we create in our brain), the more automatic the process becomes and the less effort it takes to perform the new skill. From that moment on, when the process becomes more automatic, we free up more space in our brain for other cognitive activities, meaning we have more energy left over for other tasks. This also explains why learning something new demands so much energy and why developing the skills to build authentic confidence requires conscious and committed action. Acquiring new habits takes a long

101 Listen for example also to this highly informative podcast by Dr Andrew Huberman: https://hubermanlab.com/how-to-learn-skills-faster/

time and much repetition, and lots of commitment and motivation, too. Lally and colleagues (2009)[102] found that the amount of time this takes can range from 18 to 254 days at the individual level. So, basically, this implies that you must stick at the learning process for quite some time - at least a few weeks - if you want to form a new habit. This is particularly relevant when you are in the process of developing authentic confidence by using new tools and learning new skills. It takes time and dedication (committed action) if you want to be serious about it. And it is a two-way street: not only will you be learning something new, but you will also be rewiring and replacing old connections.[103]

Neuroplasticity

> ***"You can't teach an old dog new tricks"***
>
> **old English proverb**

We have all probably heard this saying many times in the past. Today, however, we know that it does not hold true, thanks to cognitive neuroscience. Scientists have long since discovered that the human brain continues to develop and evolve regardless of age. As a matter of fact, even in old age you can change your brain and make it behave like a 20-year old's if you train it in a disciplined and focused way.[104]

In essence, what the insights in the previous sections tell us is that we can rewire our brains, at least to a certain extent. Much of our behaviour is guided by systems like the amygdala, striatum[105] and basal ganglia.[106] However, all of these systems are strongly linked to the neocortex and we can use the neocortex to alter them. We can also

102 https://centrespringmd.com/docs/How%20Habits%20are%20Formed.pdf

103 For more technical details please see: https://www.ncbi.nlm.nih.gov/pmc/articles/PMC4972342/ and https://www.ncbi.nlm.nih.gov/pmc/articles/PMC523074/ and for deliberate forgetting https://www.ncbi.nlm.nih.gov/pmc/articles/PMC4045208/ ; additionally: Dr Andrew Huberman's podcast about building strong habit's may be an interesting source for those interested in learning more about the science of habit formation and habit elimination: https://hubermanlab.com/the-science-of-making-and-breaking-habits/

104 https://www.ncbi.nlm.nih.gov/pmc/articles/PMC3983066

105 Which is part of the basal ganglia.

106 We discussed amygdala and basal ganglia in the previous sections.

alter the activities of the subcortical areas to rewire the neocortex (for example, through meditation[107]). Behaviour, practice, deeper examination, experience and even *un*focus can rewire the brain. For example, meditating and daydreaming can change the brain's anatomy. And doing something scary (by stepping outside your comfort zone) can make a challenge easier the next time around. Doing a scary thing triggers fear and that prompts an emotional reaction from the amygdala. And when we find the courage to do the scary thing we are rewarded with a shot of dopamine. In most cases we also learn that nothing terrible will happen as a result. And the ultimate reward is the creation of a new, positive memory (neural network), which makes the scary thing much easier to face the next time.

More on the neuroscience of great leaders can be found in the book *Your Brain and Business* by Srinivasan S. Pillay (2011). A detailed reference can be found in the resources at the end of this book. Finally, for those of you interested in deep dives into the neuroscience of learning, stress and change, we highly recommend the podcasts by Dr Andrew Huberman: https://hubermanlab.com/, in particular: (1) Erasing Fears and Traumas based on the modern neuroscience of fear and (2) Build strong habits.

2.2.3 How language influences our confidence – the theory

Special contributions from Dr Jacqueline A-Tjak, clinical psychologist, researcher and ACT peer -reviewed trainer

> **"Sixteen thousand—that's how many words we speak, on average, each day. So, imagine how many unspoken ones course through our minds. Most of them are not facts but evaluations and judgments entwined with emotions—some positive and helpful (I've worked hard and I can ace this presentation; This issue is worth speaking up about; The new VP seems**

107 See Newberg, A. B.; Wintering, N. A.; Hriso, C.; Vedaei, F.; Stoner, M.; Ross, R. Alterations in Functional Connectivity Measured by Functional Magnetic Resonance Imaging and the Relationship With Heart Rate Variability in Subjects After Performing Orgasmic Meditation: An Exploratory Study. Front. Psychol. 2021, 12, 708973. https://doi.org/10.3389/fpsyg.2021.708973. and Tang, R.; Friston, K. J.; Tang, Y.-Y. Brief Mindfulness Meditation Induces Gray Matter Changes in a Brain Hub. Neural Plast. 2020, 2020, 8830005. https://doi.org/10.1155/2020/8830005

> **approachable), others negative and less so (He's purposely ignoring me; I'm going to make a fool of myself; I'm a fake)"**
>
> **David & Congleton, 2013**[108]

In section 2.2.1 we learned how our inner critic comes to life and influences us in our professional setting. In section 2.2.2 we explored the neuroscience behind our inner critic, stress, thoughts and constructed emotions. Our thoughts pose a significant challenge to our sense of authentic confidence and they develop in different ways, as we have already seen in the previous section. But why are our thoughts so tenacious? Why do we find it so hard to shake them from our mind? An explanation can be found in the relational frame theory developed by Hayes et al. (see Hayes et al., 2012). It explains how we use language to learn new things by building relationships between words and the world around us. In this section we will try to provide a very simple summary of this theory, which because of its brevity will of course not do justice to the great work done by Hayes and his colleagues (see the references at the end of this book for much more detail and nuance).

The core argument of this theory concerns the process we use to make relationships between words and the world around us. For example, we learn that a little toy that looks like a puppy is called a 'puppy'. So we form a relation between the word 'puppy' and the toy. That relation also works the other way: if we hear the word 'puppy', we think of the toy as well. This is how we start learning at a very early age. The act of naming the relationship between the word and the toy is called 'relational framing'. We can then take this a step further: if we learn that the 'puppy' makes a 'woof' sound, we automatically associate the toy and the word 'puppy' with this word and the sound 'woof' and vice versa. This is known as a derived relationship. We will not link the sound 'moo' to the toy puppy because we have probably already learned that that sound belongs to a cow. So we learn that the relationship goes from A (the toy puppy) to B (the word puppy) and from B (the word puppy) back to A (the toy puppy). When we make one link (the toy is called puppy) we immediately derive the opposite as well (puppy is equal to the toy). The upshot of all this is that we can make numerous derivations. For example, if you have 19 stimuli, you can make 361 relationships (from A to B and from B to A for all 19). Adding one extra stimulus into the mix (making it 20) will increase the number of relationships to 400 (an additional 39!).

108 https://hbr.org/2013/11/emotional-agility

FIGURE 10: RELATIONAL FRAME THEORY

Example 1: Derivations with three stimuli and two given relations (4 derived relations)

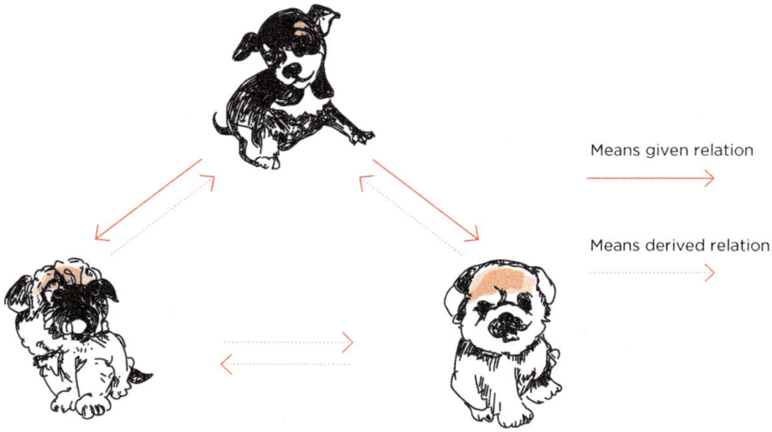

Example 2: Derivations with four stimuli and three given relations (9 derived relations)

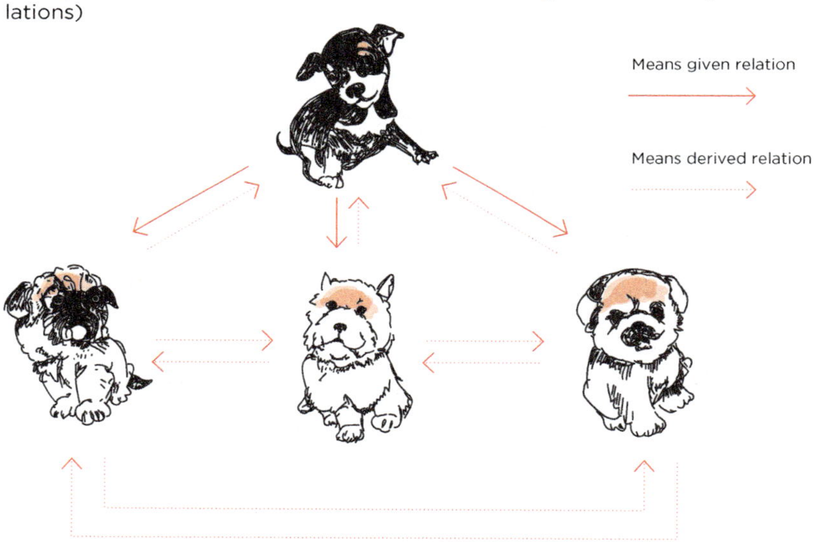

Source: Dr Jacqueline A-Tjak, key contributor to this section

The introduction and illustrations above provide a very simple explanation of how we develop relational frames. We develop these frames for everything we learn and, as human beings, we can also add the feelings and emotions we experience with regard to a specific relational frame in a specific context. For example, if we learn that 'needle' is related to 'doctor' and a 'painful experience', the next time we hear the word 'needle' we might immediately think of the 'painful experience'. This is an example of a three-way relational frame and it involves both a conscious and an unconscious process. We all look at the world through the different lenses of relational frames we have learned throughout our upbringing, education, experiences, the religion we were taught, spirituality and so on. This is, of course, not a bad thing; it is how we learn and how we stay out of trouble. If we learn that we need to drive slowly when it is icy outside to avoid accidents, that keeps us out of trouble. The challenge only really starts when the concept of value is introduced: e.g., this is better than that. Problems can arise when certain thoughts or emotions get in the way of what is important to us. Thoughts like 'you are stupid', 'you cannot do this' or 'you will fail and lose your job' can be related to so many complicated triggers and networks of thoughts that we sometimes don't even know where to start or how to explain why we feel a certain way.

If we have unhelpful thoughts or painful emotions, coping mechanisms can be triggered that do not help us to move towards what we regard as important. One coping mechanism that we often use is pushing a thought to the back of our mind. We do not want to have the thought in our mind because it makes us feel uncomfortable or causes us pain. If you have tried to do this in he past, we probably don't need to explain why this particular coping mechanism never works. For those who are still not sure, try the following experiment:

Observe your thoughts for the next few minutes and try NOT to think about a White Polar Bear.

Did you manage to NOT think about the polar bear? Probably not. In a study carried out by Wegner and colleagues (1987)[109] a group of people were asked a similar question. During the experiment, each time they thought of the white polar bear they had to ring a bell. The researchers found that the participants who were asked not to think about the white polar bear thought about it much more often than those who were asked to think about the animal from the start. This study and many others that followed concluded that it is impossible for us to *not* think about something. If we want to suppress negative thoughts, worries and anxieties, the last thing we should do is try to ignore them.

109 https://www.apa.org/monitor/2011/10/unwanted-thoughts.aspx

A second coping mechanism we often use is distraction. We try to find other things to do to keep unwanted thoughts from our minds. We know that it is impossible not to think of a difficult situation (the polar bear effect). However, trying to think of something else can cause us to build a relational frame between the distressing thought or emotion from which we are trying to distract ourselves. The result is very counterproductive: we only end up extending the network of negative relational frames to include yet another trigger. Even if we try to distract ourselves by thinking of a red car, we often end up seeing a white polar bear in the red car! So that doesn't work either.

A third coping mechanism is trying to avoid the situation related to the thought. For example, if we think we will fail to deliver during a big presentation, we may try to find ways to *not* do the presentation. Initially all you will feel is relief because you didn't have to stand up in front of the board and perform and someone else did the job for you instead. However, if the ability to give a presentation is important to you (e.g., to boost your career or reputation), you will eventually feel that you have missed an opportunity to learn and grow. Furthermore, chances are that the thoughts and painful emotions will simply return the next time you are asked to give a presentation.

A fourth coping mechanism involves another variant of avoidance: you try to 'numb' the painful feeling of anxiety or stress by eating, smoking, taking drugs, drinking alcohol, etc. This only ever leads to a double punishment: you do not learn anything and the emotions and thoughts just return each time you find yourself in a similar situation. Worse still, you can even end up developing a serious and harmful addiction.

For many people, one or more of these four coping mechanisms may appear to be effective for a relatively long time. However, they are all suboptimal solutions and may in fact result in the opposite effect: developing stronger negative relationships between triggers and unwanted emotions. In the next section we will bring the different perspectives of psychoanalysis, neuroscience and humanism together in a practical work perspective. If these four coping mechanisms are ineffective and even counterproductive, what can we do instead?

2.2.4 An integrated perspective for the new world of work

At work we are usually reluctant to show our anxiety or lack of confidence even though it is clear that everyone has to deal with these feelings at some time or other. It is often argued that there are no benefits to being vulnerable and open about insecurities at work. Stephan Lewandowsky claims that 'research into the credibility of expert witnesses has identified the expert's projected confidence as the most important determinant in judged credibility.'[110] This specific study showed how credibility was largely determined by how confident the expert appeared to be. Kay and Shipman (2014) describe various studies of overconfidence conducted by Anderson and colleagues. In one study (Anderson et al., 2012) they found that students with a high level of self-confidence enjoyed a higher social status, even when they were less competent: "translated into the work environment, he says (Anderson, JB/NvD/AvW) that a higher status means you are more admired, listened to, and have more sway over your organization's discussions and decisions" (Kay and Shipman, 2014: 22). This provides a strong case for developing confidence skills as a professional.

However, there is an important danger zone that should be noted. Confidence without authenticity and true awareness of one's own capabilities can lead to overconfidence, which is defined as the difference between confidence and accuracy. This is the so-called Dunning-Kruger effect, as explained in the much-debated study by Kruger and Dunning in 1999.[111] Overconfident people, according to this definition, lack capability but they truly believe they are competent and so they are unconsciously incompetent (see Kruger and Dunning, 1999). Research has also found that the character trait 'extraversion' is a predictor of overconfidence (see Schaefer et al., 2004). In the Anderson study (2012) this did not lead to negative consequences. Instead, it brought a lot of benefits for the overconfident students (such as higher social status). However, there is a cost attached when confidence and competence get too far out of balance and we have seen plenty of examples of this overconfidence trap in the business context.

The development of metacognitive skills (the ability to think about thinking) can be expected to support a more realistic estimation of one's own performance, as shown in the study by Kruger and Dunning (1999). Developing emotional flexibility skills to build authentic confidence increases the likelihood of you staying out of the

110 https://www.weforum.org/agenda/2014/11/whats-link-intelligence-confidence/

111 https://www.weforum.org/agenda/2014/11/whats-link-intelligence-confidence but see also: https://www.mcgill.ca/oss/article/critical-thinking/dunning-kruger-effect-probably-not-real

danger zone of overconfidence. It can also help you to find the authentic confidence required to challenge colleagues in your organisation who always seem to be so self-assured in their opinions.

Bringing together what we now know about confidence and the newly emerging world of work, we can see that there is an obvious area of tension. As human beings we are wired to critically analyse (predict) every change (in a matter of seconds and ahead of time) to see if it might pose a potential threat to us, our family, our career, our identity and so on (by continuously matching what we know with incoming information).[112] Entering the new world of work, where change is the new normal and nothing is certain anymore, requires us to train ourselves to remain focused on what is important and deal with the possible threats we may face along the way. Developing the emotional flexibility skills needed to support authentic confidence will be essential if we want to realise our full potential.[113] So how do you develop those skills? In the next chapter we will introduce an evidence-based model and a detailed toolkit.

112 In the next chapters and in the toolkit we will keep our writing as simple and straightforward as possible for the sake of readability. The underlying principles and insights of neuroscience will still apply but we won't elaborate too much on these in Part II.

113 See, e.g., also: https://www.mckinsey.com/business-functions/people-and-organisational-performance/our-insights/future-proof-solving-the-adaptability-paradox-for-the-long-term and https://www.mckinsey.com/business-functions/people-and-organisational-performance/our-insights/the-organisation-blog/its-time-to-future-proof-skill-sets-for-the-decade-ahead?cid=app and https://www.forbes.com/sites/joyburnford/2020/02/01/building-authentic-courage-the-essential-foundation-for-successful-diversity-and-inclusion/ and https://www.harpercollins.com/products/deliberate-calm-jacqueline-brasseyaaron-de-smetmichiel-kruyt?variant=40244138344482

CHAPTER 3

3. EMOTIONAL FLEXIBILITY AND AUTHENTIC CONFIDENCE

In their book *The Confidence Code* Kay and Shipman state that 'having talent isn't merely about being competent; confidence is actually part of that talent. You have to have it to be good at your job.' (Kay and Shipman, 2014: 24) We will use this observation as a springboard for a question we are often asked: '*How* do you become more confident?' There is a set of skills that can help you to develop and maintain authentic confidence and which we will explain to you in this chapter. These skills can be summarised in two words: emotional flexibility. Emotional flexibility is what you achieve when you learn to deal effectively with your emotions. At its core is emotion regulation. By 'effectively' we mean that you continue to move towards what is important for you in life regardless of the emotions that might get in your way or distract you from your goals.

The therapy related to developing emotional flexibility is called ACT, which stands for Acceptance and Commitment Therapy.[114] ACT was developed by Steven Hayes and his colleagues in the late 1990s for clinical psychology settings and has been applied with great success to treat depression, anxiety, burnout and other mental health issues.[115] Thanks to its contextual focus it can also be applied in many other settings outside clinical psychology, which has been happening more and more in recent times. In this book we apply an ACT-based approach to the work context of the highly educated professional. We have already used this approach and researched its effectiveness in the professional context and published our findings in the scientific journal *PLOS ONE*.[116] We chose not to change the original names of the six practices[117] associated with ACT's emotional flexibility concept, as developed by Hayes and colleagues, in order to stay close to its original authentic content (instead of coming up with fancy names for the sake of marketability). We believe that these

114 Also described as 'Acceptance and Commitment Training', all of it is based on Relational Frame Theory.

115 For more information please see: https://contextualscience.org/

116 See: https://journals.plos.org/plosone/article/authors?id=10.1371/journal.pone.0237821

117 ACT refers to these practices officially as 'processes'.

skills are so essential to the process of becoming good business professionals that we have tried to build bridges instead – i.e. between the underlying literature of clinical psychology and the world of business that we operate in every day. This way we can connect more easily with the scholarly ACT literature, both now and in the future.

Before we detail all six practices of emotional flexibility, we will first explore an example of a typical professional journey inspired by ACT. In Figure 11 we have visualized the typical journey of a working professional on the road towards the purpose or goal that is important to them. There is an underlying assumption here that work is part of your larger journey in life and that the work you have chosen is aligned with your life goals.

FIGURE 11: YOUR PROFESSIONAL JOURNEY TOWARDS WHAT IS IMPORTANT TO YOU

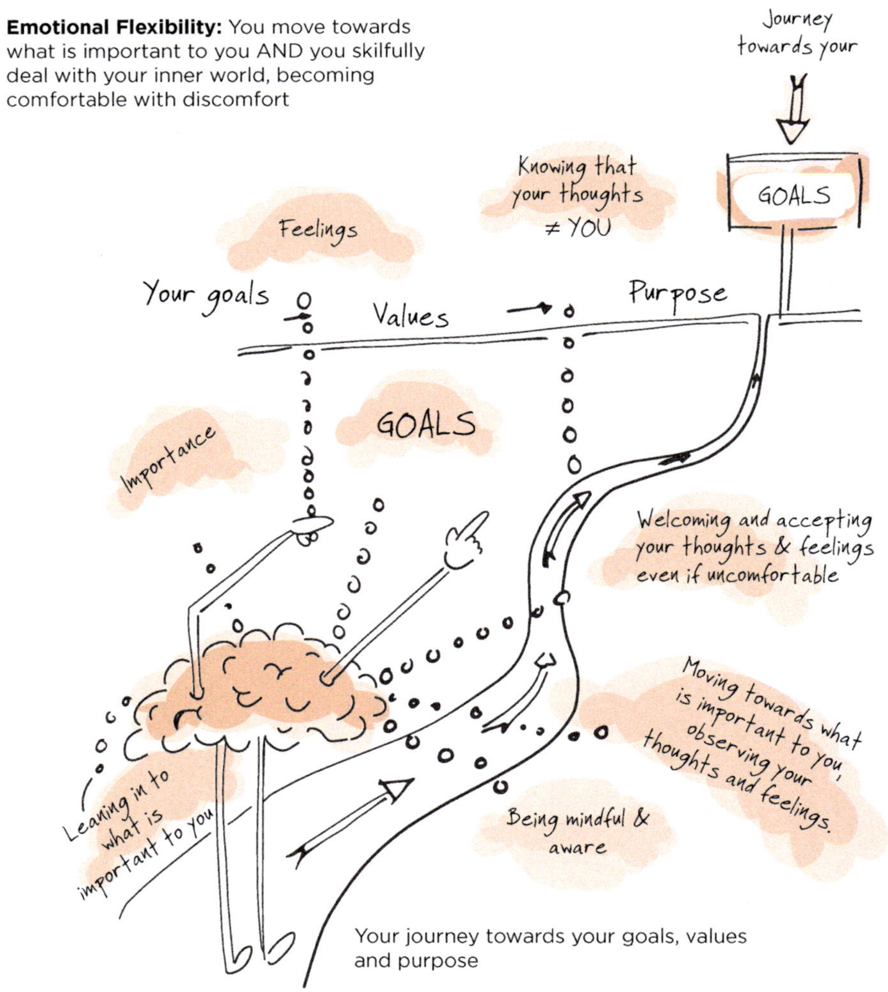

Understanding what is important to you (your purpose, goals and values) is a fundamental basis for deciding which challenges you are prepared to take on. If you understand what matters to you, you will be more able to make conscious and tailor-made choices along the journey of your career (and life). Of course, what matters to you might change over time, so it is an ongoing process of refining and reconfirming your priorities. What we focus on in this book is building emotional flexibility on your ongoing journey towards what really matters to you. If you feel a lot of insecurity and uncertainty in combination with a lack of confidence in your current job, we can offer you the tools to examine why you are in that job and whether this is indeed the place where you should be spending your time. If, through this process, you become aware that you are, in fact, in the right place, we will delve further into where your lack of confidence may come from and what you can expect on your journey. The focus will be on how your thoughts influence your actions.

What we often see is that people are not aware of what is really important to them. As a result, they end up living a life that is not intrinsically theirs. For example, you become a lawyer because your father was a lawyer but you don't actually like being a lawyer or, at best, have resigned yourself to the situation. Either way, the path you are on does nothing to maximise your potential. Sometimes people do know what is important to them but they fail to pursue their goals on a daily basis because they are overwhelmed by fears and worries. For example, if you believe it is important for your career to learn how to lead a meeting, you shouldn't turn down the chance to chair a meeting at your local sports club when the opportunity presents itself (because you are too scared to do it yourself and think you need to observe another person's performance first before taking on the task). Instead of asking someone else to chair the meeting, lean in and view this 'safer' option at your sports club as the perfect learning experience.

Of course, there are many shades of grey on the continuum between black and white - there is no 'one-size-fits-all' remedy - and there is no ultimate goal that you ought to aspire to. Every day will be different and your goals may well change over time. Which is perfectly fine. The world is dynamic and so is your life. However, you will become more aware of what and where you are, who you want to be and where you want to go. The insights and tools offered in this book are aimed at helping you to acquire the skills to develop authentic confidence and move dynamically and flexibly along this journey in a way that is fulfilling and enjoyable and, during the inevitable tough times, bearable too.

To help you on your journey towards what matters most to you, the Acceptance and Commitment Training[118] approach offers six useful practices. They are summarised in the figure below: (1) Purpose and Values, (2) Mindfulness, (3) Acceptance, (4) Defusion, (5) Self-as-

118 We use the word 'training' here because in this book we are not focusing on therapy or clinical settings.

context, and (6) Committed Action. In this book we prefer to use the word practice to emphasise the importance of the process that is required to develop authentic confidence. You will become more able to use the tools when you are committed to building a deliberate programme of practice. Some of the tools might sound strange when you read them for the first time, and stranger still when you put them into practice. But think back to when you learned how to ride a bicycle. The first time you got up on a bike you were sure you would never be able to cycle without someone's help. This feeling endured until you learned how to keep your balance. Eventually you were able to cycle without giving it a second thought. The same applies to the tools in this book. If you really want to develop authentic confidence - and in particular the emotional flexibility skills that help you achieve that - you have to give them the chance to grow and subsequently become, however slowly, habits and routines.

FIGURE 12: EMOTIONAL FLEXIBILITY - SIX PRACTICES TO BUILD AUTHENTIC CONFIDENCE

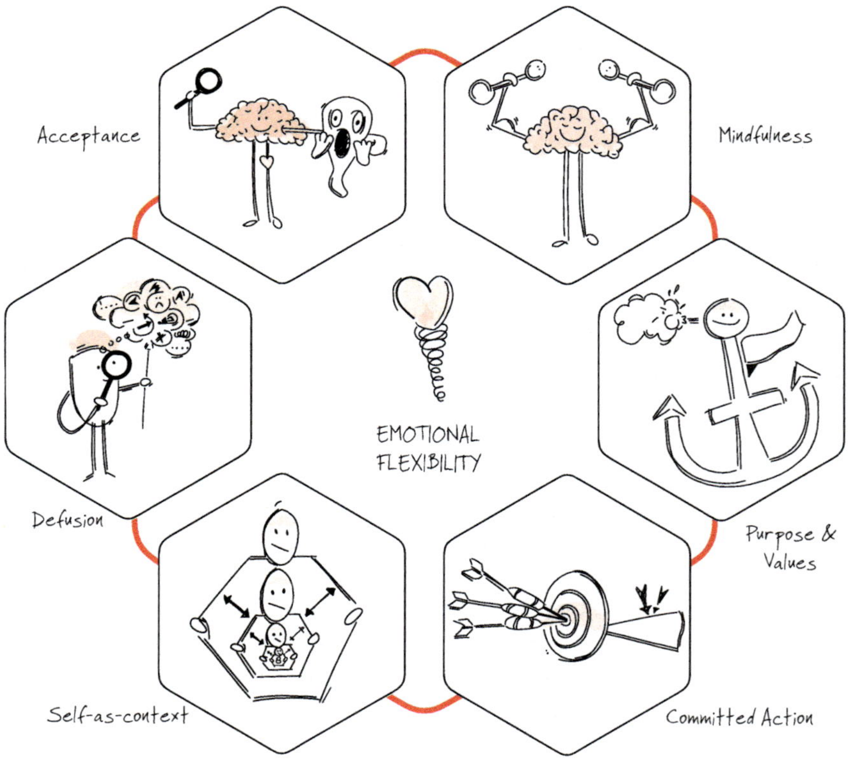

Based on the Hexaflex or the ACT model from Hayes et al. (2012)

We will explain each practice in detail in the chapters that follow. First, however, we will briefly summarise each one. It is important to note that we do not believe there is a natural sequence for this model when used in the workplace. You will learn that it is best to apply the different tools when they become relevant and in whatever order you deem to be most convenient or effective. That said, many people find it helpful to reflect on their purpose and values as a kind of foundation.

Purpose and Values

The basis for building authentic professional confidence is understanding your purpose and why you show up at work to do what you do day in, day out. What makes it worth your while getting out of bed and spending your day the way you normally do? Your purpose is supported by your values or guiding principles in your role as a leader, which we refer to as your 'leadership standards'. Being conscious of your purpose and values is important, as this forms your inner compass, especially during those moments when you are put to the test. Revisiting your purpose and values when faced with tough challenges will make it easier for you to take them on. Reflecting upon them on a regular basis will keep you fully aware of their importance and help you to stay on course.

At the same time, revisiting your 'why' also helps you to keep track of and evaluate the progress you are making. When you lack clarity on either of these you can feel like you are adrift in a little boat on a wild sea. In the absence of a beacon that you can focus on when faced with a tough challenge, your self-confidence is eroded even further, triggering a vicious circle. The tools you need to deal with such situations generally travel the high road in your brain and are based in the prefrontal cortex. They help you to reflect on what is important to you and engage your rational brain in the process.

Mindfulness (Present moment awareness)

Mindfulness (the way we explain it in this book) is all about creating a single-minded focus in your daily activities. It is about building mental strength through meditation and physical exercises so that you can stay focused and calm and able to perform at your peak in all kinds of situations: during difficult meetings, on stage, while conducting surgery or in whatever role you play in your working life. This practice lies at the heart of all the other practices in the framework and the tools related to this dimension help you to deal with the kind of stress and anxiety that travels the high or low road. Mindfulness (in conjunction with exercise and sleep) forms a terrific support system for your mental health. It helps to prevent strong emotional reactions in challenging situations and enhances your ability to keep calm in an emergency situation (for example, by doing breathing exercises).

Acceptance

Becoming more authentically confident in our abilities and in who we are is more or less impossible if we don't have the skills required to face our fears and move out of our comfort zone. When we are fearful we often try to avoid difficult challenges at work because we are afraid to fail or make mistakes. This is entirely understandable: we do not like to feel pain and try instead to bury it. We ask others to chair the meeting, lead the tough negotiation or manage the difficult project, and we stay in our comfort zone. However, growing and becoming more confident requires us to move out of our comfort zone and tackle the tasks that matter to us. There are two important aspects to acceptance: making a conscious choice to leave the safety of our comfort zone and then seizing the chance to learn. Acceptance is also about facing fear head on when we hit a bump in the road or are faced with above-average anxiety or a stress reaction. It's about looking fear in the eye, accepting the negative emotion for what it is and observing what this means in a non-judgmental manner. Doing this will substantially reduce the negative impact of fear. The tools related to this dimension will help you to deal with the kinds of fear that travel both the low and the high road in the brain.

Defusion

This part of the model is all about being aware of the triggers[119] in our environment that lead to anxiety and allow it to invade our nervous system. An angry board member, a dissatisfied client, a nasty email from a colleague, the 'what if' thoughts that occupy your mind – they can all trigger worry and anxiety. Defusion is about learning how to keep potential dangers, which are not yet real but feel real, at a distance (thereby avoiding the impact on your nervous system they normally would have). You learn that reality is never as bad as it seems and acting upon that insight helps to defuse the bomb, hence the name defusion. You distance your system from the potential danger, not by ignoring it but by changing your relationship with it. You avoid the kinds of anxiety and fear that can affect your nervous system so that you can focus on the task at hand and tackle the problem in a calm manner at the right time. The tools linked with this practice help you to address the anxiety or fear that travels to your

119 and predictions related to this.

brain via the high road and also helps you to recover after an immediate stress response.

Self-as-context

Developing the ability to view challenges from a distance - instead of trying to keep them at arm's length - is a skill that is essential for every leader. We often get so caught up in our day-to-day activities that we lose sight of the bigger picture. This applies not only in the professional context but in our personal lives, too. Learning to zoom out and look at our feelings from a distance (the helicopter view) helps us to understand what is happening and why we might be experiencing certain feelings. Putting things into perspective in terms of our purpose, values and goals helps us to assess their importance. It is often useful to create space in our lives and to take the time to reflect on what we are doing. The tools associated with this practice focus primarily on dealing with anxiety by travelling the high road in the brain through your thoughts and decision-making.

Committed Action

As with any next step that you plan to take, developing authentic professional confidence via emotional flexibility requires careful consideration of the changes you can integrate into your daily life. A very important element of this practice is the personal operating model - the modus operandi that you intend to use to achieve your objectives. It is not about defining intentions but about creating a very clear and feasible plan, with micro-level actions and a support network that you can immediately integrate into your life. This can involve taking on a challenge that you have been avoiding for a long time or deciding to follow a daily programme of meditation.

Developing your 'flexibility muscle' so that you can deal with potential obstacles along the way will help you to build the kind of authentic confidence required to surmount those obstacles. The tools connected to this practice focus on bringing all the other elements together in order to reach your maximum potential. You can tailor the focus of your personal operating model or development plan to fit the nature of your key challenges and adjust it along the way if required.

Emotional Flexibility

As already mentioned, this model is not a step-by-step process. It is a framework that brings three areas together: (a) your vision on what is important to you, (b) how to manage your thoughts and emotions, and (c) taking concrete action to move towards where you want to be. This is what makes the model very pragmatic and applicable in a work context. You can use the insights and tools in this book to deal with a variety of challenges, including the major ones related to your career or job and the smaller obstacles you face in your more trivial day-to-day activities.

Depending on your own immediate needs or opportunities for growth, you can choose to include practical steps and tools that can be leveraged along the way. Some people will already be very conscious of their purpose and values and so will benefit more from learning about mindfulness or dealing with worries the moment they arise (acceptance and defusion). Others might already be very good at facing their fears but have never given enough thought to what is really important to them and so find themselves trying to steer a course without an inner compass (purpose and values). Our online assessment tool, which we will continue to develop in the future, can help you to identify where your focus should lie if you want to build authentic confidence by developing the required emotional flexibility skills.[120]

Emotional flexibility and authentic confidence

One key question which we have not yet answered is how emotional flexibility integrates with authentic confidence. Authentic confidence comes from knowing that what you do is aligned with what is important to you, and from knowing that when you struggle along the way as a result of the anxieties you experience, you have the tools to deal effectively with those challenges. Your sense of confidence is authentic because you dare to be your true, authentic self and be comfortable with your own vulnerability. This comes from developing the emotional flexibility required to deal effectively with the stress that impacted your performance and work experience in the past. We also found this result in a study that we carried out among knowledge workers.[121] Figure 13 provides a brief overview of each practice and what they entail, as well as what the opposite implies. The list of examples is not exhaustive, of course, but hopefully the contrast will help you to form a clear picture of each practice.

Emotional flexibility and physical health

Before we conclude this chapter, one more brief reflection. We referred earlier to our recent research in which we found that when

120 www.reachingyourpotential.org

121 See: https://journals.plos.org/plosone/article?id=10.1371/journal.pone.0237821

knowledge workers develop emotional flexibility their self-efficacy (confidence) rises, too. In the same study we also looked at the physical health of these knowledge workers by examining their heart rate variability (HRV). HRV is an indicator of resilience and health.[122] We found that knowledge workers who developed their emotional flexibility (and through that their self-efficacy) also showed an improved HRV. More research is needed, of course, but these initial results show that developing emotional flexibility skills can have a positive effect on our overall health and sense of well-being.[123]

122 See https://www.health.harvard.edu/blog/heart-rate-variability-new-way-track-well-2017112212789

123 Our first paper for this study can be found here: https://journals.plos.org/plosone/article?id=10.1371/journal.pone.0237821

FIGURE 13: EMOTIONAL FLEXIBILITY VERSUS EMOTIONAL INFLEXIBILITY

	WHAT IS IT?	WHAT IS THE OPPOSITE?
	**Purpose and Values** • I know what is important to me and what I want to do • I let my values guide me in setting my boundaries • I feel supported by what's important to me when making decisions	**Lack of contact with purpose and values** • No compass. directionless • I often don't have the time to focus on the things are very important to me • I often forget the things that are important to me in the course of my day-to-day activities • I often forget my priorities when I feel stressed
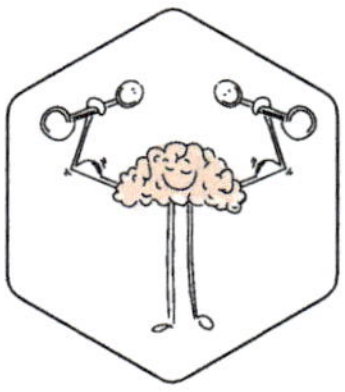	**Mindfulness (Present moment awareness)** • I am fully present in my tasks, meetings and at work • I engage fully and am able to observe my thoughts • I try to remain aware of my thoughts and emotions	**Lack of contact with the present moment** • I constantly worry about the past and the future • I am unaware of my thoughts and feelings • I go through my day without paying attention to how I feel
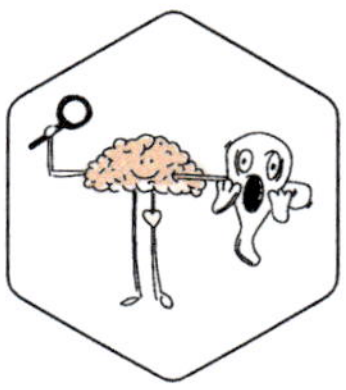	**Acceptance** • I face my fears • When I have a troubling thought I try to embrace it instead of pushing it away • I accept my own feelings, both good and bad	**Experiential Avoidance** • When I have a troubling thought I try to distract myself and push it from my mind • I push my anxieties away or just try to ignore them • I push my fear and feelings away and keep going
	**Defusion** • I see thoughts for what they are: just thoughts • I notice my thoughts and emotions calmly without becoming overwhelmed by them • I consciously observe my thoughts	**Fusion** • I identify with my thoughts, I 'am' what I 'think' • I let criticism hurt my heart • I let failure hurt me and I hold myself back
	**Self-as-context** • I am able to create a 'helicopter' view throughout the day • I can see things in the perspective of their context • I am able to take a step back and reframe situations	**Self-as-content** • I am not able to view things from a distance • It is hard to view things in perspective and context • I find it hard to reframe the way I look at situations
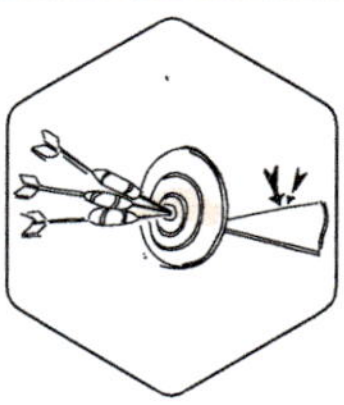	**Committed Action** • I have a set of clear, simple actions I will take to grow • I know what I need to do to develop my next career steps • I keep moving towards what is important to me, even when things get difficult	**Inaction** • Negative feelings often prevent me from taking action • When I feel stressed I am unable to do anything • I can easily feel overwhelmed by negative thoughts

Source: The authors, freely adapted from the concepts in the assessment in Chapter 4

CHAPTER 4

4. ASSESS YOUR EMOTIONAL FLEXIBILITY SKILLS – TAKE THE SURVEY NOW!

Up to now we have sought to examine the new world of work and how developing authentic confidence can help you to build a meaningful and fulfilling career. Before we dive deeper into the details, it may be helpful to take a survey so that you can see how you are already applying the skills associated with emotional flexibility in your daily life.

4.1 The survey

Please use the following instructions to complete the questionnaire:

1. Go to our free survey at http://www.reachingyourpotential.org/[124] under the heading Authentic Confidence. This test is based on a validated survey for emotional flexibility and inflexibility (Rolffs et al., 2016).[125] The QR code is:

2. When you submit your answers follow the instructions to receive your results.

124 Many thanks to Dr Martina Bender for facilitating the development of this website and to C.J. Wever and S.J.A. van der Voort, students of Computer Science and Engineering at the TU Delft, The Netherlands for the update, development and activation of the questionnaire and automatic reports. Many thanks also to Paul Stroet, PhD Candidate Business Data Science at VU Amsterdam, The Netherlands, for his continuous support in maintaining and updating the website. www.paulstroet.netlify.app

125 https://couples-research.com/wp-content/uploads/2017/06/Rolffs-Rogge-Wilson2016.pdf and https://www.researchgate.net/publication/303471074_The_Multidimensional_Psychological_Flexibility_Inventory_MPFI

4.2 Reading the results

Now that you have your results, how should you interpret, understand and use them? If you look at the results, for every process you will see a score somewhere between five and thirty points. The minimum number of points that you can score per dimension is five, the maximum is thirty. Your score is based on the five questions you answered about a practice, both for the flexible and inflexible side. For each question you can score a maximum of six points, that is, if you agreed fully with a proposition. However, if you completely disagree with a proposition, you receive only one point. If you neither agree nor disagree, you get three points. An average of more than fifteen points means that you agree more often with the propositions linked to a practice. In other words, in your experience you are likely to exhibit more of the characteristics of that practice in real life. If your score is under fifteen, it means you disagree more often with the various propositions and you probably exhibit less of the characteristics of that specific practice. The example in Figure 14 shows the results for a fictitious participant, D.

The results in Figure 14 reveal a trend among the participants in our survey. To be clear: the results do not represent a benchmark. You can take the results (including your own) at face value and see what they mean to you specifically. Up until now we have seen that most participants score higher for purpose and values and for committed action compared with the other processes (and at the same time lower for their counterparts on the emotional inflexibility side). Our experience is that the participants in our workshops find it harder to apply the processes of mindfulness, acceptance, defusion and self-as-context. Out of these four practices, they are most familiar with mindfulness and self-as-context but they tend not to apply them very well. They are not skilled in the tools and/or are unaware of the connection between these practices and how they support the development and maintenance of authentic confidence. Acceptance and defusion are usually new concepts for the majority of participants. It is no surprise therefore that the scores for the other practices are relatively low compared with meaning and values and committed action. However, it is still useful to collate all of the results for the different practices because it is important to be able to understand the connections between them. As we have already pointed out, knowing what is important to you helps you to stay on track and to understand why you wish to take on certain challenges. It also supports your choices regarding committed action. The beauty of this model lies in the fact that it brings all of the different practices together.

Interpreting the results

Below we will use the actual survey questions to tell a story about a fictional professional and use it to explain and illustrate the different practices. Let's assume that the fictitious participant D from Figure 14 is a female professional in a senior position. The first spider diagram in Figure 14 shows her emotional flexibility with the various dimensions and the second her emotional inflexibility.

FIGURE 14: RESULTS SPIDER GRAPH - FICTITIOUS PARTICIPANT D

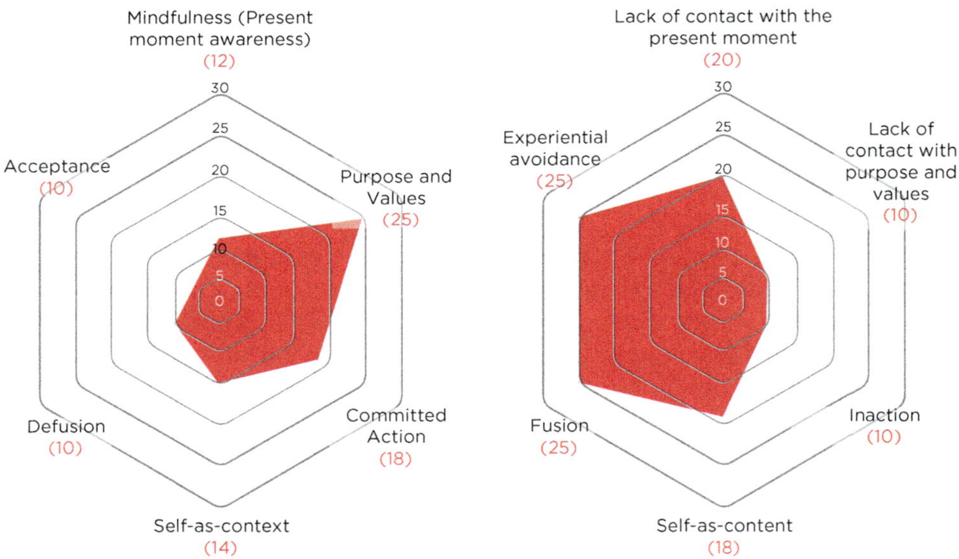

We first look at her highest score, namely for purpose and values and its counterpart, lack of contact with purpose and values. This professional agrees more often than not with the proposition that she has a clear idea of what is important to her in life. At work she makes decisions that are in line with the things that are important to her. She recently completed a leadership development programme where this issue was discussed. It has given her new energy and she uses her new insights regarding what really matters to her as an inner compass to guide her decision-making and takes the time to reflect regularly on that process. Her role in the company is in line with the company's values - as Director of Sustainability her focus is on the sustainable impact of the organisation. She agrees that family and friends are all-important and she finds life very much worth living. She feels supported by others and realises that their actions are the result of their own choices. She believes her life to be relatively in balance. And while she can still grow in this process (to a maximum of thirty points), she has come a long way so far with her 25 points. Although emotional inflexibility is not the exact counterpart of emotional flexibility (psychometrically, the correlation is not a perfect 100 per cent), a contrasting pattern can often be identified. Research suggests that increased emotional flexibility is strongly related to increased well-being, whereas lower emotional inflexibility is more associated with lower psychological stress (see, e.g., Stabbe et al., 2019; Rogge et al., 2019; Peltz et al., 2020).[126] Exercises for improving emotional flexibility can also be very useful for reducing emotional inflexibility. A contrasting pattern is visible here, too. Our professional's score for the opposite of values (lack of contact with values) is a below-average ten points. This indicates that she rarely loses sight of her priorities and values. It amplifies the total score and shows that she has a strong foundation when it comes to this particular practice.

Participant D's second highest score is for committed action. With eighteen points out of thirty she is more often in agreement with the propositions than she is in disagreement. We can assume that she has a clearly defined way of working and that she continually appraises her methods in order to keep them in line with what is most important to her. In her role as a senior professional, this may mean that she has a clearly defined working model that is focused on what she finds important and which roles she wishes to fulfil at work, as well as on how she can best renew and use her energy to achieve this. She seeks out new experiences and learning opportunities to meet the changing demands of markets and customers. She is good at dividing long-term goals up into short-term opportunities. She likes to take on new challenges and make concrete plans for her role and career. If she wants to achieve something at work, she just goes for it. Consequently, her score for inaction is quite low (ten points). This means, according to this survey, that she doesn't allow herself to become distracted by negative feelings or thoughts and knows how to keep herself on track.

126 Stabbe, O. K., Rolffs, J. L., & Rogge, R. D. (2019). Flexibly and/or inflexibly embracing life: Identifying fundamental approaches to life with latent profile analyses on the dimensions of the Hexaflex model. Journal of Contextual Behavioral Science, 12, 106-118. And https://www.sciencedirect.com/science/article/abs/pii/S2212144718302229; https://www.sciencedirect. com/science/article/abs/pii/S2212144719300274; https://www.ncbi.nlm.nih.gov/pmc/articles/PMC7382960/

Participant D scores low for both acceptance and defusion: ten points out of thirty. At the same time, her scores for the counterparts of these practices are quite high (both 25). In the case of acceptance this means that she probably has trouble dealing with difficult thoughts and feelings. She is aware of this and does not feel confident enough to show her real feelings, which is why she hides those feelings not only from her colleagues at work but also from herself. She does her best to avoid negative experiences and believes that thoughts ought to be kept under control (experiential avoidance). She tries to ignore her inner critic, which is very tiring because it is always distracting her. Her thoughts and feelings prevent her from performing at her peak. Participant D often feels overwhelmed by her thoughts and is insufficiently in the here and now to be able to focus on the task at hand. She tries to listen to what others say but often doesn't really hear them and finds it difficult to make connections on the right level with others. Her tendency to worry is a major obstacle but she refuses to confront her own worries and fears. She also tends not to listen to or act upon feedback because she finds it scary and difficult to do so. Participant D spends a lot of time casting doubt upon the opinions of others. She doesn't like recalling unpleasant experiences at work (for example, mistakes she has made). Whenever negative thoughts rise to the surface she just pushes them back down under. She blocks out painful feelings at work because she is afraid they might otherwise never go away. Participant D worries a lot about things that went wrong in the past and things she could have done better.

The scores for defusion are also relatively low for participant D (correspondingly, the results for fusion are quite high). Defusion is closely related to acceptance. These two practices can often be combined and sometimes go hand in hand. Given her low scores for acceptance and defusion, participant D probably finds it difficult to deal with harsh comments from colleagues or customers and to observe them from a distance without becoming overly emotional. She can get very upset by comments made by others. She sometimes finds it difficult to perform well when she experiences distressing thoughts and feelings. This makes her feel insecure and, as a result, she finds it hard to concentrate, which makes it harder for her to focus fully on what is being said in meetings. Her emotions get in the way of her performance. She suffers from the feeling that she can't see the forest for the trees anymore and can react quite strongly to her own negatives thoughts, firmly convinced that they are true. If someone makes an unpleasant comment at work, it can have a lengthy emotional impact on her. She often identifies with her loudest inner critics and is quick to make a mountain out of a molehill.

The scores for mindfulness and self-as-context are also not very high (with a corresponding pattern for their counterparts). The results for mindfulness or present moment awareness indicate the extent to which you are able to concentrate and whether you are often distracted by your inner voice. They show whether you are able to be fully present at work and remember the most important things that have been discussed in a meeting as opposed to being constantly distracted. Can you be 'in the moment' and mentally present when you have to focus on a task? Are you able to clearly articulate your beliefs and opinions at work and focus on what is happening in the here and now? Can you find the words to describe your thoughts easily? The answers to these questions reveal your ability to stay focused at work and remain in a state of mindful flow. It appears that participant D is less successful in this regard. She is aware that she is often mentally preoccupied either with the past (what went wrong) or the future (what could go wrong) instead of the here and now (lack of present moment awareness).

The dimension self-as-context relates to the ability to view things from a broader perspective. Given her relatively low score, participant D obviously finds it hard to accept her failings. She suffers from tunnel vision and that makes it harder for her to put things into perspective. She finds it difficult to zoom in and out. She needs to distance herself from the details sometimes and take a helicopter view of the situation. Participant D also focuses too much on her negative self-image. She would benefit from a better understanding of who she is as a person, independent of her job title or the role she plays at work. It's also about being compassionate towards yourself (which also involves acceptance) by understanding who you are. The counterpart self-without-context scores higher. Participant D often criticises herself and finds it hard to see things from another angle. Taken together, participant D's scores indicate that improving her emotional flexibility would be of great help to her, as it is strongly related to many positive work outcomes, including performance, emotional well-being, self-efficacy[127] and reduced anxiety (see also Brassey et al., 2020, and Flaxman et al., 2013 for a comprehensive review).

127 We have already discussed self-efficacy. It is more or less an academic term for 'self-confidence'. Work-related self-efficacy refers to the belief in your capability to perform a certain task.

Working on improving these skills in the context of your professional life can help you build the authentic confidence required to spot and avail of the opportunities that come along in the course of your career, as well as to lean in at work, speak up during meetings, give feedback when you need to or go on stage and give a presentation in front of a large audience. Knowing that you can use these practices and tools when you are feeling anxious or lacking in confidence can give you the energy to meet your challenges even when they make you feel uncomfortable. This can be very empowering. In the next chapters we will introduce a toolkit that is linked to these six practices. Of course, there is more to building authentic confidence than just dealing with your thoughts and emotions and you can learn other important skills, too. In Chapter 11 we will discuss a number of additional key skills that will help you tackle the tasks that many people try to avoid when they lack confidence, as we found in our research. These skills are related to (1) lifelong learning, (2) courageous conversations, (3) providing feedback, (4) speaking up in meetings, and (5) effective presentation tips and techniques.

How can I leverage my survey results?

The results of your assessment hold up a mirror to you, one in which you can see which practices in the field of emotional flexibility are worth developing. Our expectation is that people will benefit most from a holistic approach (instead of choosing just a few of the practices and then hoping for the best) simply because the six practices form a web in which they can interact with each other. That is why we advise you to take all of the practices into consideration and to focus initially on the ones you find most difficult. Figures 15 and 16 can help you to identify the problematic situations you wish to work on.

FIGURE 15: THE PROBLEM SITUATION: PLAIN SAILING, BUMPY RIDE OR SUDDEN CRASH?

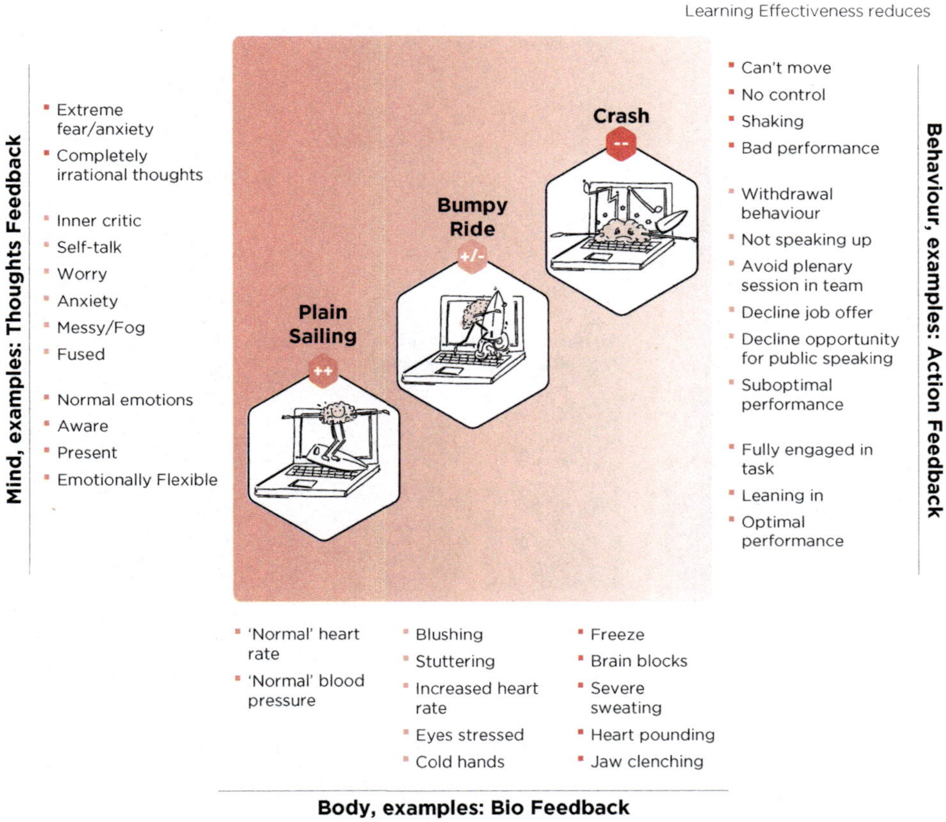

Source: the authors

The figures show the interaction between mind, body and behaviour. Becoming aware of what is happening in your mind and how it interacts with your bodily sensations, feelings and emotions, as well as the behaviour you exhibit in certain situations, is an important step in the process of reflecting on whatever challenge you are facing. Hopefully you will eventually find yourself in the plain sailing zone more often, but there will always be lots of bumpy rides and even sudden crashes along the way e.g., when you predict that you may be in danger.

FIGURE 16: WHAT IS THE SITUATION IN WHICH YOU WANT OR NEED HELP?

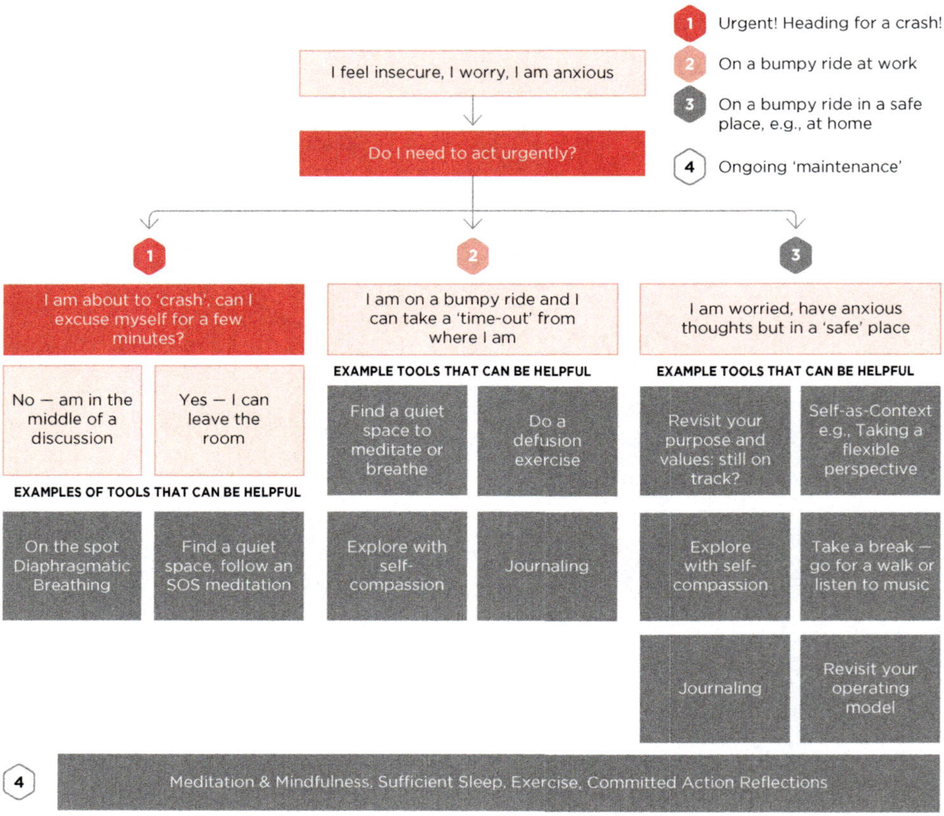

To locate where you stand in Figures 15 and 16, answer the following questions:

1. Looking again at your survey results, in which areas could you benefit the most? Where are your lowest scores?

2. When you reflect on your most challenging situations, where are the bumpy rides and when are you most in danger of a sudden crash?

3. If you have identified a problematic situation that you want to focus on, reflect on how quickly you need to act: do you have to intervene urgently or do you have the space to take a time-out?

Next, with the answers to this set of questions in mind, look at the overview provided in Figure 17, which presents all of the tools in the playbook described in Part II of this book. If you are used to experiencing potential sudden crashes at work every now and then (moments when you really have to move out of your comfort zone or when stress levels become very high), you will benefit most from the tools related to the processes of mindfulness, acceptance and defusion. However, you should note that these tools work best when you also pay enough attention to developing your overall mental and emotional flexibility or emotional fitness. Developing a comprehensive maintenance system using the exercises in category 4 (see Figure 17) can be very helpful.

FIGURE 17: WHICH TOOLS ARE MOST HELPFUL FOR YOUR SITUATION?

	TOOLS DESCRIPTION	TOOLS MOST HELPFUL WHEN:
PURPOSE & VALUES	5.4.1 Becoming self-authoring	3 4
	5.4.2 Ikigai	3 4
	5.4.3 Core values	3 4
	5.4.4 Best self aspiration	3 4
	5.4.5 Strengths	3 4
	5.4.6 Gratitude reflections	2 3 4
MINDFULNESS	6.4.1 Pause button	1 2
	6.4.2 Diaphragmatic breathing	1 2
	6.4.3 Mindfulness for busy people	2 3 4
	6.4.4 Mindfulness throughout working day	2 3 4
	6.4.5 Mindful voice techniques	2 3
	6.4.6 Sleep	3 4
	6.4.7 Exercise	3 4
ACCEPTANCE	7.4.1 Growth vs fixed mindset	2 3
	7.4.2 Self-Compassion	2 3
	7.4.3 Year of Yes	3 4
	7.4.4 Anxiety reappraisal	2
	7.4.5 Acceptance in action	1 2

TOOLS DESCRIPTION	TOOLS MOST HELPFUL WHEN:	
8.4.1 Observe thoughts and let go	1 2	DEFUSION
8.4.2 Naming inner critic	2	
8.4.3 Bubble technique	2	
8.4.4 Psychological halloweenism	2	
8.4.5 Voice techniques for defusion	2 3	
9.4.1 Journaling everywhere you go	2 3 4	SELF-AS-CONTEXT
9.4.2 Your iceberg	3 4	
9.4.3 Ambidexterity	2 3	
9.4.4 Taking a flexible perspective	2 3	
10.4.1 Matrix for advancing authentic confidence	3 4	COMMITTED ACTION
10.4.2 Operating model to develop authentic confidence	3 4	
10.4.3 Mitigating excuses	3 4	
10.4.4 Personal board	3 4	
10.4.5 Employ a coach	3 4	

1 In need of urgent help! You might be heading for a crash!

2 On a bumpy ride at work, in a meeting, in the performance arena

3 On a bumpy ride, but in a safe/private place

4 Search for ongoing maintenance tools

The next part of this book will guide you through the practical tools attached to the six practices of emotional flexibility that support the building of authentic confidence. You can regard the second part of the book as a 'self-help' toolkit (or use it together with your professional coach).

At certain periods in your life you may need additional help in developing these skills, often as a result of negative experiences. This is entirely normal. Many business executives, top athletes and successful artists regularly consult an external coach or therapist to help them take the required steps forward. If you are interested in getting extra support, please read our section about finding a coach (10.4.5). This book is meant to assist you on your personal development journey towards authentic confidence. It is not meant as a replacement for mental health care. If you are experiencing mental health problems, we recommend that you seek professional help.

PART II
TAKING ACTION

SIX PRACTICES AND ADDITIONAL SKILLS

"The most effective way to do it, is to do it."
Amelia Earhart

INTRODUCTION

Introduction to the practices and tools

In the following chapters you will find several tools for each of the six practices for building emotional flexibility, as well as an additional chapter on other skills relevant to developing authentic confidence. Each tool will be described in a synthesized manner. However, there is often much more information about a tool that is worth sharing and where that is the case we have added relevant sources for further exploration. We recommend that you read the introduction sections of each practice first to find out where you are likely to benefit the most. There is no need to read through all of the tools from start to finish. You can travel through the chapters in whatever order you like and start with those topics that resonate most with you. In this iterative process the results of your assessment and your own immediate needs are a good starting point. It is also a good idea to keep a personal journal containing your thoughts and reflections as you go along. We have provided space at the back of this book where you can take notes. Or you can use your own separate personal journal if you wish.

CHAPTER 5

5. PRACTICE 1 – PURPOSE AND VALUES

let go
of all your leaves
before spring arrives.
it takes a bare soul
to bloom again.
|soils. |

you are built
to stay firm
but your light
is supposed
to take you
places.
| a lighthouse
is not a home. |

maybe the construct of
happiness is so abstract
we need to keep breaking
it to feel
what it's made of.
| under
construction. |

the salt
in you
keeps you afloat
but will always
sting your wounds
every time
you hit
rock bottom.
| drifting away. |

when their sins
get you down
on your knees
and draw you closer
to the soils
you spring from
it is mother nature
who works in mysterious ways
rooting for you
when you have nothing left
to lose.
| you grow
at breaking points. |

i am like water.
I can burn
and still be
the one thing
you cannot
live without.
|keep it cool. |

grow wild
and nurture your roots
a hungry heart
does not become
full
when fed
into insecurities.
|wall flower. |

they will come
into your life
and make you feel
you are at a point
of no return.
| do not change
a point
into a circle. |

to some
these words
mean nothing.
and they are read
simply out of curiosity
of what could go on
inside another's head.
some will take these words
and mock the existence
of the writer.
some will pick up on these words
and weigh them up to their
material value.
some will take them
places where they
hit rock bottom.
these words
have given me
everything
i lost
when i saw them
lying
on the lips of those
whose voices
turned silent when
i needed them to be heard.
|when the world
conspires to
turn you into
someone you
never dared to be.
catharsis. |

Noor Intisar, former Campus Poet, University of Antwerp

5.1 What do we mean by the practice of purpose and values?

If you do not know where you are going, what is important to you and what you are good at, every challenge, worry and anxiety will cost you energy without bringing you any nearer to your goal. Knowing what matters to you is the foundation for personal effectiveness and fulfilment. Hayes et al. (2012) describe this practice as one that is primarily focused on forging a connection with your values. Values are at the core of this and they are closely connected to your purpose and an understanding of your strengths.

For the purposes of this book, we have chosen to address not only the subject of values but also to include other elements like purpose, vision of success, strength awareness and gratitude as well. When we talk about purpose we are referring to the reason for adopting a holistic way of living. In our opinion, your purpose should be one that covers all aspects of your life: who you want to be as a business professional, as a family member, as a parent, as a community member, as a friend and so on.

It's about understanding why you get up in the morning (Ikigai), how you want to fulfil the different roles in your life (your core values) and connecting these to where you believe you are heading in life (your vision of your best self). Affirming this and the things you are grateful for on a daily basis helps you to stay tuned in, aware and focused. In the next section we will present a broader framework for your personal development as a professional. It is your job to figure out what is important to you within that framework.

5.2 Why develop skills to define your purpose and values?

> **"If you don't know where you are going, any road can take you there."**
>
> **Lewis Carroll,** *Alice in Wonderland*

The above quote pretty much sums up why the element of emotional flexibility is so important when building authentic confidence. Taking ownership of your life and career is the best favour you can do yourself, all the more so because you are the best person to ask why you are here to do the work you do. If you let others make decisions for you, you will eventually end up somewhere you would rather not be in your career. Conversely, spending your life in places where you feel lots of energy and passion is more likely to make you happy and fulfilled. In their work, the adult development psychologists Robert Kegan and Lisa Lahey (2009) describe the five stages of development that can help to clarify the transformation required to achieve a high and stable level of authentic confidence: (1) the impulsive mind, (2) the imperial mind, (3) the socialized mind, (4) the self-authoring mind, and (5) the self-transforming mind.

According to Kegan and Lahey, around 58% of the population have not (yet) reached stage 4[128], which refers to the self-authoring mind.[129] This is visualized in Figures 18 and 19. The first figure shows the different stages of adult development, as defined in two studies conducted by Kegan (1998). Adults develop at different stages over time. The vertical axis shows the level of mental complexity that is required in each stage. In the words of Kegan and Lahey, "the complexity of a mindset is a function of the way it distinguishes the thoughts and feelings we have (i.e., can look at, can take as object) from thoughts and feelings that 'have us' (i.e., we are run by them, are subject to them). Each different level of mindset complexity differently draws the line between what is subject and what is object.

---

128 As you can see in Figure 18, both studies add up to around 58% for everything below the flat curve in stage 4, the self-authoring mind. Study A had an *n* of 342, and the percentages are presented above the curved line in the graph: 5%+8%+14% and 32%= 59%. Study B, with an *n* of 497, is presented below the curved line: 1%+2%+8%+47%=58%.

129 We want to emphasise that these studies were carried out some time ago; we don't have updated evidence to show what these percentages would be today.

Greater complexity means being able to look at more (take more as object). The blind spot (which is subject) becomes smaller and smaller." (Kegan and Lahey, 2009: 61, E-book version).

When you are at the stage below the self-authoring mind you are strongly influenced by what others think (authority, knowledge and other external standards and sources of information, including friends, family members and colleagues). In this stage you are able to understand what you want and who you are, but you are still living your life according to what others expect of you and are heavily impacted by your surroundings. This is not the only stage where you can experience worries and anxiety, but it may be the stage where your behaviour is most affected by your worries and insecurities. This can happen consciously and/or unconsciously. If you are living your life primarily in this stage, becoming aware of that fact is the first step towards the next stage of development (and 'freedom'): the self-authoring mind.

FIGURE 18: STAGES OF ADULT DEVELOPMENT

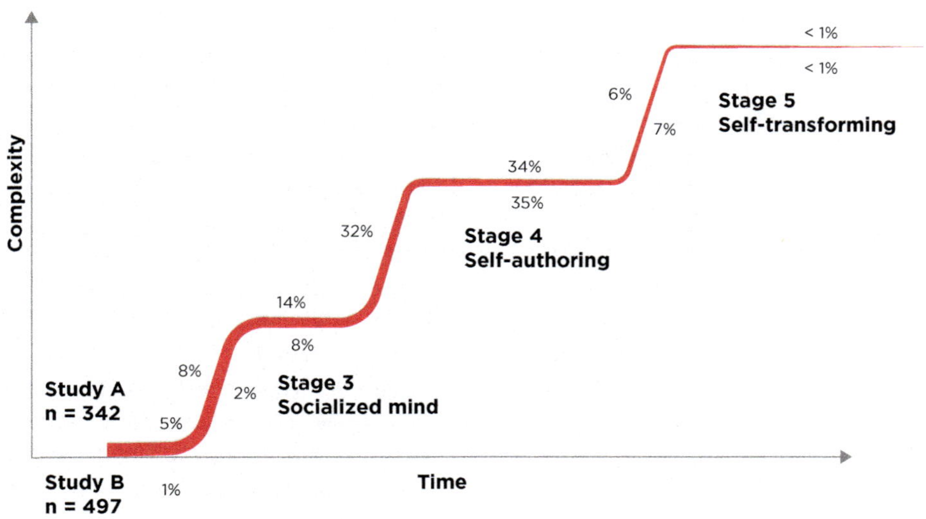

Source: Kegan and Lahey (2009: 28)

FIGURE 19: DESCRIPTION OF THE STAGES OF ADULT DEVELOPMENT

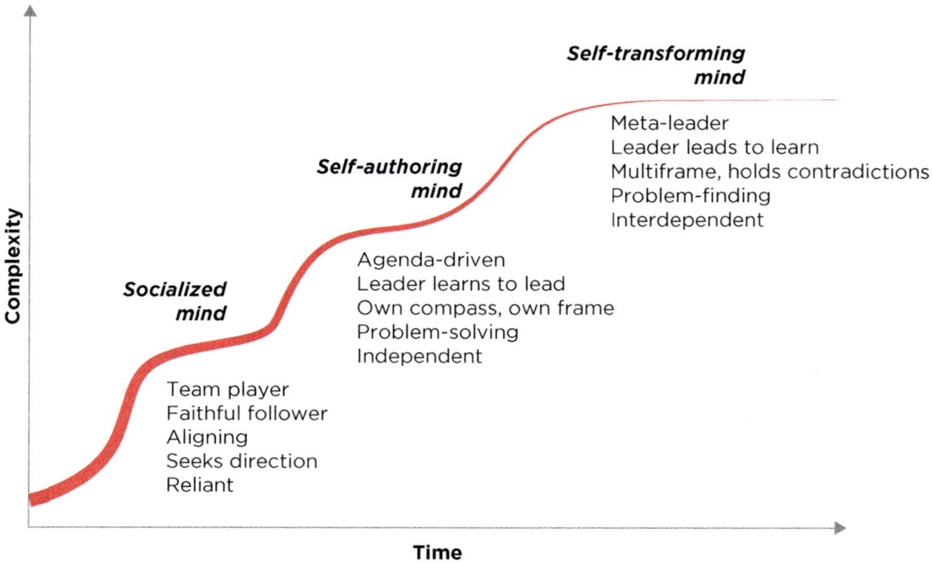

Source: Kegan and Lahey (2009: 16)

In the self-authoring mind stage we find ourselves more in control of our own life. We become more independent from the external world and what others tell us. We can define who we are without being defined by other people, institutions or knowledge. We take this information on board, but we decide who we are ourselves. We become more autonomous and the author of our own life. According to Kegan and Lahey, around one third of the adult population is self-authoring. Who we are is determined more by who we want to be ourselves and not by what the world tells us we should be. We separate ourselves from what the outside world thinks and form our own opinions by looking at our lives in an objective manner. To reach this stage it is important to understand your purpose, values and strengths in such a way that you can distance yourself from everything that happens around you. This keeps you grounded and calm in the middle of the storm and helps you to use your purpose, values and strengths as guiding principles when making decisions.

According to Kegan and Lahey, only 1% of the population can be said to have moved to the next level: the self-transforming mind.[130] The self-transforming mind is the next evolutionary step of the human mind as it interacts more with its surroundings, but then in a manner that is focused not only on what is important to us personally but also on what is important to others. In this stage you focus more on what you can do to make things better for *everyone*. Our hypothesis is that the challenges involved in building authentic confidence apply primarily to those of us who operate at the level of the socialized mind. The tools we present in this context are aimed at supporting the transition from the socialised to the self-authoring mind.

To complement Kegan and Lahey's stages of adult development, we would like to explore the neuroscientific explanation of why this element of emotional flexibility is so powerful when it comes to developing authentic confidence. Understanding your purpose, values and strengths, and reaffirming them on a regular basis, helps you to stay focused and give you a frame of reference when challenged. Worries and fears that travel the 'high road' often lead a life of their own. As explained above, if we do not intervene, they can eventually result in the activation of a stress response.

You will discover that some of the tools concentrate on reframing and seeing things in (a different) perspective, basically adding to the different options for what could be true and extending the prediction repertoire, whereas others focus on being in the moment and mindful. It is for these moments, when we create mindfulness or reframe our thoughts,[131] that having clarity regarding our purpose, values and strengths, as a strong inner anchor, will help us to stay on course and focused and continue to engage our prefrontal cortex. This will help us to manage or reduce (the impact of) worries and to avoid the build-up towards increasing anxiety and eventually a possible stress response.

130 We are not aware of a recent update of this research, perhaps these percentages have moved as a result of the last couple of years in which we have found an increase in attention for topics related to this book, awareness, mental health and well-being.

131 Please note that we are not suggesting that you should 'dispute' your own thoughts. According to the ACT approach, it is important not to suppress our thoughts but to pay them the attention they deserve instead. We will explain this in more detail throughout the toolkit.

5.3 Purpose and Values: 'From > To' behaviours and thoughts

When considering the transformation needed to clarify your purpose and values, it helps to think in terms of the behavioural changes you want to achieve - the so-called 'From > To' behaviours. This involves moving away from behaviours that keep you in the stage of the socialized mind towards behaviours that enable you to perform with a self-authoring mind. Figure 20 shows a number of 'From > To' changes that may help you. These examples are provided merely as a source of inspiration; you are the only one who knows what is right for you. The tools in this chapter will help you to understand what those behavioural changes might be in your case.

FIGURE 20: PURPOSE AND VALUES - 'FROM > TO' EXAMPLES

From	To
EXAMPLE OF BEHAVIOUR	
Being unclear about what is important to you	Knowing what you are here to do, your purpose and values
Not really understanding what you're good at	Understanding your strengths
Following whatever project you are asked to do	Making conscious choices for your path
EXAMPLES OF THOUGHTS	
"I'll take on this task because I've been asked to"	*"I'll take on this task and I know why this matters to me and I can leverage my strengths"*
"I am not sure what I want to achieve in life"	*"I know how these challenges will bring me closer to what I want to achieve"*

5.4 Tools for defining your purpose and values

We offer six tools that can help you to define your purpose and values or to continue to be closely connected to them, for example through practicing gratitude. You will also find extra references and recommendations at the end of each section.

5.4.1 Reflections on becoming self-authoring

Description of this tool	**What will this tool enable for you:**
With this tool you will create awareness with regard to being self-authoring versus having a socialized mind.	• An understanding of where you are with regard to becoming self-authoring • Inspiration to challenge yourself

Introduction

This tool enables personal reflection and helps to create awareness. We have already described the different stages of adult mental development as defined by Kegan and Lahey (2009) in the introduction to this chapter: (1) the socialized mind, (2) the self-authoring mind, and (3) the self-transforming mind. This model shows that, given the increasing complexity of the working environment, there is a growing need for professionals to move from the level of a socialized mind to that of a self-authoring mind in the way they function. Kegan and Lahey's research shows that the majority of the workforce still functions on the basis of the socialized mind and not the self-authoring mind, even at the most senior levels within organisations.

From the perspective of the three stages identified by Kegan and Lahey, we can see a clear link with the development and growth of authentic confidence and emotional flexibility. Becoming self-authoring requires clarity concerning your inner compass and a clear picture of what is important to you in terms of purpose and values. We often think of colleagues who are not afraid to speak up or push back during a meeting as 'self-authoring'. However, it is important to realise that this is not always the case. Even people who appear to have strong opinions and are able to express themselves well can still be very much embedded in a socialized mind. In fact, the things they say may even be determined largely by what they think others want to hear. The focus in this chapter, therefore, is on developing the courage to act upon what is important to *you* and to become self-authoring, even if this means going against the grain and following a different path from the rest.

In the spirit of emotional flexibility, however, we wish to emphasise that we are not asking you to ignore your fears and insecurities. On the contrary, we encourage you to embrace them, while continuing to move towards achieving what is most important to you.

> **"I realized a clear shift around the age of forty when I felt truly confident. I was starting to make my own independent decisions (not decisions influenced by others); it went better and better. I wish I had known this at a younger age. And even though others or your parents tell you these things, it only becomes real when you are ready for it and go through it yourself."**
>
> **Abbe Luersman,** CHRO, EVP and Chief People Officer, Otis Elevator Co.

The first step in moving from the socialized mind to the self-authoring mind is becoming aware of your values and purpose and knowing where you are at this moment and why. To this end we have included a tool for creating self-awareness in our playbook that is linked to Kegan and Lahey's three stages of adult development.

Reflections on the self-authoring tool

Figure 21 shows the relationship between different themes at work and the three stages of adult development. For each theme there is a socialized, self-authoring and self-transforming description of behaviour. Reflect on where you believe you are right now with regard to each theme (that can also be a point between two different descriptions, of course, as it is a sliding scale).

FIGURE 21: THEMES AT WORK AND STAGES OF ADULT DEVELOPMENT

	SOCIALIZED	SELF-AUTHORING	IN TRANSFORMATION PHASE TOWARDS SELF-TRANSFORMING
INNER COMPASS	I follow what others find important; no strong inner compass; difficult to prioritize what I say yes to	I am very clear of what is important to me; this helps me to prioritize what I focus on, what I spend energy on	I am clear about what is important to me but I am not a prisoner to these thoughts — I am open to exploring other ideas and matching them with mine
WHO LEADS	I join 'the car' as a passenger, following where we go	I drive the car, being clear about the direction in which to go	I am considering the situation and flexible as to who drives the car or what directions will be best, given the situation — aware of what is important to me but open to the situation and prepared to adjust
SPEAKING UP	I assimilate to the group, I may speak up but hold back from sharing my own true opinions or important observations if they deviate from the norm	I speak up with a focus on my own agenda and what is important to me — even if this deviates from the group norm	I speak up with the intention to understand the situation, engaging in finding the best answer for the moment, being aware of my own beliefs and the limitations of my own beliefs as well
LEANING IN	I avoid leaning in or creating new opportunities to follow if this deviates from what the 'group' or system appreciates	I lean in to new opportunities or create them, linked to what is important to me — and I remain focused during this	I lean in to what is important to me, with an open mind to absorb the ongoing changing environment and being aware that I might need to change along the way, following what is needed (for me) in this moment and in this situation

Source: Developed by the authors with input from Prof. R. Kegan.

> **"One of my mantras is: 'you are what you think' - in other words: 'I control my own destiny'. It helps me in making decisions in difficult situations like one time, for example, when I was working with a challenging boss. I had to reflect on whether I wanted to stay or not, or to ignore it, but then I took control over my situation. In my current role (at Unilever), I am totally not stressed about the content of my work; the stress or the biggest challenge comes from the relationships and politics**

> **that come with this job and the level of responsibility. It is very important then to have an inner anchor and know what is important to you and what you stand for."**
>
> **Jan Zijderveld,** at the time of the interview member of the Unilever Executive Team and President of Unilever Europe

Next, we would like you to open your personal journal and write down your thoughts on each theme, including examples that support your score. Write down also why you think you are currently exhibiting this behaviour.

> **"If something becomes very complicated, I am conscious of my behavior that I would move on to the next thing if it becomes half-difficult; for example, if someone else would come with something new and I thought I could add value, I would jump on to that; and so I end up being a gatherer of jobs or tasks, and not a deliverer of anything. I end up spinning twenty plates at once, and I cannot control them at all; I am continuously obliged to follow through and therefore I don't have time to think about what I value because I am too busy living up to what other people want."**
>
> **Senior Executive,** anonymous contribution

Return now to your answers for Figure 21 and recall how you scored on the various propositions. If you scored below self-authoring on all or a few themes, take a moment to reflect on how you can use this to define your purpose and values and how the tools in this chapter can help you to move towards becoming more self-authoring. Remember, small steps can make a huge difference. For example, the next time you notice that your behaviour is preventing you from becoming more self-authoring, you will be able to take a step back and reflect on how you want to deal with the situation. You can then either accept the situation for what it is or change course.

Young people often find it very hard to be self-authoring when they are just starting out in their career, but the challenges involved also apply to the more complex and senior roles in an organisation. Self-authoring does not mean focusing only on those things you enjoy doing, even at the micro level. Not even those in senior roles have the power to do this. Becoming self-authoring implies that you follow your inner compass at each level of seniority in the organisation. In more junior roles this involves not being afraid to speak up in meetings when you believe that something is not entirely right. Having an opinion and expressing it are important in every role. Our research has shown that young people have an overwhelming tendency not to speak their mind if they feel uncertain or lack confidence. They are often afraid that what they have to share will be considered dumb and may have a negative effect on how people see them. This train of thought, albeit a very logical one, has a very *socialized* focus. Learning to detach yourself from that way of thinking and speaking your mind at every level within the organisation can help you to move towards becoming self-authoring. The key is to clarify your circle of influence and, within that circle, to move towards what is important to you in a self-authoring manner.

> **"Being self-aware is very important to me. It helps to reflect on who you are when you are in difficult situations, to focus on what is right and what is important."**
>
> **Michelle Roborg-Sondergaard,** Senior HR Executive

> **"A situation in which I felt very confident: I remember at grad school I had a funny interaction with a senior faculty member. I was told he was good at career advice. In my second semester, I set up a meeting with him to get his feedback. I appreciate content feedback on my work or on my skills-set the most when it comes from people who are generally disagreeable or tough and they don't throw out praise regularly, so it means a lot more because it must mean you have really impressed them. He looked at my vita and told me I was doing way too much, and I would be shocked if I could even achieve a quarter of the things I had on my plate; I was going to fail miserably if I did not cut all these projects. Instead of taking it all on board and agreeing with this feedback, the funny thing was that I came out of this conversation feeling motivated to prove him wrong. I felt like 'who is this guy, he doesn't know me, he doesn't know how much energy I have or what my work ethic is and so how could he predict what I could accomplish? So, I set my mind to proving him wrong and when I finished grad school and I had a meeting with him a couple of years later and he said, 'You know I was wrong; I underestimated you.' I came away from this meeting thinking that I have enough motivation or enough skills that made me successful in this field and this was a great**

> **source of affirmation for me to find out that the very guy who doubted me, now thought that I could pull it off."**
>
> **Adam Grant,** Professor of Management and Psychology, The Wharton School, University of Pennsylvania

In this section, we introduced the theme of the socialized mind versus the self-authoring mind. Kegan and Lahey have studied this for many years and published a book called *Immunity to Change* that provides much more detail. If you want to read more of their work, please consult the reference list.

5.4.2 Defining your ikigai (your purpose): what is really important to you?

Description of this tool	**What will this tool enable for you:**
Ikigai is a Japanese concept. They believe that every person has a reason for being. This tool will help you discover your 'reason for being', or in other words: your meaning in life, your purpose.	• An understanding of your purpose and meaning in life in a holistic way. • Reflecting on potential opportunities or gaps.

Introduction

Ikigai is a Japanese word that means 'reason for being'. It is a concept that helps you to reflect on the things that really matter to you, starting with an essential question: what gets you out of bed in the morning? Before you continue reading, we would like to invite you to watch a short inspirational video on YouTube that explains this concept a little further. You can use the QR code below or follow this link: https://youtu.be/_X7LQZXIlUk

QR-code #IWAKEUPFOR

> **"If you make mistakes in my profession, the impact can be enormous: it can be the difference between life and death. I remember one time we had complications with a patient. I was only a young assistant. This really impacted me and my**

> **confidence. I ended up blaming myself. In those days there was not much emotional support for medical staff but today the situation is much better. I experienced times when I questioned whether I had chosen the right profession, whether I really liked my job. But each time I quickly realised that this is what I had to do, that this was my purpose. That helped me through the tough times."**
>
> **Jan J. Wever,** MD, PhD, Vascular Surgeon, Haga Hospital, The Hague, The Netherlands

> **"When I am really passionate about a project I don't stop to think 'can I do this?' My enthusiasm always propels me forward."**
>
> **Adam Grant,** Professor of Management and Psychology at the Wharton School, University of Pennsylvania

Ikigai tool

Picture this: your alarm clock goes off in the morning, telling you it's time to wake up. A new day awaits you. You open your eyes and...

What usually happens next in your case? Do you jump out of bed full of anticipation for the day ahead? Or do you dread getting out of bed and wish you could stay under the covers all day? The first moment of the day can be very informative. It tells you whether you are focusing on the right things in life, whether your job is really the right one for you or whether you should consider a change. Most of us dedicate more than 40 hours of our week to our work. So it is imperative that we make it worthwhile and meaningful, as well as enjoyable and exciting.

In this tool we will guide you through some self-reflection questions on the concept of ikigai in order to identify the source of value in your life and the things that make your life worthwhile. The concept is visualized in Figure 22.

FIGURE 22: FINDING YOUR IKIGAI (YOUR PURPOSE)

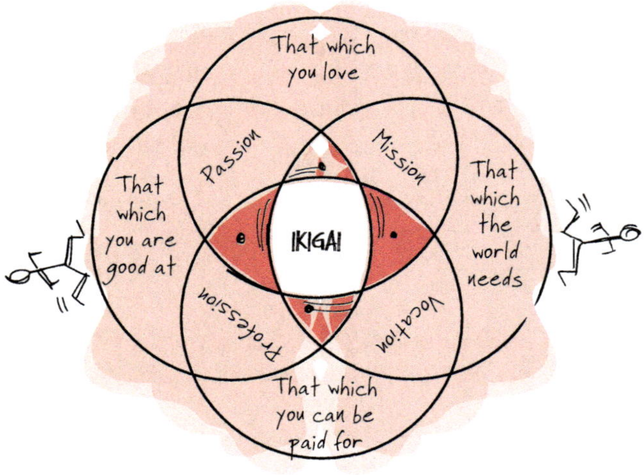

Source: based on García and Miralles (2017:9).

Reflect on the following four questions to discover your ikigai:

1. *What do you love?*
   Irrespective of all other factors, what are the things you love doing? You are probably aware of these things already, but you may not know how you should go about doing them.
2. *What does the world need?*
   A lot, when you think about it. There are many problems in the world that need to be solved. If you can find one that interests you, use it to guide you.
3. *What can you be paid for?*
   Pretty much anything, in theory. However, you have to find people who need what you are offering or selling. You may need to be a bit creative, but there might just be something of monetary value in the things you love and that the world needs.
4. *What are you good at?*
   Everyone has some trait or skill they excel at. It is critical to know your unique strengths, as well as areas for personal growth and development.

It is at the intersection of all these insights where you can find your ikigai. Of course, this is a journey in itself and some people need a lot of time to discover their ikigai. The purpose of your work depends on how you view your work and your motivation to work, as well as the objective of your work.

> **"I am very clear nowadays about my purpose and what role I want to play in this world. Together with my values, this is truly my inner compass for when situations get tough and difficult decisions have to be made. I love my company and the people working here so much, and my focus is entirely on serving them and the business for the greater good. That is my ikigai."**
>
> **Leena Nair,** former Chief Human Resources Officer (CHRO), Unilever; current CEO of Chanel

Why is it important to understand your ikigai when building authentic confidence? Understanding your ikigai helps you to stay on the right course when you are challenged or when you are offered different opportunities. When you feel afraid it helps you to lean in to a specific challenge. It helps you to understand that you accepted that challenge because it is related to your purpose - the one you thought so long and hard about. It also enables you to say no to requests that are outside of your ikigai because although the requests might be very interesting and flattering they will distract you from what you want to focus on. This gives you an inner sense of direction; it supports the move from the socialized to the self-authoring mind (because you follow what is important to you) and provides you with an inner compass. Of course, this does not mean that your ikigai never changes. Things are always changing in your life. Your surroundings or your self-awareness can change along the way. The key is to stay aware of your ikigai so that it can support you in feeling confident about your focus in your day-to-day activities.

> **"I went on a vision quest later in my career. I was at Unilever. This was a huge eye-opener for me. A big shock to my system and a total reset."**
>
> **Tex Gunning,** CEO, Leaseplan

> **"I remember having been in a very tough job where we had to fundamentally shift direction if we were to survive and I felt like I was swimming upstream constantly and had to go against the stream. A toxic senior leader did not understand the need for change. I connected with my deeper purpose and why this was so important to the business and to me. It helped me to deal with my emotions. I was still anxious, but I knew why I was doing it. I had created a groundswell of support which also helped me to stand tall in the boardroom. The board were very**

> **receptive, and I realised during a factory visit that my value proposal was similar to those used in the biggest factory in the group. It was tough, but it worked over time. We made a transformation for the better."**
>
> **Karen Rivoire,** Competence Flow Leader, Inter IKEA Group

If you would like to read more about this concept, please check the reference list for García and Miralles and their book *Ikigai.*

5.4.3 Prioritising your core values: defining an inner compass

Description of this tool	**What will this tool enable for you:**
We don't always reflect on our values or consciously affirm them. This tool helps you to reaffirm the ones you want to adopt as your core values and inner compass.	• A clearly chosen set of core values that you choose to live by. • An inner compass to guide your decisions when you are challenged.

Introduction

> **"If you are authentic and driven by your values and focused on always doing the right thing, then the worst thing that can happen is that you, yourself, can get hurt. And if you feel confident that you can recover, the worst thing that can happen is that you may lose your job. But if you think you can recover from that, then you can become more confident. This is self-talk. No-one can do that for you, you must do this yourself! I have told myself that I will never avoid doing something out of fear. I will only avoid doing something because I feel it is not right or isn't going to add value."**
>
> **Abbe Luersman,** CHRO, EVP and Chief People Officer, Otis Elevator Co.

This tool is an extension of the Ikigai exercise but is more focused on your core values. Knowing and choosing the values that you want to live and work by will help you stay anchored if you get challenged at any point during your career. Reflecting also on the consequences of choosing those values helps you to have the courage to live by them. For example, if you are very sure about a certain value and why you choose to live by that value, then you may feel more confident to speak up when that value is violated, irrespective of the consequence of speaking up.

Tool for prioritising your values

This tool is based on an exercise from Russ Harris' book *The Confidence Gap: From fear to freedom*.[132]

If you have already reflected on becoming self-authoring (tool 5.4.1), you will have had the time to think about what it means to become more inspired by leading 'from the inside'. Developing an inner compass is necessary if you want to be able to lead from the inside and knowing what is important to you is crucial to that process. One of the ingredients is your values. Your values represent what is most important to you; they determine how you want to lead your life, who you want to be as a person, how you want to do your work, the type of colleague or friend you want to be and so on. In order to become authentically confident, it is essential to understand these values because they can help you get through challenging moments and make important decisions. Being clear about your values will help you feel confident when you need to perform or make a decision and understand the consequences.

> **"It is our inner compass, our inner resilience, our inner game that gets us through the most difficult of times. I was facing a very difficult situation not so long ago and what got me through it was entirely my inner game. I went to the temple. I walk or jog to the temple every Sunday for 45 minutes. I pray for half an hour, meditate and think about the week that has passed and the next week that is coming, and then I walk back home. So, I get a few hours of good exercise and thirty minutes of decompressed thinking about the topics that matter to me. That is what got me through this difficult situation as well: the inner compass of my purpose and my values."**
>
> **Leena Nair,** former Chief Human Resources Officer (CHRO), Unilever; current CEO of Chanel

> **"I remember a situation that I got into a while ago, which was the result of letting things linger too long where my intuition already had told me that I had to take steps. I learned from that to trust my gut more and immediately face the challenge, discuss things, and not to let it go on for too long. As leaders we are often biased to think that things will work out for the best.**

132 Used with permission of the author.

> **I learned that if my gut tells me that something is not right, I should trust it and act straight away in line with my beliefs."**
>
> **Paul-Peter Feld,** CHRO, Enexis

> **"I had a troubled upbringing and had to deal with a lot at a young age. I often have had to revisit my values in my career. Taking this experience of my past with me helped me to keep putting things in perspective. Don't get me wrong: I also want to get to the top of my career, and I will do my best for that. But in the end, I will survive if I don't get there and the same goes for a lot of things that I enjoy. I can do without. At McKinsey, I feel I can be totally myself and focus on creating impact for clients. I am not worried about bringing the tough messages."**
>
> **Beltrán Simó,** Partner, McKinsey & Company, Bogotá, Colombia

> **"My wife and I make a circle of life balance about twice a year: that cycle includes different parts like health, work, family, friends, house and so on. We discuss if we feel it is balanced or if we need to change anything; this helps me to stay focused and calm."**
>
> **Sebastiaan Besems,** Chief Commercial Officer, Burg Group, The Netherlands

Values are not about what you want to receive or achieve. Instead, they are about how you want to behave or act on an ongoing basis. There are lots of different values, but the overview below provides a list of the most common ones.[133] Study the list, reflect on each value and circle your response to each question: (A) how important the value is to you and (B) to what degree you live by this value. When you deduct A from B you will immediately see where you have a potential gap (value gap) and an opportunity for change. The greater the difference, the greater the gap. You can either adjust this value in terms of its prioritisation or consider taking value-focused action.

---

133 We thank Russ Harris, who allowed us to use the values from *The Confidence Gap: A Guide to Overcoming Fear and Self-doubt* as the basis for this exercise. See the reference list at the back of this book for more details.

FIGURE 23: OVERVIEW OF VALUES

	A. Important to me 1 = not 5 = very	B. I live by this 1 = not 5 = very	Value gap A minus B
Acceptance: To be open to and accepting of myself, others, life etc.	1 2 3 4 5	1 2 3 4 5	
Beauty: To appreciate, create, nurture or cultivate beauty in myself, others, the environment etc.	1 2 3 4 5	1 2 3 4 5	
Connection: To engage fully in whatever I am doing, and be fully present with others	1 2 3 4 5	1 2 3 4 5	
Adventure: To be adventurous; to actively seek, create, or explore novel or stimulating experiences	1 2 3 4 5	1 2 3 4 5	
Caring: To be caring towards myself, others, the environment etc.	1 2 3 4 5	1 2 3 4 5	
Contribution/Impact: To contribute, help, assist, or make a positive difference to myself or others	1 2 3 4 5	1 2 3 4 5	
Assertiveness: To respectfully stand up for my rights and request what I want	1 2 3 4 5	1 2 3 4 5	
Challenge: To keep challenging myself to grow, learn, improve	1 2 3 4 5	1 2 3 4 5	
Conformity: To be respectful and obedient of rules and obligations	1 2 3 4 5	1 2 3 4 5	
Authenticity: To be authentic, genuine, real; to be true to myself	1 2 3 4 5	1 2 3 4 5	
Compassion: To act with kindness towards those who are suffering	1 2 3 4 5	1 2 3 4 5	
Cooperation: To be cooperative and collaborative with others	1 2 3 4 5	1 2 3 4 5	
Courage: To be courageous or brave; to persist in the face of fear, threat, or difficulty	1 2 3 4 5	1 2 3 4 5	
Creativity: To be creative or innovative	1 2 3 4 5	1 2 3 4 5	
Curiosity: To be curious, open-minded and interested; to explore and discover			
Encouragement: To encourage and reward behaviour that I value in myself or others	1 2 3 4 5	1 2 3 4 5	
Equality: To treat others as equal to myself, and vice-versa	1 2 3 4 5	1 2 3 4 5	
Excitement: To seek, create and engage in activities that are exciting, stimulating or thrilling	1 2 3 4 5	1 2 3 4 5	

	A. Important to me 1 = not 5 = very	B. I live by this 1 = not 5 = very	Value gap A minus B
Fairness: To be fair to myself or others	1 2 3 4 5	1 2 3 4 5	
Fitness/Health: To maintain or improve my fitness; to look after my physical and mental health and well-being	1 2 3 4 5	1 2 3 4 5	
Flexibility: To adjust and adapt readily to changing circumstances	1 2 3 4 5	1 2 3 4 5	
Freedom: To live freely; to choose how I live and behave, or help others do likewise	1 2 3 4 5	1 2 3 4 5	
Friendliness/Kindness: To be friendly, companionable, or agreeable towards others	1 2 3 4 5	1 2 3 4 5	
Forgiveness: To be forgiving towards myself or others	1 2 3 4 5	1 2 3 4 5	
Fun: To be fun-loving; to seek, create, and engage in fun-filled activities	1 2 3 4 5	1 2 3 4 5	
Generosity: To be generous, sharing and giving, to myself or others	1 2 3 4 5	1 2 3 4 5	
Gratitude: To be grateful for and appreciative of the positive aspects of myself, others and life	1 2 3 4 5	1 2 3 4 5	
Honesty: To be honest, truthful, and sincere with myself and others	1 2 3 4 5	1 2 3 4 5	
Humour: To see and appreciate the humorous side of life	1 2 3 4 5	1 2 3 4 5	
Humility: To be humble or modest; to let my achievements speak for themselves	1 2 3 4 5	1 2 3 4 5	
Industry: To be industrious, hard-working, dedicated	1 2 3 4 5	1 2 3 4 5	
Independence: To be self-supportive, and choose my own way of doing things	1 2 3 4 5	1 2 3 4 5	
Intimacy: To open up, reveal, and share myself – emotionally or physically – in my close personal relationships	1 2 3 4 5	1 2 3 4 5	
Justice/Integrity: To uphold justice and fairness	1 2 3 4 5	1 2 3 4 5	
Kindness: To be kind, compassionate, considerate, nurturing or caring towards myself or others	1 2 3 4 5	1 2 3 4 5	
Love: To act lovingly or affectionately towards myself or others	1 2 3 4 5	1 2 3 4 5	

	A. Important to me 1 = not 5 = very	B. I live by this 1 = not 5 = very	Value gap A minus B
Mindfulness: To be conscious of, open to, and curious about my here-and-now experience	1 2 3 4 5	1 2 3 4 5	
Order: To be orderly and organised	1 2 3 4 5	1 2 3 4 5	
Open-mindedness: To think things through, see things from other's points of view, and weigh evidence fairly	1 2 3 4 5	1 2 3 4 5	
Patience: To wait calmly for what I want	1 2 3 4 5	1 2 3 4 5	
Persistence: To continue resolutely, despite problems or difficulties	1 2 3 4 5	1 2 3 4 5	
Pleasure: To create and give pleasure to myself or others	1 2 3 4 5	1 2 3 4 5	
Power: To strongly influence or wield authority over others, e.g., taking charge, leading, organizing	1 2 3 4 5	1 2 3 4 5	
Reciprocity: To build relationships in which there is a fair balance of giving and taking	1 2 3 4 5	1 2 3 4 5	
Respect: To be respectful towards myself or others; to be polite, considerate and show positive regard	1 2 3 4 5	1 2 3 4 5	
Responsibility: To be responsible and accountable for my actions	1 2 3 4 5	1 2 3 4 5	
Romance: To be romantic; to display and express love or strong affection	1 2 3 4 5	1 2 3 4 5	
Safety/Security: To secure, protect, or ensure safety of myself or others	1 2 3 4 5	1 2 3 4 5	
Self-awareness: To be aware of my own thoughts, feelings and actions	1 2 3 4 5	1 2 3 4 5	
Self-care: To look after my health and well-being, and get my needs met	1 2 3 4 5	1 2 3 4 5	
Self-development: To keep growing, advancing or improving in knowledge, skills, character, or life experience	1 2 3 4 5	1 2 3 4 5	
Self-control: To act in accordance with my own ideals	1 2 3 4 5	1 2 3 4 5	
Sensuality: To create, explore and enjoy experiences that stimulate the five senses	1 2 3 4 5	1 2 3 4 5	
Sexuality: To explore or express my sexuality	1 2 3 4 5	1 2 3 4 5	
Spirituality/Faith: To connect with things bigger than myself	1 2 3 4 5	1 2 3 4 5	

	A. Important to me 1 = not 5 = very	B. I live by this 1 = not 5 = very	Value gap A minus B
Skilfulness: To continually practice and improve my skills, and apply myself fully when using them	1 2 3 4 5	1 2 3 4 5	
Supportiveness/Service to others: To be supportive, helpful, encouraging, and available to myself for others	1 2 3 4 5	1 2 3 4 5	
Trust: To be trust worthy; to be loyal, faithful, sincere, and reliable	1 2 3 4 5	1 2 3 4 5	
Knowledge: To continue developing insight and knowledge	1 2 3 4 5	1 2 3 4 5	
Family: To ensure close family connections; spend enough time with family	1 2 3 4 5	1 2 3 4 5	
Friendship: Nurture friendship relations; make enough time for friends	1 2 3 4 5	1 2 3 4 5	
Achievement: Achievement at work, in career; progress in life; delivering on projects; winning in sports games	1 2 3 4 5	1 2 3 4 5	
Privacy: Having space for myself; sufficient privacy	1 2 3 4 5	1 2 3 4 5	
Commitment: Delivering on commitments; Following through on promises	1 2 3 4 5	1 2 3 4 5	
Loyalty: Being loyal to friends, family and people I work with	1 2 3 4 5	1 2 3 4 5	
Excellence: Strive for the best; continuous improvement	1 2 3 4 5	1 2 3 4 5	
Balance: Keeping a balance; not a person of extremes	1 2 3 4 5	1 2 3 4 5	
Harmony: Seeking harmony, avoiding conflict	1 2 3 4 5	1 2 3 4 5	
New Value:	1 2 3 4 5	1 2 3 4 5	
New Value:	1 2 3 4 5	1 2 3 4 5	

You can also identify your top six values to create more focus and prioritisation. Once you have identified these values, reflect on how they are relevant to you in your work situation (use a journal to write down your thoughts). Is it possible to live up to these values all of the time? Where do you see possible areas of friction? Think of those times when you felt you were lacking confidence. In those situations were any of your values compromised? How can these values help you face your fears and insecurities?

> **"A core value and important way for me to manage stress is what I call 'Pass the Monkey'. It is a combination of skill and mindfulness. This is about clearly setting your boundaries and knowing what your responsibility is and where it ends. Holding others accountable for their contribution and not taking it all on your own shoulders. A senior leader is a conductor; (s)he doesn't need to be able to play all the instruments. I see people taking on other people's responsibilities too often and they suffer big time. It is not an easy thing to do well. It requires skill and experience, and I am convinced it should be part of any senior leader's tool kit."**
>
> **Jan Zijderveld,** former CEO, Avon Inc. and President of Unilever Europe

> **"Humility is key: none of us is as smart as all of us and so as a leader you must be able to act humble enough to include others and ask for help."**
>
> **Tex Gunning,** CEO, LeasePlan

> **"The only reason I am doing what I am doing is for the cause and purpose that drives me in the work I do and that gives me the confidence to make difficult decisions."**
>
> **Chet Kuchinad,** Chief People Officer, Save the Children International

5.4.4 Defining your best-self aspiration - a visualization technique[134]

Description of this tool	**What will this tool enable for you:**
A visualization of 'your best self' at different levels of what you want to achieve: (a) a particular behaviour change or (b) a particular holistic view on who you want to be in a certain period of time.	• A picture (and vision) of yourself when you are at your best. • Inspiration for the future you want to work towards.

134 This section includes special contributions from Dr Srini Pillay, Harvard-trained psychiatrist and brain researcher; Chief Medical Officer and Co-founder of Reulay and CEO of Neurobusiness Group.

Introduction

> **"The man who says he can and the one who says he can't are both correct."**
>
> **Confucius**

Many athletes and actors openly admit that they use visualization techniques before a big performance and that they swear by them. They visualize the activity from start to finish, including success. According to Srini Pillay,[135] a Harvard-trained psychiatrist and brain researcher, when we visualize an activity, overlapping brain regions are stimulated that are similar to those aroused when we actually perform that same activity. This means that visualization 'warms up' the brain so that we can perform better when we actually do what we have first visualized. This is why we have included an exercise to allow you to visualize your best confident self before performing a task. It will help you to think and feel more efficiently and make the required changes in your brain.[136] Visualizing success can help you to successfully carry out the task in real life. The interviews we conducted also showed that many business leaders use this technique or a variation thereof.

> **"I remember a situation where I felt really great. It was during my university days. We all had to give a presentation at a seminar before a very tough but also very fair professor. I prepared well and made sure I focused on the main points. I got great feedback from the professor! In addition to being well prepared in terms of the material, I had also prepared myself visually. The president of the college was an excellent speaker and I had seen her speak at a forum a week earlier. Right before my presentation I channelled her. I closed my eyes and thought about how she gave her presentation and tried to do the same. Seeing it very clearly helped me to be successful. Channelling someone else's best self has become a very helpful tool for me!"**
>
> **Consultant,** anonymous contribution

135 https://hbr.org/2014/03/to-reach-your-goals-make-a-mental-movie

136 See, e.g., https://www.ncbi.nlm.nih.gov/pmc/articles/PMC5226947/ and https://www.ncbi.nlm.nih.gov/pmc/articles/PMC5767265/

Tool for visualizing your best self
Below is a description of various visualization techniques presented in the form of guided visualizations. You can record the instructions yourself or ask someone to guide the visualization session for you. During your visualization it is important to observe what goes on in your mind (thoughts), what you feel (emotions and senses) and what you do (action) to make the experience of visualization as real as possible.

Visualization option 1: Set your aspiration for your best self

- We invite you to perform an exercise in which you will envision your best self in a future scenario.
- Sit down on a chair; back straight, legs uncrossed, make yourself comfortable. Put your hands in your lap and plant your feet on the ground.
- Relax your body... relax your shoulders... relax your jaws (this is where we often hold stress). Be aware of your breathing; breathe in... and out, in... and out...
- Reflect on the following question: Which specific behaviours or activities do you tend to avoid because you don't feel confident enough? Please think of one specific behaviour or activity that you have avoided today but that would be a great help to you if you could find the courage enough to do it. Write it down.
- Now, imagine you are at home sitting on the couch, one year from now. You are completely relaxed and enjoying a nice evening in. You feel content and fulfilled.
- You start thinking about how the past year has been at work since you started working on building your authentic confidence. It has been an amazing time. You find it hard to believe what you have accomplished in only one year and you feel a huge sense of pride! You have achieved extraordinary results.
- You were able to adjust that one behaviour you really wanted to change and you did so very successfully. You managed to move beyond the fears that had been holding you back; you took risks, stepped out of your comfort zone and did the things that you previously never dared to do. You have learned so much and achieved what you once thought was impossible.
- Watch this 'movie' in your head keeping the following in mind:
  - What is the end result of what you have achieved? In what situation do you find yourself now?
  - What did you manage to do that you previously believed was beyond you? When did you do it? Who was there with you? What did you do exactly?

  - Which thoughts did you have? What went on in your mind? Which emotions did you feel?
  - How did you feel? What biofeedback did you receive?
  - What was the eventual outcome of this situation?
- Close your eyes for a few minutes to reflect.
- When you open your eyes again, find a quiet spot for yourself and draw a picture of what you saw in your head (your vision). Feel free to use your imagination. There is no right or wrong way of doing this. It is all about what you see in your mind; it represents your best self. Then write down in a few sentences what your drawing represents. Give yourself plenty of time to do this exercise. Spending an hour or even longer on it can have a very powerful effect.
- Hang up the drawing you have made at home or keep it in your diary. You can then revisit it on a regular basis and keep your vision alive.

In the above exercise you may have experienced moments when you did not feel confident enough. Try to imagine what you could do to perform better at those moments. You could imagine yourself overcoming a tough challenge and becoming really good at the task involved. This is called 'motivational general mastery imagery', a type of imagery that helps to improve confidence.[137]

Visualization option 2:
- Make sure you have first done a mindfulness exercise or something else to relax. Stress makes it difficult for your brain to imagine things.
- Choose an image that represents a key aspect of your future. For example, if you imagine yourself as more confident, you might picture yourself doing something that you fear but that you have also identified as being important to you. Something like delivering a presentation to an important group of colleagues, your team or the board of directors.
- Use your imagination as vividly as possible and add as many senses as you can. In the case of a presentation to your colleagues, you might be able to smell the coffee served in the room, see the colour of the curtains and feel the floor under your feet. (Activating multiple senses can leave a stronger impression on your brain.)

137 https://www.tandfonline.com/doi/abs/10.1080/02640410802315419?src=recsys&journalCode=rjsp20) and https://www.ncbi.nlm.nih.gov/pubmed/19191065

- Feel how this all fits with your actual self. If it doesn't match, adjust the image until it is believable. Make it stronger and stronger and allow yourself to feel the pleasure embodied in what it represents.
- Imagine in the first person and the third person. That is, see yourself in the image, then *be* there in the image and take in everything around you.
- Imagine how you got to this point step by step: first, a project that you rounded off well and that earned you this new role; then the transformation that you executed well and which created a lot of support for you as the new leader of the team. (This support also helps to improves your confidence.)
- Close your eyes and refine and internalize the image. Become deeply familiar with it.
- Each time you return to the image you can fine-tune it.
- Then, when you have reflected and have opened your eyes again, find a quiet spot for yourself and draw a picture of what you saw in your head (your vision). Feel free to use your imagination. There is no right or wrong way of doing this. It is all about what you see in your mind; it represents your best self. Then write down in a few sentences what your drawing represents. Give yourself plenty of time to do this exercise. Spending an hour or even longer on it can have a very powerful effect.
- Hang up the drawing you have made at home or keep it in your diary. You can then revisit it on a regular basis and keep your vision alive.

If you want to read more about the power of using mental imagery to enhance the effectiveness of implementation intentions, please consult the work of Srini Pillay, *Your Brain and Business: The neuroscience of great leaders* (page 142). See the references at the back of the book.

5.4.5 Identifying your strengths: what gives you energy?

Description of this tool	**What will this tool enable for you:**
To reach your maximum potential and be at your best, it is important to understand and leverage your strengths: what you are naturally good at. This tool will help you discover them.	• Understanding of your strengths: what you are naturally good at and what gives you energy. • Practical understanding of how to integrate this insight into your career and life.

Introduction

> **"Everybody is a genius. But if you judge a fish by its ability to climb a tree, it will live its whole life believing that it is stupid."[138]**

In this tool we will elaborate on how you can use insights and reflections on your strengths to support the development of authentic confidence. Various studies have shown that the use of your strengths in the work context can be linked to work engagement (see, e.g., Harzer & Ruch, 2012, 2013; van Woerkom et al., 2016). Van Woerkom discovered that employees who were able to use their strengths on a weekly basis at work reported higher levels of self-efficacy and proactive behaviour.

Strengths are related to your natural talents and to what you do best. There are multiple tools available on the internet that can be used for exploratory purposes.[139] Strengths are categorised according to different talents and they describe your natural tendency to achieve your goals through certain talents. Your top talents are the ones that give you the most energy. When you draw on your strengths you can do what you do extremely well and with pleasure.

This tool is just one of many tools that can help you gain an insight into what you are good at and/or what gives you energy at work.[140] It helps you to choose the projects and roles that are right for you and develop your authentic confidence as a result. You may think certain roles are right for you until an honest appraisal of your strengths makes you realise that a different role or project might allow you to leverage your strengths more effectively, thereby redu-

138 This quote is often attributed to Albert Einstein but it first appeared in a book by Matthew Kelly (2004). The original quote appears to stem from 1898 (https://futurism.com/internets-epidemic-fake-quotes-real-scientists/). Irrespective of its source, we believe this quote is highly relevant to this section and so we decided to include it.

139 For the sake of completeness we would like to stress that many online tools are not properly scientifically validated and we therefore recommend using them only in an exploratory manner to help you to reflect on your journey to self-discovery.

140 Of course, you should remain careful not to confuse the challenge of learning something new and a lack of skills in a certain area with a lack of 'strengths' in that area – learning something new requires effort and related strengths may also evolve over time.

cing the risk of negative motivation and erosion of your self-confidence.

Using your strengths requires a level of self-awareness that helps you to understand what you are good at, what you enjoy and what you should focus on in relation to your purpose and values.

> **"I once had to take on the position of interim director after it suddenly became vacant. It was an opportunity for me to show my worth, as I was also one of the candidates for this role. The stress was considerable during that period because there was a lot going on, but I knew that everything would turn out fine. I was familiar with the content and soon I found myself in a positive flow. Knowing my worth and strengths fuelled my confidence. In the end, I got the job."**
>
> **Pieter Waasdorp,** Director of Entrepreneurship, Ministry of Economic Affairs, The Netherlands.

> **"I have a clear understanding of my strengths and my gaps. And I also make sure I learn how to fill in the gaps. I use a learning mindset to find out what I need to know and that is how I am able to build a narrative to support what I want to achieve."**
>
> **Chet Kuchinad,** Chief People Officer, Save the Children International

Tool for defining your strengths
There are many tools that you can use to discover your strengths. You can explore the various options and see which one suits you best. In this section we will ask you a number of self-reflection questions aimed at identifying your strengths and underpinning them with anecdotal evidence from your own experiences and those of your colleagues.

1. **Follow the energy**: When you feel on top of your game, record your thoughts in a journal.
2. **Form a balanced image**: Ask relevant stakeholders, peers or friends and family what they regard as your top three strengths; what do they think you are good at?
3. **Reflect**: How can you translate this into an overall image of what is important to you in work and life (ikigai) and your values.

4. **Act**: If necessary, decide which changes you would like to make to your current role (or to the new role you are about to take on) so that you can integrate most of your strengths.

> **"I believe that all of this [building authentic confidence] should start with an understanding of who you are, what your natural gifts are, the areas you are average in and the areas that you are less good at. An important part of developing confidence is repositioning your sense of insecurity in order to understand who you are and what your gifts are and then spend more time on becoming the best version of yourself and to really leverage your strengths."**
>
> **Rick Goings,** former CEO and Chairman Emeritus, Tupperware

> **"I often felt an oddball case at McKinsey. I was a creative person, but not the one that should lead the heavy-duty modelling piece of a project. So, I learned how to gravitate towards those projects that would require creative problem solving (with less emphasis on linear or root-cause problem solving), and there I would shine. And where I knew I had weak spots, I would find ways to work with people who complemented my skills."**
>
> **Joanna Barsh,** Senior Partner Emerita, McKinsey & Company

> **"I joined a consulting company later on in my career. Then I experienced my confidence was challenged. I was extremely impressed by the profile of people I worked with and I realised that my past was only my entrée ticket. Now I had to prove myself again within this new organisation. I looked around and saw all of them very accomplished and bringing such impressive backgrounds. I seriously questioned why they hired me there. Of course, after a year of landing in the job, I saw things again in perspective and realised that all of us had something that we were good at and we were adding value to the business in our own unique ways. I had to 'reconnect' with my strengths and what I bring to the mix."**
>
> **Ron van der Jagt,** Senior Executive

5.4.6 Daily gratitude reflections

Description of this tool	**What will this tool enable for you:**
This tool offers a way to reflect on a daily basis on what you are grateful for. It helps you to regularly check in on what is important to you.	• Reflections on a daily basis on the things you are grateful for. • Affirmation of your Purpose and Values.

Introduction

Gratitude has been proven to support subjective well-being. Counting your blessings every day makes you happier and can have a positive impact on the quality of your sleep (see, e.g., Emmons and McCullough, 2003). A study by Chen and Wu (2014) found that gratitude enhanced self-esteem in athletes when they had a higher affective trust in their coaches. Previous research suggests that gratitude interventions can increase the gratitude of an individual (Wood et al., 2010) and that interventions to increase gratitude can lead to an increase in self-esteem and well-being (Lin, 2015).

These are all great reasons for practicing gratitude daily. We have included the tool in this section on purpose and values because it helps to reflect regularly on where you are vis-à-vis what is important to you. An exercise in gratitude can help you to become aware of all the great things that happen every day and facilitates a personal check-in moment in which you can examine whether you are on track in terms of your purpose and fully aligned with your values. This kind of tool is also useful for other emotional flexibility practices but we decided to include in it in this section because we have found it to be fundamentally linked to the things that are most important to you.

In *CEO Excellence* (2022:285) the authors Dewar, Keller and Malhotra explain that one of the six mindsets that distinguish the best leaders from the rest is the 'perspective practice', which includes gratitude. "There is no question that great CEOs are productive, successful and confident... The best CEOs proactively take steps during their tenure to maintain a humble perspective". In their work, they refer to the important role of remaining humble and embracing servant leadership – "the best CEOs keep their job and themselves in perspective by ... never making it about themselves (Dewar et al., 2022:276)" – as well as practicing gratitude.

> **"I try to find satisfaction in my work in the smaller things."**
>
> **Jan J. Wever,** MD, PhD, Vascular Surgeon, Haga Hospital, The Hague, The Netherlands

Tool for reflecting on gratitude

At the end of each working day - for example, on your way home in the car or on the train - take a moment to follow these steps:

1. **Pause** - Take a deep breath and see yourself in the moment, right here, right now.
2. **Gratitude** - Think about all the things you are grateful for that happened during your working day today. If you can, write them down: "I am grateful for ..."
3. **Reflect** - Look at the things on your list and reflect on how satisfied they make you feel. Also, think of your values and your purpose: how are they related to what is important to you?
4. **Awareness** - Be aware of how this reflection makes you feel, what you are feeling right now and what your thoughts are. Observe everything, take a few deep breaths and then let go of your thoughts.

If you feel this exercise resonates with you, you can consider doing it in the evening too and including the part of your day that plays out after work. Some people do this exercise with their children at bedtime. The exercise is not about ignoring the difficult stuff, it is actually the opposite. As you will see when you explore this toolkit and the model of emotional flexibility, the main idea is to let the 'bad' things be present as well. For the purposes of this exercise, however, we ask you to focus on the things that you perceive as blessings.[141]

> **"Every evening my youngest son and I write down three things we are grateful for today."**
>
> **Leena Nair,** former Chief Human Resources Officer (CHRO), Unilever; current CEO of Chanel

141 There are also many apps that can help you with daily 'gratitude reflections', including ones where you can include pictures of things, situations, etc. you have seen during the day that made you feel grateful.

CHAPTER 6

6. PRACTICE 2 – MINDFULNESS

breathe
breathe
breathe.
a poem
came to being
through taking
breaths.
breathe
when you feel
like there is nothing
left to lose
and the world
will give you
what
you need to
survive on.
|the brain functions
better on oxygen. |

hold it
higher
higher than your
heart
hold on
and let go
when the winds
start to blow
your way.
|feel. feel like there is
nothing left
to lose
with all you have. |

listen
what do you feel
what is your heart
telling you
this very moment?
don't talk back
your heart is speaking in volu-
mes.
write.
|this is how you know. all the
answers.
you need.
to stop searching for. |

Noor Intisar, former Campus Poet, University of Antwerp

Special contributions by Barbara Doeleman-van Veldhoven, founder and director of BFC Compassionate Care & Mindful Medicine, expert in mindful and compassionate leadership[142]

142 For more information about Barbara and her work: www.ccmm.care

> **"When we get too caught up in the busy-ness of the world, we lose connection with one another - and ourselves."**
>
> **Jack Kornfield**[143]

It is impossible to make the right decisions for ourselves, for our business and for the projects we are involved in without the required level of focus and clarity of mind. Allowing ourselves to be distracted by everything around us negatively impacts our mental resilience and amplifies our fears and anxieties, which is the opposite of being mindful. Mindfulness is at the very heart of developing emotional flexibility and building authentic confidence.

6.1 What do we mean (for the purposes of this book) by the practice of mindfulness?

> **"Mindfulness is the capacity and the willingness to meet every experience and every situation with curiosity, care and mildness"**
>
> **Barbara Doeleman-van Veldhoven,** founder and director of BFC Compassionate Care & Mindful Medicine, expert in mindful and compassionate leadership

For the purposes of this book and in support of developing authentic confidence, we have decided to add a few areas to focus on in this chapter to help you achieve the kind of mindfulness described above. We will illustrate the topics that we discuss in this chapter by telling three short stories.

The first story is about **in the moment attention**. Remember that CEO you worked with or that senior leader who always exuded power whenever (s)he entered the room? They are rare, but they do exist. There is no senior leader anywhere who is not always extremely busy and who doesn't have to deal with conflicting demands. And yet there are leaders who are still able to give you their full attention when you meet them to discuss a problem. These rare specimens are focused, empathetic, caring and sharp, and they always inspire you to keep moving forward and overcome your challenges. When

143 https://tinybuddha.com/wisdom-quotes/when-we-get-too-caught-up-in-the-busyness-of-the-world-we-lose-connection-with-one-another-and-ourselves/

their mobile phone rings they ignore the intruder. They have already decided that when they enter into a conversation with you they will give you and the topic of discussion their full attention. These leaders are the ones who have mastered mindfulness. They operate completely in the moment and are never bothered by what happened an hour ago or what might happen in the next few hours or days. They 'see' you and make you feel special. More importantly, they are very good at helping you to solve your problem.

The second story concerns **sleep**. A few years ago, Adriana Huffington published a book called *Thrive* in which she opened the eyes of the world to the detrimental effects of sleep deprivation. Because of exhaustion and lack of sleep, she had a nasty fall at work, broke her cheekbone and injured her eye badly. She explains that we are going to need a different definition of success if we wish to be able to maintain a sustainable working life. And, of course, she is right. Sufficient sleep is not only essential to staying healthy, fit and present during the work day, it is also an essential ingredient - or more accurately a necessary condition - for developing and maintaining authentic confidence and emotional flexibility, as we will explain in the next section.

The third story has to do with the mental benefits of **exercise and sports**. Many successful and confident business leaders maintain a disciplined exercise regime. They often participate in extreme sports like marathons, iron man races and so forth. However, taking part in extreme sports is not really necessary because even moderate exercise can have tremendous mental health benefits (and is perhaps even more healthy, being less injury-prone).[144]

> **"I am a runner and learned a lot from breathing exercises. It taught me to relax. For example, I practice 'block breathing',**

144 Of course, we are aware that sleep and sports are not mindfulness exercises; we include them here nevertheless because they support a healthy brain and body as well as mindfulness and developing authentic confidence. We want to make a similar comment regarding a few of the other tools we have included. For example, breathing techniques or voice techniques for restoring a sense of calm cannot be classified as mindfulness techniques as such, but these techniques do support becoming more mindful and increase your ability to apply emotional flexibility when developing authentic confidence.

> **which means that you hold your breath between breathing in and breathing out for a few seconds."**
>
> **Ron van der Jagt,** Senior Executive

The stories above encapsulate what we have identified in this chapter as the essential aspects of mindfulness. It's all about creating mental fitness and sharpness so that you can remain in the moment and focus fully on what you are doing at any given moment during your busy working day. The different elements of mindfulness - e.g., meditation, mind-wandering, sleep and sports - all contribute to the development of a healthy and focused mind. In the next section we will explain in more detail why this is the case.

6.2 Why develop mindfulness skills?

Many studies have confirmed the benefits of mindfulness and meditation practices. There are many ways to develop mindfulness skills, including by practicing mindfulness meditation (e.g., learned through protocolised mindfulness trainings) and other variations, as we will explain in this chapter. From a neuroscientific perspective, mindfulness practices, particularly in the form of a programme of eight weeks of mindfulness-based stress reduction (MBSR), have been found to change specific areas of the brain that support the development of authentic confidence, as we describe in this book.[145] Researchers have identified changes in the areas that are important for learning, memory and emotional regulation, all related to the cortex. They have also observed a decline in brain cell volume in the amygdala. The participants in a study reported that they felt less stress as a result (see, e.g., Singleton et al., 2014; and Hölzel et al., 2011). There are many other benefits related to meditation, including an increase in positive emotions and less anxiety and stress.[146] All in all, meditation can have a positive effect on the cortex and may reduce the likelihood of an amygdala-driven response (Pittman and

145 Research is still evolving here, see, e.g., https://www.psychologytoday.com/us/blog/the-athletes-way/202205/mindfulness-doesn-t-change-our-brains-in-ways-once-thought

146 https://www.psychologytoday.com/us/blog/feeling-it/201309/20-scientific-reasons-start-meditating-today

Karle, 2015).[147] It is also an important foundation for the other practices associated with emotional flexibility.

> **"I have trained myself so well through years of weekly meditation that it helps me to face my fears."**
>
> **Leena Nair,** former Chief Human Resources Officer (CHRO), Unilever; current CEO of Chanel

6.3 Mindfulness: 'From > To' behaviours and thoughts

What are the transformations you will go through when you practice mindfulness and meditation to support the development of authentic confidence? The benefits can be very impactful, including a switch from ruminating and worrying to being more present at work. You will be much more capable of engaging fully in meetings and displaying an interest[148] in your clients.

During a business call, instead of constantly thinking about what happened yesterday or last week or what might happen tomorrow or next week, you will be able to stay in the here and now. Your mind will move away from destructive thoughts likes 'they will think I am stupid' and become actively engaged in your work.

You will be more capable of developing a crystal-clear focus in meetings and during conversations with clients. This will help you to use the tools and techniques presented in the next few chapters. Practicing mindfulness and being present in the moment in an open and curious manner are not only fundamental to other processes. They also enable you to leverage, actively apply and lean in to what is important to you (your purpose and values). The next figure visualizes a number of 'From > To' examples that are relevant to this chapter.

147 In other words: it becomes easier to remain calm and present when there is a stress experience or a prediction of something unexpected.

148 Curiosity is an important part of emotional flexibility and mindfulness – Jacqueline Brassey spoke about this in a podcast with the authors of the book *The Curious Advantage* which you can listen to here: https://ludicconsulting.com/news/new-podcast-the-curious-advantage-ep-1

FIGURE 24: MINDFULNESS - 'FROM > TO' EXAMPLES

From	To
TYPES OF BEHAVIOUR	
Worrying	Being present
Ruminating	Fully engaging, curious
Thinking about past or future	Being in the here and now
TYPES OF THOUGHTS	
"I hope the Board will not think I'm stupid once I've done my presentation"	*"Let's focus fully on this presentation now, on how I can make it better"*
"I don't dare to speak up - I might come across as stupid"	*"Let's focus on the problem that we are solving..."*

6.4 Tools for developing mindfulness

We offer seven tools in this chapter but they do not include the already very well-established tools associated with meditation. It would not be of any value to include meditation exercises here as there are so many tools widely available, as well as easy access to training. Instead, at the back of this book is a list of apps that can help you get started with meditation. What we intend to focus on in this section are the mindfulness tools that have strong links to emotional flexibility and authentic confidence.

We strongly recommend giving meditation a try for a longer period of time, say about eight weeks, to experience its benefits in terms of developing authentic confidence and emotional flexibility. We would like to recommend a free online resource based on Jon Kabat-Zinn's MBSR training: https://palousemindfulness.com/. This training, organised and led by Dave Potter, offers a self-paced programme and an opportunity to obtain a certificate of completion afterwards that is valid for many follow-on teacher trainings. Practicing meditation and mindfulness is essential to the development of authentic confidence, leaning in to what is important to you, reaching your potential and boosting your overall sense of well-being.

6.4.1 Finding and using the pause button at work

Description of this tool	What will this tool enable for you:
This tool helps you to build awareness about the interplay between thoughts, body and action and how to 'pause' and choose your response.	• Increased awareness of the interplay between your thoughts, body and behaviour. • Empower you with a 'pause button'.

Introduction

> **"Forces beyond your control can take away everything you possess except one thing, your freedom to choose how you will respond to the situation. You cannot control what happens to you in life, but you can always control what you will feel and do about what happens to you."**
>
> **Harold S. Kushner,** in Viktor Frankl (2014: X)

An important step in developing authentic confidence is building awareness of the external and internal triggers that undermine our confidence. The quote cited above is all about stimulus and response. It tells us that we always have a choice in how to respond to the circumstances we find ourselves in and the stimuli we experience, whether they be internal or external. If we start believing this and become skilful at putting it into practice, we will start to feel empowered because we will have climbed into the driver's seat of our life. With this tool we will explain how to do exactly that.[149]

> **"Down through the years I have learned to recognise my inner critic when it speaks up and to use the experience to better understand myself and learn from it. I know now when it is about to happen. In some situations it is easier to deal with than in others, but the fact that I can recognise it means that I**

149 Thanks to new insights from neuroscience, we now know that this is based on developing better awareness in the moment and the capability to be more adaptable when 'predicting' options, combined with the ongoing cycle of incoming new information – as explained in Chapter 2.

> **can choose how to deal with it - for example, by taking a step back or diving into the discussion."**
>
> **Abbe Luersman,** CHRO, EVP and Chief People Officer, Otis Elevator Co.

Pause button tool
Before introducing and explaining the pause button tool, please take a moment to explore your thoughts. Set a timer on your smartphone for one minute. Keep a pile of Post-Its® close at hand. During this minute, write down every single thought that you have, one thought per Post-It®. Don't skip this step!

When the minute is up, lay out all your notes on the floor or on a table. As you will probably see, you can have a lot of thoughts in only one minute. These are the kinds of thoughts you usually have during your day and often you are not even conscious of them. In addition to the thoughts you have just written down, there are also lots of other thoughts that come and go unconsciously. On the cover of her book *Emotional Agility* (2016) Susan David writes: "Every day we speak around 16,000 words - but inside our minds we create tens of thousands more."

This means there is a lot of stuff going on in your brain that can have an impact on you. Becoming aware of this is step number one. But what should you do with this flood of thoughts? First of all, most of these thoughts do not require you to do anything. Thinking is part of being human, after all. Some thoughts, however, do not help us but can be a potential hinderance. We have to learn to be more aware of such thoughts and to press the pause button so that we can give ourselves the time to decide how, if at all, we will let these thoughts impact us. Some thoughts can lead to an emotional reaction, as already described in Chapter 2. Knowing how to (a) become aware and (b) change the impact of our thoughts will empower us to stay on the course we wish to follow.

Becoming aware of your triggers
Think of the moments when you become insecure or lack confidence. You can also reflect on the framework that was provided in Chapter 2 for mind, body and action feedback. Triggers often have their origin in one of these categories: something you think, something you feel in your body or an emotion, or an action that you take or something you avoid. Triggers are messengers, they are not the cause of the discomfort you may feel.

> **"Having faced many challenges before has made me more aware of situations where I need to take action immediately."**
>
> **Paul-Peter Feld,** CHRO, Enexis

Achieving an understanding of what triggers your lack of confidence, including by writing down the different triggers you experience over time, can help you to become more present in the moment and more aware of when these triggers appear. When you practice mindfulness you build up 'muscle' and you cultivate skills that can help you to become aware of these trigger moments, which often appear very suddenly, as if out of nowhere. When you learn how to become aware of these moments you can manage your response much more quickly.

Identify your inner critic

You can also do an exercise to make yourself aware of the inner critics that are related to trigger moments or causes. If you are constantly hearing critical messages in your head, it can help to explore the source of those messages and to understand the inner child that learned these messages from early experiences. A well-known example of this kind of inner voice is 'I am not good enough'. This is a regular visitor for many people and we will discuss it in other exercises as well. We all have inner critics and if you would like a few tips on how to identify them, have a look at this YouTube video: https://www.youtube.com/watch?v=XHGBeg6AnMo.

Becoming aware of your inner voices, which are often triggered when you are at work, is step one in the process. Here are a few examples of the thoughts that appear in the above YouTube video:

"I am not able to do what is expected of me."
"I am not as good as I should be."
"I am unlovable."
"I am a failure, and my patient will soon realise that too."
"I am never going to open my mouth again."

The people quoted in the video all are professionals, so the chances are high that our colleagues at work have similar thoughts, too. How does that impact what we do and how we perform? Do we hold ourselves back? Do we avoid leaning in during meetings? Do we avoid telling the truth to a client (because we believe our inner voice) when in fact if we did tell them the truth, we would be doing them a great service? Now that you are reflecting on your triggers, your inner critics, your thoughts and the possible causes, the question is: how should we act when they present themselves?

Take a pause

Taking a pause might sound a bit self-indulgent to some, but when you become aware of a trigger moment taking a pause does not mean you have to take a long break to ponder your next action. Taking a pause means using the moment of awareness to consciously choose your action. You take ownership of your response in the moment. This is not easy because automatic reactions happen so quickly. However, if you learn to become more mindful and more aware of these moments, you will also learn to change your usual response into one that you deliberately choose yourself. This requires practice, but it is possible. A pause can be as simple as taking a few deep breaths, observing what is happening and holding back momentarily before you react. For example, during a meeting you could say, 'Let me think about this for a moment' and then take the time to make up your mind. Similarly, you can wait until the next morning before responding to an email or, if you literally want to take a break, go for a quick cup of coffee.

When you pause to reflect on a trigger moment you become aware of how you feel at that moment and can describe the emotion to yourself. In psychology this is known as labelling your emotion. This helps you to become more aware of what goes on inside you at any given moment. "Along with the importance of precisely labelling our emotions comes the promise that once we do give them a name, our feelings can provide useful information." (David, 2016: 168) You may simply notice that you are feeling angry, sad, happy or joyful. People can experience many emotions throughout the day without even being aware of them. Becoming aware of the triggers and the emotions you feel at that moment can help you to be more mindful about your responses. There are so many different human emotions possible and sometimes we don't even know what to call them. Previous studies have identified 27 different emotions.[150] This act of noticing and describing your emotions can be carried out very quickly during and shortly after the moment in question. And it can be done without anyone noticing that you are taking a little pause.

Choose your own action

The action that you choose to take depends entirely on what you think is best in that moment after reflecting on the experienced trigger and the emotion. During your pause and when you have described the emotion to yourself, you can use other tools from the toolkit too (including some that we will discuss later on in this book). For example, you can decide not to respond to the question asked during the meeting because you are aware that if you respond now you will give an emotional answer and not the answer that you would give if you had more time to react. A pause can be long or short; the crucial thing is that you take ownership of the moment and do not let the trigger that you notice or experience force you into an emotional reaction.

If you learn to recognise your triggers and related (emotional) responses, take a pause and choose your own action, you will start to develop the meta-skill of observing the situation, which is something we will also discuss in relation to many of the other tools that follow. You can learn to do this if you focus on developing the basic skill of mindfulness. The more you practice, the better you will become at it, as scientific research shows that people who develop mindfulness skills become better at self-regulation.[151] This moment of 'awareness, pause and choosing your own action' is also essential when you want to take the time to reconnect with what is important to you (your purpose and values). These steps can help you to decide what your response will be and which action you should choose.

150 For more information about this study, please go to http://www.dailymail.co.uk/sciencetech/article-4862846/Scientists-discover-27-DIFFERENT-emotions.html or https://www.pnas.org/doi/abs/10.1073/pnas.1702247114. You can explore an interactive map of emotions here: https://s3-us-west-1.amazonaws.com/emogifs/map.html

151 See, e.g., Tang, Y. Y., Holzel, B. K., & Posner, M. I. (2015a). The neuroscience of mindfulness meditation. Nature Reviews Neuroscience, 16(4), 213–225. https://doi.org/10.1038/nrn3916 and
Tang, Y. Y., Posner, M. I., Rothbart, M. K., & Volkow, N. D. (2015b). Circuitry of self-control and its role in reducing addiction. Trends in Cognitive Sciences, 19(8), 439–444. https://doi.org/10.1016/j.tics.2015.06.007

> **"I practice mindfulness and have also introduced it into my team. It has helped me to be calm and in control. I have also introduced other tools related to resourcefulness that have helped the team to understand themselves both as individuals and as members of a team, and to become aware of the emotional triggers and their impact. This has enhanced our collaboration and has made our more supportive of each other in our daily interactions."**
>
> **Michelle Roborg-Sondergaard,** Senior HR Executive

> **"I got into mindfulness later in life and I find it very helpful. I do it regularly, especially when I get tense about stuff. I find getting into the moment, as opposed to worrying about what may happen tomorrow, a very useful technique, also to get to sleep. I am involved in a very difficult job at the moment. To get it off my mind, I practice mindfulness before I sleep. I force myself into the moment. I also recommend it to my children. This is something I have only learned in the last few years."**
>
> **John Brand,** Consultant, Bowmans, South Africa

6.4.2 Diaphragmatic breathing in the boardroom and beyond

Description of this tool	**What will this tool enable for you:**
This tool helps you understand how to breathe well for authentic confidence. It is the basis tool for emotional flexibility and SOS situations.	• You will master the 'right' technique for breathing.

Introduction

Breathing is at the core of being calm and taking charge of your life. We describe breathing not only in terms of its necessity for our survival but also as a skill. People are often unaware that there are different ways of breathing deeply and that some ways of breathing can actually do us more harm than good. In this tool we will look at the important skill of controlled breathing.

> **"When I feel extreme stress, I try to get my breathing under control again. That calms the whole system down."**
>
> **Jan J. Wever,** MD, PhD, Vascular Surgeon, Haga Hospital, The Hague, Netherlands

Diaphragmatic breathing tool

This technique can help you at all kinds of moments and is particularly effective when you experience an SOS moment. It reduces stress and calms you down when you are about to experience 'crash' mode or extreme stress. The technique is used by the military and by athletes to focus, gain control and manage stress. It helps you to deal with worry and nervousness and during moments when you need to become calm, for example just before a performance on stage or when leading a meeting.

When you are stressed it feels as if your breathing is originating in your chest area or higher up in your body. You may notice your breaths are shorter than usual and perhaps you are not taking the time to breathe out fully or calmly.[152] This type of breathing can actually amplify the feeling and experience of stress. The trick to becoming calm again is to learn to breathe from your diaphragm, which is the lower part of your belly just under your rib cage, as shown in Figure 25 below.

Caroline Goyder, a leading voice coach, provides a very powerful explanation of the workings of the diaphragm. In the Greek language, the word for this is 'Phrenos' or 'phren' which in Ancient Greece represented the mind, heart and diaphragm (Goyder, 2014: 88). It is important to reflect on this for a few moments, especially since our focus is on developing authentic confidence. Breathing from the diaphragm automatically involves the mind and heart, which closes the circle if you reflect again on what we said in Chapter 2 about the sympathetic nervous system (activated when we are stressed) and the parasympathetic nervous system (activated when we calm down).

When we become stressed and anxious and are feeling an immediate stress response or a strong emotional reaction, the sympathetic nervous system (SNS) is activated, as already explained. The SNS 'is made up of neurons in the spinal cord that connect with nearly every organ system in the body, which allows the SNS to influence

152 There is a disbalance in your breathing pattern.

dozens of responses, from pupil dilation to heart rate. The role of the SNS is to create the fight-or-flight response' (Pittman and Karle, 2015: 23). In order to calm the SNS down, the parasympathetic nervous system (PNS) needs to be activated. An example of when you activate your PNS is when you are lying in the chair at the beauty salon or when you are receiving a massage. Sometimes you will even hear your stomach rumble. This is an indication that you are moving into a deep mode of relaxation and that your PNS has been activated. Deep diaphragmatic breathing supports the activation of the PNS and calms down the SNS, taking you out of the potential fight, flight or freeze mode. This allows you to regain control of yourself.

The mind and heart are also involved from a philosophical viewpoint through our purpose and values and they inform the choices we have to make at important moments. There are also physical aspects that are relevant to this area of our body. Like our heart and lungs, the diaphragm moves when we breathe. The moment we breathe in, it descends and pushes the stomach out while the other organs move down. In other words, it is a powerful natural inner massage of your torso that helps to relax your body and mind if you do it well.

There are five easy steps:[153]

1. Place your hand just below where your ribs start. This is your abdominal area. Focus on this area when you breathe in and out.
2. Breathe in while counting 1 - 2 - 3 - 4 (feel your abdomen expand).
3. Stop and hold your breath while counting 1 - 2 - 3 - 4.
4. Exhale while counting 1 - 2 - 3 - 4 (feel your abdomen deflate).
5. Repeat 3 to 5 times and visualize the numbers as you count.

Variations on this exercise include exhaling for longer than you inhale (for example, exhaling for 6 seconds instead of 4) and the 'physiological' sigh, as explained by Dr Andrew Huberman.[154] A physiological sigh refers to a "pattern of breathing in which two inhales through the nose are followed by an extended exhale through the mouth."[155]

153 https://www.med.navy.mil/sites/nmcphc/Documents/health-promotion-wellness/psychological-emotional-well-being/Combat-Tactical-Breathing.pdf

154 You can find an explanation here: https://hubermanlab.com/how-to-build-endurance-in-your-brain-and-body/ (Eliminating 'side cramp' With Physiological Sighs).

155 Further described here: https://scopeblog.stanford.edu/2020/10/07/how-stress-affects-your-brain-and-how-to-reverse-it/

> **"What I do when I am stressed or nervous: I breathe deeply from my belly, three or four times, in via the nose... hold it briefly... and out via the mouth... and then I am calm again."**
>
> **Jan Zijderveld,** former CEO Avon Inc. and President of Unilever Europe

FIGURE 25: DIAPHRAGMATIC BREATHING

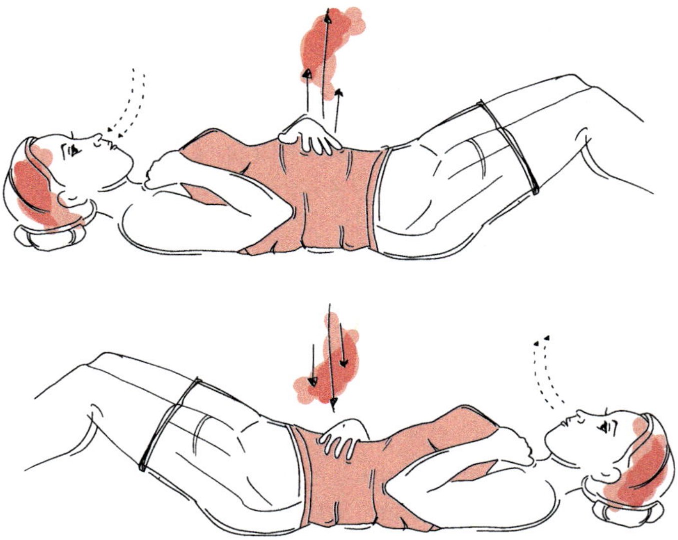

> **"When things get very difficult, I pause and breathe and connect with my purpose and values."**
>
> **Joanna Barsh,** Joanna Barsh, Senior Partner Emerita, McKinsey & Company

6.4.3 Mindfulness for busy people

Description of this tool	**What will this tool enable for you:**
Learn how to practice mindfulness even if you think you are too busy. The truth is: no one is too busy for mindfulness!	• You will understand the fundamental principles of mindfulness and how to apply them in a busy schedule.

Introduction

Professionals often say that they don't have the time for mindfulness. However, when you dig deeper you find out that they actually don't know how to practice it or believe that mindfulness almost requires you to become a full-time monk. When you explain all the variations of mindfulness they often have an 'aha' moment and realise that mindfulness is accessible to all of us. In this tool we will be exploring mindfulness for busy people.

The Oxford English Dictionary defines mindfulness as 'the quality or state of being conscious or aware of something,' and 'a mental state achieved by focusing one's awareness on the present moment, while calmly acknowledging and accepting one's feelings, thoughts, and bodily sensations, used as a therapeutic technique.' It's all about maintaining awareness and the intention to take care of the experiences and situations you are aware off. Mindful attention is intentional and relational to all experiences, even when you are very busy.

For this tool to be effective, regular mindfulness and meditation practice is essential. We ourselves define meditation as cultivating focus to see all kinds of experience, including bodily sensations, sounds and thoughts. We define mindfulness as a mental state achieved by focusing one's awareness on the present moment, while calmly acknowledging and accepting one's feelings, thoughts and bodily sensations, used as a therapeutic technique. We will be referring to both concepts in this section.

> **"I have moments when I am anxious, but I don't spend my nights lying awake. I am able to let go of these things easily and I enjoy focusing on different activities at the weekend. Staying in the moment and letting go really helps."**
>
> **Lex Meijdam,** Professor of Economics, Tilburg School of Economics and Management, Tilburg University

> **"I realised that I had to invest time and effort in getting to know myself better, in the ability to reflect on my own intentions and attitudes. I actively participate in the practices of the Brahma Kumaris. Once a year, I go on a leadership retreat where we reflect and meditate for three or four days. Their philosophy is to live your daily life from the inside out, to connect with the good and bring that mental model of service to the role you need to play. It is their spiritual wisdom that we should**

> **live our lives guided by our inner voice or what they call the 'soul'."**
>
> **Tex Gunning,** CEO, LeasePlan

Mindfulness for busy people (tool)

Busy people come in many different shapes and sizes. They have families and careers and multiple jobs or they combine a full-time job with caring for aging parents, and so on. Nowadays, we all appear to be busy. Life is said to be much busier now than when our parents were our age. Whether this is actually the case or not is another matter, but the fact is that the modern 24/7 society we live in makes it feel that way. And there is no doubt that we are more easily distracted today because of the Internet and the constant availability of information and entertainment on our smartphones, tablets, laptops, smartwatches, etc. Research by Killingsworth and Gilbert (2010) showed that the participants in their study were 'lost in thought' 47% of their time on average. In other words, for 47% of their time, the participants' mind was not in the same place as their body (what they were doing). And the same study found a strong correlation between moment-by-moment awareness and contentment or happiness. There is potentially a lot to gain here,[156] as this is entirely the opposite of being mindful.

If you think that the only way to become mindful is by sitting on a pillow with your legs crossed and humming mantras for an hour each day, then you are mistaken. Of course, exploring and making time for meditation on a regular basis is important and certainly not a luxury. But, in reality, this is not always possible for everyone. So, another way to build mindful awareness during the day is to find activities in your busy programme that you can transform into mindful moments. If you start exploring what those moments could be, you will find lots of candidates. We will name a few here just to get you started, but you will be able to think of many more yourself, too.

Our first example is 'brushing your teeth in a mindful manner'. We assume you brush your teeth twice a day for at least one or two minutes. These minutes can be used to brush your teeth *and* to create a moment of mindfulness. When you are brushing your teeth, take a deep breath and examine how your toothbrush is touching and cleaning your teeth. Other thoughts may pop up, just observe them and let them go. Focus again on brushing your teeth and observe

156 https://www.science.org/doi/10.1126/science.1192439

every move you make. The second example is 'getting dressed in a mindful manner'. You are never too busy to get dressed for work each day. When you step out from under the shower (which is another potential mindful moment) and start getting dressed, observe each move you make while putting on your clothes. Observe how the fabric of your clothes touches your skin. Other thoughts will come along, they always do; observe them and let them go. Observe and engage with the process of getting dressed and be there in the moment.

We trust you get the point by now and that you can think of many other potential moments of mindfulness, such as eating your breakfast or travelling to work. There are multiple moments during your busy day that you can transform into mindful moments if you choose to do so. It is a muscle you can start flexing right away. Use these moments to do a breathing exercise and to examine what happens in that moment. There are many books and apps that can help you explore all of this. Please check our references at the back of this book. In 2016, for instance, Hougaard and Carter wrote a short article about this subject in *Harvard Business Review*. If you are interested in reading the article, you can use this link:
https://hbr.org/2016/03/how-to-practice-mindfulness-throughout-your-work-day.

There are all kinds of ways of introducing mindfulness into your working day. Many mindfulness and meditation apps offer the option of sending you notifications during the day (on your smartphone, watch or laptop) reminding you to breathe, to feel the tips of your toes or think about how you are sitting on your chair. They can also ask you questions that help you to stay in the moment. You can explore some of these apps using the references at the back of this book.

> **"I once had to give a really important presentation in front of a large audience of CEOs, entrepreneurs and even our Prime Minister. I prepared well, but more importantly, I found a quiet space to focus on the presentation, to rehearse and to be in the moment. It went very well. I usually find these things very difficult, but I discovered that preparing well and taking the time to be alone can make all the difference."**
>
> **Pieter Waasdorp,** Director of Entrepreneurship, Ministry of Economic Affairs, The Netherlands

Here's a link to a funny and informative clip called 'How to train your 'monkey mind': becoming 'mindful' everywhere and anytime' on YouTube:

How to train your monkey mind

https://www.youtube.com/watch?v=4PkrhH-bkpk

6.4.4 Mindfulness throughout your working day

Description of this tool	**What will this tool enable for you:**
This tool explores how you can apply mindfulness when you have to perform: in a meeting, during a presentation or when focusing on an analysis.	• Understand what you can do at critical moments during your work day to bring a mindful focus to your work.

Introduction

With this tool you can learn how to be mindful during moments that matter in your working day. For example, when you are about to chair an important board meeting or give a presentation to a large group of industry leaders or clients, or when you have to appear on national television to represent your organisation and give your expert opinion. What these moments have in common is that your performance is of critical importance and, of course, that you will probably be very nervous and worried about failing. You will feel your stomach churn, the palms of your hands will become sweaty and you will find you can only remember half of the two-minute speech you prepared. These are the moments when your brain starts going crazy. So what can you do to calm yourself down, stay focused and deliver a good performance? We will explore this in the next section.

> **"One of the most important things I have learned over the last few years is to be clear about the intention with which I am going into a conversation. If I reflect on this before a conversation, it really helps to lead the conversation along the right lines. It makes me more effective."**
>
> **Paul-Peter Feld,** CHRO, Enexis

Becoming mindful during your working day (tool)
As we have already said, you don't have to spend hours upon hours practicing meditation or mindfulness every day. Setting aside around ten minutes each day as part of your standard *modus operandi* or operating model (which we will discuss in Chapter 10) can help you to leverage the enormous benefits of meditation. When you start practicing mindfulness and become more and more aware of your 'prediction pattern' or, to explain it in a more classical[157] manner, of the triggers that cause you to react emotionally, you will become more conscious of what goes on in the moment when that happens. For example, in a meeting or when you receive an upsetting message. There are a number of things you can do in those moments.

In this playbook we refer frequently to breathing. Breathing is the foundation of becoming mindful and aware in the moment, which in turn supports the feeling and state of becoming authentically confident. If you have only a few minutes to do your breathing exercises, or even less, remember to breathe from the diaphragm. You might not always be able to do the diaphragmatic breathing exercise we described earlier, but if you focus on your breathing using the lower part of your belly, as opposed to your chest, and exhale for (a bit) longer than you inhale, you will find that this works too, as does a physiological sigh.[158] It is something you can even do in the middle of another activity. When you feel stressed or tense you can always do a breathing exercise on the spot to calm you down. And no one else needs to know.

1. **Setting your intent**. Before you have a meeting with someone, think about what the purpose of the meeting is. You can do this while you are on your way to the meeting. The same applies to the presentation or workshop that you have to lead or any other performance you are about to deliver. Breathing deeply in and out, ask yourself: "What is my intent, how do I want to show up, how do I want to present myself, what do I have to give, and what

157 By 'classical' here we mean what most of us still see as happening: a situation, a trigger and how we respond. We now know through new insights from neuroscience that this is based on our own predictions of what is possibly going to happen - along the way we will include little comments on this to help you become more aware of the opportunity to expand your prediction repertoire and frames, which will help you become more emotionally flexible.

158 See: https://www.youtube.com/watch?v=rBdhqBGqiMc and find more relevant links via hubermanlab.com

do I want to achieve, how do I want to connect, who do I want to be?" Visualize achieving your goal in your mind. If you have more time, you can also write down your intent and do a few minutes of meditation or mindfulness beforehand. Reflecting on your intent and visualizing success (however you define it; see also Chapter 5) will give you the calm confidence you need to improve your chances of success.

2. **Become aware of the sensations in your body**. Just before your big performance, examine what you feel in your body: feel your feet on the ground and feel the sensations in your stomach. Add a helping of honest curiosity to the experience; where is it, how does it feel? Allow these sensations to be there, feel where they are and be aware of them. When you feel comfortable, you can try breathing some calmness into the parts of your body where you still feel some tension.
3. **Reflect on your actions**. Reflect on how you feel in general (your breathing, your intention and the sensations in your body) and visualize yourself leaning in to the challenge. In that moment, connect with your purpose and values (Chapter 5), in other words, the reason why this is important to you, and make a conscious decision to either lean in to the challenge or to engage instead in avoidance.

> **"Currently, I am really on top of my game because I have so much experience in my field compared with the people I work with – it's all about skill and competency. I also tend to slow things down and to listen carefully before trying to say something, and I don't feel as much responsibility for jumping in and saving the day. Instead, I tend to sit back, listen more and be mindful. It gives me more time to deal with challenging situations."**
>
> **John Brand,** Consultant, Bowmans, South Africa

There are also small mechanisms that you can integrate into your busy working day that will remind you to be mindful or can help you to correct your actions when stress threatens to take over. We all remember situations in which we sent an email in a hurry in response to an external trigger that evoked a negative emotion.[159] You feel you must reply to the email immediately because you are in a hurry to go and pick up your kids from their sports training. And if you are

159 Because of what you know and learned, how you feel and what you predict will happen next (see Chapter 2).

late, they will be waiting out on the street. So you write a quick but slightly emotional email in reply. You hit the send button, close your laptop, pack your bag and grab your car keys. You have one foot outside the office door when it hits you that the e-mail you have just sent is not entirely accurate. You recall what a colleague told you earlier that day and you suddenly realise how everything is connected. You have jumped to conclusions a bit too quickly. You feel a knot in your stomach and start to worry that perhaps you should not have sent the quickly drafted email but you cannot turn back the clock now. You start feeling insecure about the whole episode and that feeling stays with you for the rest of the day.

This is just one example of how your emotions (that you construct yourself) can take over from your rational thinking. Larry Murphy provides an excellent example of how to put mechanisms in place that can help to prevent this from happening. He configured his e-mail programme to allow him to change his message in case he responds too fast and starts having second thoughts a few minutes after writing the email.

> **"Emails are a constant source of stress for me. And that's not just because I receive too many. More pressing on me is the worry that I'm not communicating as effectively as I would if I were physically present with the other person, and able to read their reactions so as to manage my approach accordingly. And I worry that when a substantive email I send doesn't get a timely response, I've perhaps somehow caused offense or a tension that isn't helpful. So, I second-guess a lot on emails I'm writing. To accommodate that second-guessing, for many years, I've used an automated email rule - my 'oh, s**t' mechanism - to delay the sending of my emails for a full three minutes after I hit the send button. It gives me a moment for my subconscious to go to work, to replay the email in my head, and for me to go into the outbox, open up the email and make a change before it actually goes out. Thank goodness for that functionality in Outlook!"**
>
> **Larry Murphy,** President and COO Executive Education and Lifelong Learning University of Virginia Darden School Foundation

6.4.5 Mindful voice techniques

Lead author of this section: Anneke Brouwer, Systemic Dialogic Speaker Coach, Executive Voice Expert at The House of Silence[160]

Description of this tool	What will this tool enable you:
This tool enables you to find your most deep, relaxed and powerful voice. It helps you to stay calm and feel confident while speaking.	• You will know how to breathe, prepare and use your voice before speaking in public, be it on stage or in smaller group settings.

Introduction

The human voice is part of the vagus nerve of the sympathetic nervous system (SNS), which connects the brainstem to the body. Hence, your voice is very important in calming and soothing your state of mind while speaking. Breathing is the key instrument, not only for calming yourself, but also to support your most deep, relaxed and powerful voice. When we feel stressed and tense or out of breath, we do not have a free, energetic and clear voice. Shallow breathing creates a voice that sounds constricted and lightweight. And it works both ways: when you experience that your voice is not your natural one, unpleasant feelings can arise as well. So you experience a 'double whammy'. Other unwelcome side effects are that you may leave the impression that you are hurried, insecure about what you are supposed to be doing or, worse still, unprepared.

> **"We breathe without thinking.**
> **We breathe without thinking.**
> **We don't have to make an effort to breathe. We just breathe.**
> **We breathe in and we breathe out.**
> **It is a natural process, a matter of physics. The principle of communicating vessels. The balance that arises in the dance between underpressure and overpressure, requiring no effort on our part. In... Out... In... Out... All by itself.**
> **As long as we are able to let go...**
> **We don't need to *take* a breath. We simply breathe.**
> **If we had to actually draw a breath each time we needed to breathe, we wouldn't last very long at all. Taking a breath implies making an effort to breathe. Performing an action.**

160 See also: https://annekebrouwer.nl/?lang=en; This chapter also includes special contributions by Caroline Goyder: www.carolinegoyder.com

> **But the trick when breathing is not to do anything at all. To just let it go. To let go of all the tension so that the simple act of breathing overrides any need to draw a breath.**
> **This kind of breathing is called diaphragmatic breathing, also known as belly breathing, and it forms the basis for mindful expression, for softening your frame of mind, for recovering your sense of calm and self-confidence, for relaxing, for leadership."**
>
> **Anneke Brouwer,** Systemic Dialogic Speaker Coach, Executive Voice Expert at the House of Silence

Mindful voice technique tool
There is a magical tool that will help you to find your most deep, relaxed and powerful voice. It is a tool we discussed earlier in this chapter: diaphragmatic breathing or belly breathing. This tool not only produces sufficient energy for a strong vocal presence, but it also softens the voice, giving it a warmer character. The combination of your most deep, relaxed and powerful voice and the relaxed state of your body results in a speaker who sounds calm, pleasant and confident - the way your voice sounds when you are fully relaxed. Mindful use of your voice helps you to speak with consistency, confidence and credibility. Mastering this tool will also give you confidence the next time you have to speak in public and might be nervous.

If you are not sure that you can make this tool work for you, a few words of inspiration may help:

> **"It was the Greek orator Demosthenes who proved the power of practice. He went from being called The Stammerer - the poor man couldn't even pronounce the 'r' in 'rhetoric' - to being known as a great speaker. Plutarch, the Greek historian, biographer and essayist remarked that he became 'a man who had the power and the ability to speak to both workers and leaders.' It was all down to hard work. Demosthenes built himself an underground study and practiced and practiced until he became the greatest speaker in town. He had the self-belief to change the habit and work the muscle."**
>
> **Goyder,** 2014: 87-88

At the core of mindfully mastering your voice are three steps. We build on the previous tool (sub-section 6.4.2) involving diaphragmatic breathing and introduce voice techniques along the way. These three steps are inspired by the work of Coblenzer (1993-1998) and practical experience and expertise in the field.[161]

Step 1: Locate your diaphragm
In the diaphragmatic breathing tool we visualized that breathing from your belly was one of the best ways to calm down after a strong emotional reaction. This type of breathing is also very helpful when you are preparing to speak. This can be in a meeting, on the phone or on stage. Proper breathing as the basis of great voice usage can help you to stay focused on what you want to do and can even prevent a potential emotional reaction. Before we start using the voice in this process, let us recap on the previous tool to help you to locate your diaphragm precisely:

1. Close your eyes and ground yourself while standing. Place your hand just below where your ribs start. Take three slow and deep breaths using your belly. Imagine your breath as a source of nourishment and relaxing energy.
2. Focus on your abdominal area. Feel your abdomen expand when you slowly breathe in and deflate when you breathe out. This is healthy, controlled breathing (diaphragmatic or natural breathing).

Now it's time to start using your voice.

Step 2: Find your mindful voice
A deep and relaxed voice has the power to help you stay calm and feel confident while speaking. Finding your authentic and mindful voice is therefore well worth the effort. Humming helps too. Try the following. Ground yourself while standing and breathe slowly in through your nose. Feel your abdomen expand and breathe out through your mouth while you hum. Feel how low (but warm and positive) your voice is and how easily it issues from your throat. Repeat this a few times and make the humming sound more meaningful, as if you are responding positively to someone you are listening to. Feel the resonance in your abdomen. Feel the low notes deep in your belly. This is your most relaxed voice. You sound calm, pleasant and confident.

You can become more familiar with this calm, pleasant and confident sound by using it in your daily life while listening to others. Try using this low, relaxed voice when you are in a conference call with

161 By Anneke Brouwer: https://annekebrouwer.nl/?lang=en

others. No one can see you in a conference call, so you can concentrate fully on your voice instead of also having to focus on how you appear to others in a face-to-face setting. And you can do this just before you get on stage. Use the tool to warm up your voice, find your mindful speaking voice and calm and soothe your state of mind.

However, when using this technique you will need to speak more slowly if you want to retain your mindful voice. Just try to stay in the moment (using your mindfulness techniques), in the here and now, and avoid worrying about what you have already said or what might come. Be in the now. When you notice that you are going too fast, take a moment to pause and focus on your belly breathing again. If this helps, feel how your breath travels through your nose as you breathe in and out. The deeper you breathe, the more relaxed you will feel and the more mindful your voice will sound. Your team members, colleagues, clients and even a broader audience will experience your voice as calm, pleasant and confident.

Remember that when you speak everything can feel very slow when you pause. We tend to speak much faster when we are nervous. Don't be afraid to slow things down, to pause every now and then. Breathe and enjoy your warm, calm voice. In the meantime, keep varying the tone of your voice by lengthening the vowels in the most important words. If you don't vary the tone of your voice, your manner of speaking can become monotonous and boring to listen to. Your mindful voice relaxes your state of mind and makes it much easier for others to listen to you.

Step 3: Speak mindfully
Speaking mindfully means being aware of how you speak by doing so with precision and energy. Articulate all the vowels and consonants in each word clearly. Speak your sentences from start to finish with the same energy, like you are tasting each and every word. Your listeners will then find it easy to follow your message. Speaking mindfully also means moving. Humans are made to move. Humans are not trees, we were not born to stand still. Start by grounding yourself and then move while you are speaking. Use gestures and think of them as verbal punctuation. This makes emphasising the meaning of words much easier and it helps to convey the emotion behind your words. To establish a smooth vocal rhythm and to keep speaking mindfully, use gestures that are supple. Move from side to

side calmly across the stage.[162] Think in terms of slow, powerful movements. If you are brave enough and really want to become a master in this area, you can also train the muscles in your face and mouth to support your new-found mindful voice.

Here are a number of useful tips and techniques.

1. Warm up your speech organs using your hands. Massage the muscles of your cheeks with your fingers for two minutes while chewing.
2. Practice chewing a big piece of bubble gum with your lips closed but your teeth apart and while making an 'mmmm' sound.
3. Repeat the above exercises, but now while opening and closing your mouth a few times.
4. Pout your lips while exhaling to make your lips and cheeks more supple.
5. Move your tongue from one cheek to the other in a circular manner.
6. Now speak as if you can taste each word, with exaggerated articulation. Move your lips, tongue and jaw in as exaggerated a manner as possible while speaking your thoughts out loud.
7. Start slowly and finish fast without stumbling. Repeat every sentence three times with the same exaggerated diction and speed.

Now you are ready. You have found your diaphragm and your mindful voice, and you know how to speak mindfully by articulating the words fully and with energy. Start small and experiment as you go along.

> **"When I started to study the voice (at the world-class Central School of Speech and Drama in London), I struggled. Learning how to use this wonderful instrument seemed arduous, complicated. The epiphany came when I understood that little and often, approached with lightness and ease, was the key to change. As my teacher used to tell me, the secret was to 'try less hard'. When you find physical ease, the voice – and your innate presence and charisma – opens up. And that's the challenge for my corporate clients, where most get to their roles through hard work and intellectual focus. They push through. It's a clear case of 'what got you here won't get you there'. The voice does not work like that. If you want ease and**

---

162 We are focusing here on speaking in front of an audience, e.g., on stage. However, many of these techniques (apart from walking back and forth on stage) also apply to 1:1 conversations and/or meeting settings.

presence in the spotlight, slow down, breathe and be present. 'Try less hard'. Why? Because effort tenses us up, closes us down. The voice is an instrument that works best when we open up, breathe, become free, fluid, playful. It's why my teachers told me to 'get out of my head and into the body', a lesson that I continue to be mindful of every day, twenty years on. I'm always open to any path or practice that gets me into the body - as it has a miraculous effect on my voice. Alexander technique, classical Pilates and yoga have been faithful friends over the years and have transformed my voice and presence through regular practice. And I see every day in my clients that it's when we settle into ourselves, breathe, open up, that the voice follows. And when your voice and presence open up, that's when you compel attention. You resonate in a different way when you are settled into your deepest truth. If you want to find your own voice, know that it's there, just waiting for you, ready to play. The art is to find time each day to get into the body, to 'get the motor running', as Katherine Hepburn used to say. Every morning, take five minutes to sing, move, open up, and your voice will follow. Above all trust your voice. Every human has a wonderful voice within. Get out of the head into the body (sing in the shower!), and yours will open up too. I'm walking proof because my journey took me from frustration to trust, and ultimately enjoyment in my own voice. Little and often, done with love is all it takes to find a voice you can own and enjoy. I think of two very senior leaders I've worked with this year who have found that when they let go and trust their voice, and allow who they are to shine through, that openness is what pulls audiences in."

Caroline Goyder, a leading voice coach and author of the book *The Gravitas Method* (2014); for more inspiration, please watch Caroline Goyder's famous Ted Talk, 'The surprising secret to speaking with confidence': www.carolinegoyder.com

6.4.6 The power of sleep[163]

Description of this tool	What will this tool enable for you:
This tool teaches you about the importance of sleep in relation to developing authentic confidence.	• Increased awareness of the importance of sleep. • Initial tips and tricks and further references.

Introduction

Thanks to Arianna Huffington, and many more since, we have become more aware of the importance of sleep in the last couple of years. In her book *The Sleep Revolution* (2017) she explores the subject in great detail. We all know intuitively how important sleep is to our overall well-being. 'Research has shown that sleep-deprived brains lose the ability to make accurate judgements. This in turn can lead to irrational and unjustified claims such as "I do not need sleep" or "I'm doing fine with a couple of hours of sleep".' (Van Dam and van der Helm, 2016).[164] Lack of sleep can negatively affect your optimism and self-esteem[165] and increase risky behaviour.[166] This may explain why, despite the fact that we know that sleep is important, we often tend to underestimate how important it is to our functioning and mental health at work. According to Huffington, 'lack of sleep is often the culprit behind anxiety, stress, depression, and a myriad of health problems' (2017: 25). In her book, Huffington gives multiple examples of how lack of sleep is related to increased anxiety and mental health challenges.

163 This section includes special contributions from Dr Srini Pillay, Harvard Medical School and Neuro Business Group, and Dr Els van der Helm, sleep neuroscientist

164 https://www.mckinsey.com/business-functions/organisation/our-insights/the-organisational-cost-of-insufficient-sleep

165 Lack of sleep can decrease your optimism and self-esteem: https://www.ncbi.nlm.nih.gov/pubmed/23055029

166 Sleep can increase risky behaviour: https://www.ncbi.nlm.nih.gov/pubmed/15984914 and https://www.ncbi.nlm.nih.gov/pubmed/28833531

FIGURE 26: LEADERSHIP PERFORMANCE IS HIGHLY DEPENDENT ON SLEEP

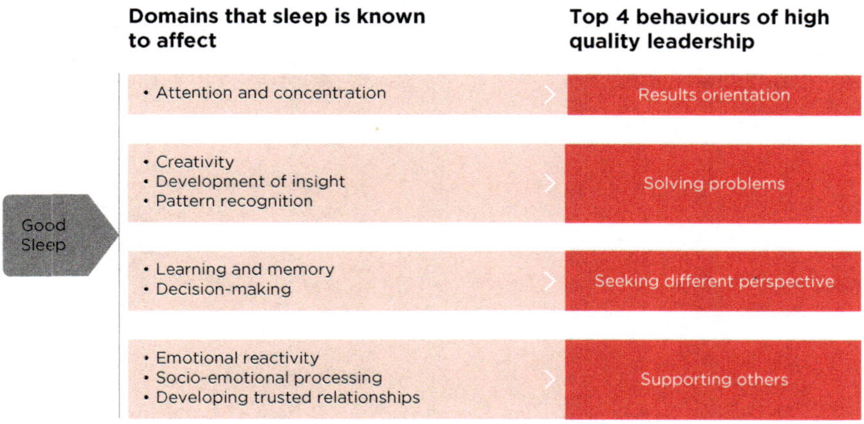

Source: McKinsey & Company (Feburary 2016). The organizational cost of insufficient sleep (see https://www.mckinsey.com/business-functions/people-and-organizational-performance/our-insights/the-organizational-cost-of-insufficient-sleep).

Leadership performance (like any performance) is highly dependent on sleep (see Figure 26). It turns out that lack of sleep actually makes you more sensitive to stress and can increase amygdala activation.[167] The prefrontal cortex is also very vulnerable when it comes to lack of sleep. Classical explanations of how the brain responds refer to the fact that if we do not sleep enough, we are driven more by the emotional centre of our brain, the amygdala, as opposed to the rational thinking part, the prefrontal cortex (see, e.g., Pittman and Karle, 2015; and Tabibnia and Radecki, 2018). However, on the basis of new insights, perhaps it is better to say that we become more alert to danger and the threshold for predicting potential danger becomes lower. Research by the University of Sydney and the Mount Sinai School of Medicine in New York (2014) has shown that not sleeping long enough is related to increased levels of stress and anxiety (Huffington, 2017: 75). Poor sleep leads to difficulty with concentrating, issues with memory and poorer health in general (Pittman and Karle, 2015). When you sleep, memories are consolidated and neurotransmitters are replenished during the REM part of your sleep. Having sufficient or more REM sleep impacts the amygdala in a positive way, as it is associated with lower reactivity in the amygdala (Van der Helm et al., 2011). So, if we get a good night's sleep, including sufficient REM, this will calm the amygdala and affect our resilience to stress during work in a positive way.

167 https://www.ncbi.nlm.nih.gov/pubmed/25325493 and https://www.ncbi.nlm.nih.gov/pubmed/21458943

> **"The number one mental health tip is sleep, a fact with which I am all too familiar. At Unilever we invested a lot in mental health awareness."**
>
> **Jan Zijderveld,** former CEO Avon Inc. and President of Unilever Europe

> **"I am very inspired by Ariana Huffington's Thrive movement. She has democratized the importance of sleep. I make sure I get eight hours of sleep every night."**
>
> **Karen Rivoire,** Competence Flow Leader, Inter IKEA Group

> **"For me, eight hours of sleep makes a big difference and I try hard to make that a priority. That's the amount I need to feel energized and excited."**
>
> **Jeff Bezos,** Founder and CEO, Amazon[168]

> **"Aetna (US Insurance company) pays its employees up to $500 a year when they can show (through Fitbits) that they sleep at least seven hours a night for a certain period of time."**
>
> **Mark Bertollini,** CEO, Aetna[169]

> **"Sleep has always been foundational for my performance. I need seven hours of sleep to perform the way I need to my current job. Of course, with intense travel and work commitments, sometimes this becomes compromised, and when that happens it comes with a cost. When I don't get enough sleep my performance suffers."[170]**
>
> **Cees 't Hart,** President and CEO, Carlsberg Group

168 Thrive Global: https://journal.thriveglobal.com/jeff-bezos-sleep-amazon-19c617c59daa

169 https://www.cnbc.com/2016/04/05/why-aetnas-ceo-pays-workers-up-to-500-to-sleep.html

170 https://hbr.org/2018/02/senior-executives-get-more-sleep-than-everyone-else

Sleep quality and awareness tool

With this tool we aim to increase your awareness of the importance of sufficient sleep and what 'sufficient' means in this context. We will provide further references where you can get more information to improve the quality of your sleep.

1. Your sleep deficit: are you getting enough sleep?

We all know people who claim they can survive on just a few hours of sleep a night. Most of them, however, are the exception to the rule. 'The vast majority of us need between seven and nine hours of sleep to function at our best' (Webb, 2016: 28). Sleep neuroscientist Els van der Helm claims that if you get woken up by your alarm clock every morning, it is an indication that you have not slept enough. You cannot sleep too much; you simply wake up when you have had enough. Many of the participants in her workshops say that they don't get enough sleep during the week. When they compare the amount of hours they think they should sleep each night over five nights with the amount they actually sleep, the difference is between five and ten hours. You cannot compensate for this by sleeping more at the weekend. Life is a marathon and not a sprint. Finding ways to ensure you get enough sleep during your busy working week will help you stay calm and more focused, and your worries and insecurities will be less likely to send you into a spin.

2. Some easy tips and techniques

There are many quick wins when it comes to increasing the quality of sleep. Some of them may be familiar to you but we often forget or underestimate their impact. Below is a list of 'low-hanging fruit' that we can make good use of.

- Avoid the blue light of your phones and tablets at least two hours before you go to bed.
- Leave phones and tablets outside of the bedroom.
- If you feel like you need help to fall asleep, use guided meditations focused on sleep that can be found in meditation and mindfulness apps such as Calm and Headspace.
- Make sure you have enough fresh air in your bedroom.
- Stick to a regular exercise pattern and a healthy diet (not too much heavy food late in the evening).

- Avoid consuming too much alcohol. It is often thought that alcohol helps us to fall asleep but it actually reduces the quality of sleep.[171]
- If you are anticipating a tough working week (lots of travel and late-night meetings), you might benefit from power naps during the day.
- If you have to travel a lot as a professional, get some advice on how to deal with long journeys and jetlag. There are many simple tips that can have a huge impact (from changes in your diet to not adjusting to local time on short trips).
- Don't drink coffee after 3 p.m.

3. Where can I get more support?

If you want to find out more about the power of sleep, we recommend the work of Arianna Huffington (*The Sleep Revolution*), Caroline Webb (*How to Have a Good Day*) and Els van der Helm. More information can be found in the references.

6.4.7 The amazing benefits of exercise[172]

Description of this tool	**What will this tool enable for you:**
This section explains the mindful benefits of exercise and how exercise can actually support a mindful, confident focus.	• It will build your understanding of the importance of exercise to support authentic confidence.

In this section we will not be presenting a specific exercise tool. Instead we will explain why certain kinds of physical exercise support the overall development of emotional flexibility and authentic confidence.

171 https://www.ncbi.nlm.nih.gov/pmc/articles/PMC4666864/ and https://www.ncbi.nlm.nih.gov/pmc/articles/PMC2775419/. Excessive alcohol use is associated with longer sleep times while less sleep is associated with worse hangovers. https://www.ncbi.nlm.nih.gov/pmc/articles/PMC5499928/.

172 This section includes special contributions from Dr Srini Pillay, Harvard-trained psychiatrist and brain researcher; Chief Medical Officer and Co-founder of Reulay and CEO of NeuroBusiness Group.

Introduction
In Chapter 2 we explained how fear, reward and habit affect the brain and the role of the amygdala. Like sleep, the amygdala can also be impacted by exercise. And there are more benefits too.

> **"Interestingly, in a career such as mine, my upbringing and the training that I had emphasized the value that 'you had to defeat your fears'. So, I did a lot of ultra-distance running and the like – I overcame my fears and confronting them has helped."**
>
> **John Brand,** Consultant, Bowmans, South Africa

How does exercise support authentic confidence?
There are many ways in which regular exercise can have a positive impact on authentic confidence. Intense aerobic exercise in particular is said to produce excellent results. Aerobic exercise includes running, walking, cycling, swimming and dancing. Engaging in intense aerobic exercise for at least 20 minutes releases neurotransmitters called endorphins into the bloodstream.[173] Endorphins can reduce pain and improve your overall feeling of well-being (Pittman and Karle, 2015). There are many types of exercise that can make you feel more relaxed and help you to process your thoughts and any stress that has built up. Most of us are familiar with the creative ideas that we have when we go for a walk or a run. This is because we are relaxed and less intensely focused on our daily activities. However, studies have shown that not all kinds of running have the same effect. Running outdoors makes you more creative than running on a treadmill.[174] Also, walking on a winding path makes you more creative than taking a stroll around the block.[175]

Exercise changes the chemistry of the amygdala (Pittman and Karle: 146). It changes the levels of the neurotransmitters norepinephrine (which improves attention, perception, motivation and arousal) and serotonin (which helps to keep brain activity under control). These neurotransmitters reduce the level of stress we experience. Exercise also reduces our sensitivity to anxiety (Smits et al., 2008). Stress changes your body's metabolism and can adversely impact your psyche. Exercise reduces the body's sensitivity to stress and there-

173 See, e.g., https://www.ncbi.nlm.nih.gov/pubmed/6091217, https://www.ncbi.nlm.nih.gov/pubmed/1553453 and https://www.ncbi.nlm.nih.gov/pubmed/3157040

174 https://www.ncbi.nlm.nih.gov/pubmed/24749966

175 https://www.ncbi.nlm.nih.gov/pmc/articles/PMC5061809/

fore reduces these negative effects.[176] Regular exercise also makes you more resilient.[177] Stress increases amygdala activity. Because exercise decreases the body's response to stress, it is conceivable that it will also lower amygdala activity. In fact, this is exactly what recent animal studies are showing. Additionally, regular exercise keeps the brain young. It supports cell growth and the neuroplasticity in our brain, which helps the brain to change (Baek, 2016).[178] The effects of regular, intense aerobic exercise can be quite long-lasting and can continue to have an effect for many weeks.

Maintaining a healthy sports regime will support your emotional flexibility and authentic confidence in the workplace. Many senior leaders know the positive effects of exercise and most of them are enthusiastic participants in sports. Running, in particular, is very popular among busy professionals. Find an exercise regime that works for you and integrate it into your operating model (we will explain the term 'operating model' in sub-section 10.4.2 of Chapter 10).

> **"I normally use exercise that really works well for me. At this moment, I have no time for it, and I know that is wrong."**
>
> **Andres Cadena,** Senior Partner, McKinsey & Company, Bogotá, Colombia

> **"I had an upbringing in which physical fitness and endurance were very present; we learned to believe we were physically invincible and that has given me courage. I often say that to people when talking about marathons; doing them gives you courage. It gives you intellectual courage as well."**
>
> **John Brand,** Consultant, Bowmans, South Africa

> **"I am a dedicated Ironman athlete, I run marathons and, if I can, I run 10K every morning. I only learned this in the last 5-6 years. And I cannot do without it; it gives me a lot of energy and helps me stay focused and level-headed."**
>
> **Beltrán Simó,** Partner, McKinsey & Company, Bogotá, Colombia

176 https://www.ncbi.nlm.nih.gov/pubmed/17148741; And https://www.sciencedirect.com/science/article/pii/S0165032721010739
177 https://www.ncbi.nlm.nih.gov/pmc/articles/PMC4013452/
178 https://www.ncbi.nlm.nih.gov/pmc/articles/PMC5091051/

If you want to read more about the neuroscience of exercise and its impact on the brain, we can recommend several scientific articles that you will find in the appendices at the back of this book. Books on this topic that might be of interest can be found in the resource section of Ratey and Hagerman's *Spark: How exercise will improve the performance of your brain* and Otto and Smits' *Exercise for Mood and Anxiety: proven strategies for overcoming depression and enhancing well-being*. You will also find some references in Pittman and Karle's *Rewire the Anxious Brain*. Detailed references for these sources can be found in this book's bibliography.

CHAPTER 7

7. PRACTICE 3 – ACCEPTANCE

how many times
did we separate
them
from their roots
to admire their leaves
knowing they weren't
meant to stay?
|rose
coloured glasses. |

the words
you push
into the back
of your throat
will turn
every other
sound
you make
into an unheard
whisper.
|pushing it
forward. let your voice
be heard. |

the sea
she will drown those
who do not know
how to swim
and those who stay
for too long.
|the weight of salt
on the surface
of self-love. |

the fears
we bury
six feet under
nurture the roots
of everything
we plant.
|narcissists
and daffodils. |

perhaps
now you
understand
why being positive
does not always
leave you
feeling good.
|projection. |

perhaps when you realize
your body is
your only house
and you are always
on the move
you will not feel
out of touch
in different places.
|fear of leaving
buildings. |

Noor Intisar, former Campus Poet, University of Antwerp

> **"If you hold onto the handle, she said, it's easier to maintain the illusion of control. But it's more fun if you just let the wind carry you."**
>
> **Brian Andreas,** Story People[179]

179 http://www.storypeople.com

At the core of acceptance is 'letting go of control' and accepting what 'is'. Facing whatever you meet on your path demands awareness, courage and skill. Becoming aware of your fears and insecurities is step one. Deciding to face them is step two. But then how do you face those fears skilfully and in such a way that you really can move past them? In this chapter we will explore this further.

7.1 What do we mean by the practice of acceptance?

"Exposure therapy is a psychological treatment that was developed to help people confront their fears. When people are fearful of something, they tend to avoid the feared objects, activities or situations. Although this avoidance might help reduce feelings of fear in the short term, over the long term it can make the fear become even worse. In such situations, a psychologist might recommend a program of exposure therapy in order to help break the pattern of avoidance and fear. In this form of therapy, psychologists create a safe environment in which to 'expose' individuals to the things they fear and avoid. The exposure to the feared objects, activities or situations in a safe environment helps reduce fear and decrease avoidance."[180]

All of the practices of emotional flexibility are important and relevant. The practice of acceptance, however, is crucial to building emotional flexibility and, with that, authentic confidence. The above quote is from the website of the American Psychological Association. It explains acceptance as the practice of exposing yourself to fear. For the purpose of building authentic confidence, acceptance is relevant on three different levels.

The first level concerns the development of helpful mindsets[181] that enable you to lean in to challenges, which also enhances your ability to face your fears.[182] Facing your fears allows you to deal with

180 http://www.apa.org/ptsd-guideline/patients-and-families/exposure-therapy.aspx

181 Mindsets matter! Those who are interested in the power of mindsets may find the work by Dr Alia Crum interesting: https://profiles.stanford.edu/alia-crum

182 You may have noticed that we use the words 'fear' and 'anxiety' repeatedly throughout the book; In this book 'fear' can apply to situations that are life-threatening but also to situations in which people are afraid but are not really in mortal danger, e.g., the fear of failure.

potential difficulties. Imagine you have decided to take on the challenge of making a presentation to a large audience, having finally found the courage to do so after spending a lot of time rehearsing and planning it. On the day itself you walk onto the stage and ... you freeze. You forget everything you wanted to say, you drop your notes or worse still you trip over on stage. You feel like a complete failure and regret ever taking on the challenge. What you need then is the mindset required to deal with this situation: a growth mindset and a mindset of self-compassion. We will discuss these further in the toolkit in this chapter.

The second level concerns making a conscious decision to seek out situations in which you will feel your fears because you are outside your comfort zone. In order to be brave enough to face them, you not only need to possess the aforementioned mindsets but also to know how to find the kinds of (out-of-your-comfort-zone) situations where you can still feel relatively safe (so that you can practice). Going too far out of your comfort zone will lead you to a space with too much distress, which will reduce the opportunity to learn.

The third level concerns learning how to physically feel and explore your fears. Understanding the triggers and signals of fear in your mind, body and behaviour and learning to observe them in the right way are critical to overcoming the negative effects of fear. We have included tools that relate to all three levels in the workplace setting. Before we discuss them, let us first explore why it is important to develop acceptance skills.

7.2 Why develop acceptance skills?

> **"Things are never as bad as they seem."**
>
> **Miss Maudie,** in To Kill a Mockingbird

At the heart of acceptance is knowing that if you avoid or ignore your fears and worries, you will not be able to learn from them or rid yourself of them. You might feel some temporary relief when you avoid a challenge, but you may not have moved past it. You have to face your fears and challenges in order to build a new relationship with them. In reality, when you move out of our comfort zone you often find the experience less scary than you envisioned. Knowing this also helps you to put things into perspective when planning to take on a challenge.

An academic study by Ainsworth and colleagues (2017) found that acceptance made a significant difference when it came to reducing intrusive thoughts characterised by worry. In an experiment they invited three groups of people (total n=77) to participate in an exercise to investigate the impact of three interventions on worry intrusion before and after the exercise. The group that applied acceptance meditation (inviting the fear in and facing it) had fewer negative thought intrusions (e.g., worrying about not meeting a deadline) after the acceptance intervention than the group that applied either a simple mindfulness exercise or a progressive muscle relaxation technique (PMR in Figure 27). Those techniques were still helpful but they were less effective with regard to reducing worry.

FIGURE 27: THE ROLE OF DIFFERENT TYPES OF BREATHING IN NEGATIVE THOUGHT INTRUSIONS

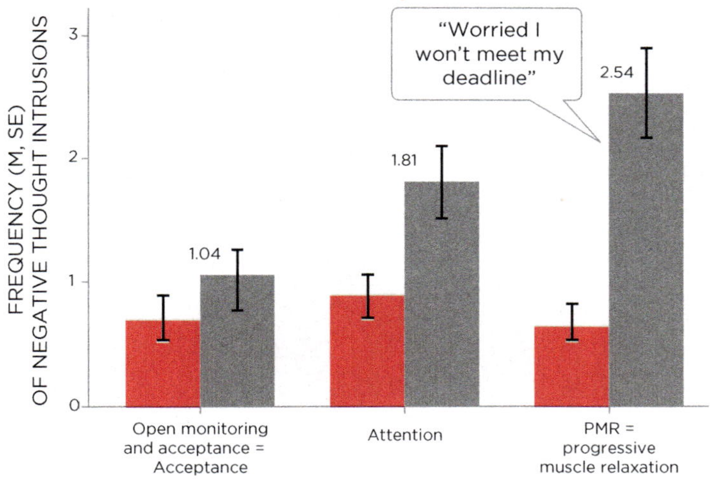

Group differences in negative thought intrusions before and after worry

PROCESS:

- Baseline measurement
- 5 mins breathing focus (either Acceptance, Attention or PMR)
- 4 mins worry focus on a current relevant worry topic
- 5 mins post-worry breathing focus (either Acceptance, Attention or PMR)

Source: Ainsworth et al. (2017: 75)

Exposing yourself to your fear is another way of explaining acceptance. From the perspective of neuroscience, effective exposure to fear can lead to a rewiring of the brain. Pittman and Karle (2015: 126-127) describe the exposure approach as follows: 'During each exposure, anxiety typically rises, often to an uncomfortable level, and then begins to subside. The key is to let the anxiety response run its course, peaking and then lowering, without escaping the situation. In this way, the amygdala begins to pair a previously feared situation with safety.' The idea is that through exposure we are giving our brain a new experience in a situation that previously felt fearful and dangerous but can now start to feel safe or, at the very least, neutral. Explaining this in the light of current scientific insights, including the theory of constructed emotions, we could say that facing our fears enables us to expand our repertoire of possible outcomes. When we see that nothing bad happens it increases the possibility that the next situation will have a similar outcome and that there may be no danger at all. This is what changes your response.

In the working context, creating those experiences that you dread the most (provided they are important to you) can help you in two ways: you will build a skill and competence around an activity that normally fills you with fear (e.g., making a presentation to a large group or chairing a meeting) and you will also gradually rewire your brain to experience the situation as safe or neutral instead of as scary and dangerous. It is important that you choose challenges where you can gradually 'stretch' yourself out of your comfort zone and avoid straying into your 'terror zone' by stretching yourself too far and too fast. We will discuss this in more detail later on in the chapter.

7.3 Acceptance – 'From > To' behaviours and thoughts

FIGURE 28: ACCEPTANCE 'FROM > TO' EXAMPLES

From	To
TYPES OF BEHAVIOUR	
Leaning back when an opportunity arises	Taking on the challenge
Trying not to feel uncomfortable	Exploring your feelings and emotions, facing them
Having a Fixed Mindset	Having a Growth Mindset
TYPES OF THOUGHTS	
"I'm scared to lead the meeting - let someone else do it"	*"I'm scared but it's important to me and I will go for it!"*
"I don't want to feel this stress - I will avoid it"	*"I will explore what I feel and where I feel it"*

7.4 Tools to develop your acceptance skills

7.4.1 Choosing your performance and failure mindset: growth versus fixed

Description of this tool	**What will this tool enable for you:**
This tool helps you reflect on a helpful mindset to build authentic confidence and the courage to lean in to challenges at work.	• Awareness about your current mindset and developing a mindset that helps you to grow and lean in to challenges.

Introduction

Carol Dweck is the founding researcher of the Fixed versus Growth Mindset movement. In her research she has found that children with a more flexible mindset and who are more open to learning from their failures performed better at school than those children who believed that intelligence and talent were fixed qualities and that you either had them or you didn't. Inspiring these kids to adopt a more growth-oriented mindset did miracles and vastly improved their performance. The key lies in the art of daring to fail, and to fail well. A lot depends on how you see yourself when you fail and whether you get back in the saddle immediately for the next ride, as opposed to avoiding the same challenge after failing at it once.[183] In the interviews we carried out for this book, we heard time and time again from senior professionals that there is no successful person who has not repeatedly failed in her or his career. It is how you deal with failure that makes all the difference.

A study by Tupperware and Georgetown University found that cultivating a growth mindset culture is very important. Workers who were told that failure is part of the road to success reported higher levels of confidence and an increased ability to overcome challenges. More confident workers are more successful at work and are more optimistic about future success than workers with less confidence. Specifically, greater confidence yielded an average of 27% more recruits and 22% higher sales. More confident workers were 16% more likely to come up with better ways of getting things done, 17% more likely to be innovative at work and 24% more likely to overcome challenges at work. Making failure part of the road to success created a growth mindset in the organisation, with amazing results.[184]

> **"Disempowering is an important word. Instead of working hard to avoid 'losing' or 'failing', it is about 'playing to win'. Once you build an environment that goes beyond disempowering failure, people play to win, they start to lean in – and they stand taller when they lean in, there is more of a strive to their actions."**
>
> **Rick Goings,** former CEO and Chairman Emeritus, Tupperware

183 See for critical reviews also: https://www.ncbi.nlm.nih.gov/pmc/articles/PMC6594552/ and https://www.scientificamerican.com/article/debate-arises-over-teaching-growth-mindsets-to-motivate-students/

184 The original study was published here: https://ir.tupperwarebrands.com/news-and-events/press-releases/2017/03-06-2017-145955783
A related paper by the same group of researchers was also published later and can be found here: https://meridian.allenpress.com/accounting-review/article-abstract/96/2/205/436091/How-Controlling-Failure-Perceptions-Affects

What is the difference between a growth mindset and a fixed mindset? The visual in Figure 29 summarises both mindsets. If you truly adopt a growth mindset, you believe that failure is an opportunity to grow. If you have a fixed mindset, you believe that failure marks the limit of your abilities. With a fixed mindset, it is easy to set yourself up for failure. We all make mistakes, after all, but if you don't acknowledge that fact, you will end up feeling badly about yourself an awful lot of the time. When you accept that mistakes are part and parcel of trying new things, adopting a growth mindset can help you to feel positive and to lean in to the challenges ahead.

FIGURE 29: GROWTH MINDSET VERSUS FIXED MINDSET

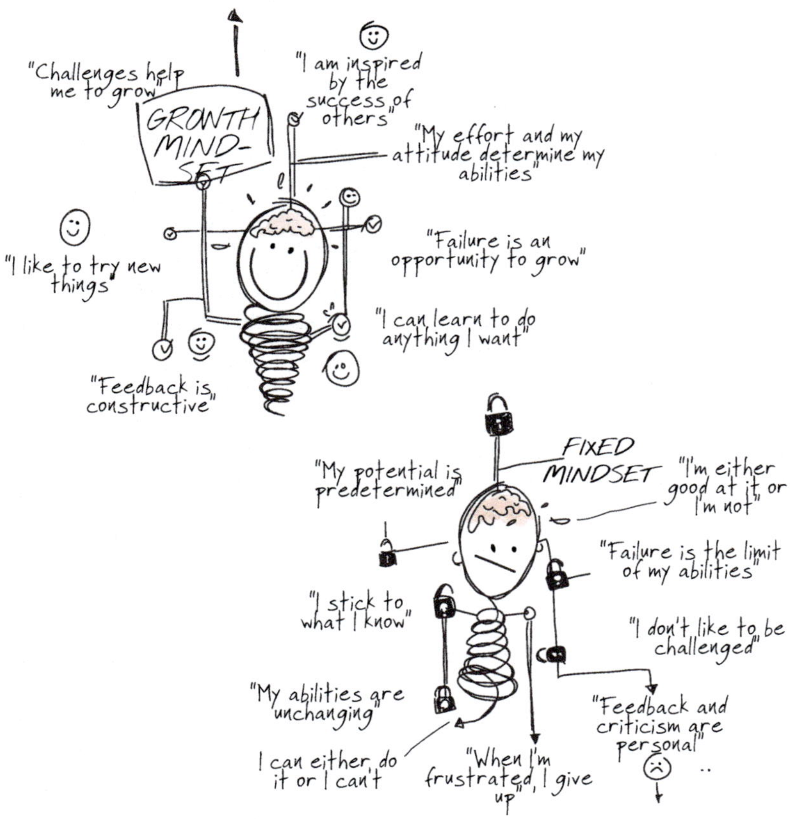

Source: Authors, adapted from and based on work of Dweck (2006 and 2017).

> **"Even the most powerful CEO is sometimes insecure. The leader of today dares to be open about lacking confidence and has a growth mindset."**
>
> **Ingrid van den Maegdenbergh,** Managing Partner The Netherlands, Egon Zehnder

> **"I am very resilient and persevere when I have a tough thing to do. I just keep plugging away and charge into the obstacles. I may cry in frustration, but besting that obstacle becomes my goal. I guess I have a lot of Grit [Grit in psychology is a positive, non-cognitive trait based on an individual's passion for a particular long-term goal or end state, coupled with a powerful motivation to achieve their respective objective]."**
>
> **Joanna Barsh,** Senior Partner Emerita, McKinsey & Company

Growth Mindset versus Fixed Mindset tool

The tool that we present here is a self-reflection tool. The questions below are adopted from Carol Dweck's work, which you can find on her website: www.mindsetworks.com. For her books on this theory, we gladly refer you to our list of references. Please take a look at the self-reflection assessment below. For each question, indicate whether you mostly agree or mostly disagree. Then refer to the key below and see how many times you mostly agreed with the questions marked with an (F), indicating a fixed mindset, versus those marked with a (G), which indicates a growth mindset. If you mostly agreed with the fixed mindset questions, reflect on how adopting a growth mindset might help you to develop your authentic confidence and how you could deploy this mindset the next time you face a new challenge.

Self-assessment: Your Mindset – Fixed or Growth? What do you believe?[185]

1. You have a certain amount of intelligence and you can't really do much to change that.
2. Your intelligence is something about you that you cannot change very much.
3. No matter who you are, you can significantly change your intelligence level.
4. To be honest, you cannot really change how intelligent you are.
5. You can always substantially change how intelligent you are.

185 For more information see, e.g., https://www.mindsetworks.com

6. You can learn new things, but you cannot really change your basic intelligence.
7. No matter how much intelligence you have, you can always change it quite a bit.
8. You can change even your basic intelligence level considerably.
9. You have a certain amount of talent, and you cannot really do much to change that.
10. Your talent in an area is something about you that you cannot change very much.
11. No matter who you are, you can significantly change your level of talent.
12. To be honest, you cannot really change how much talent you have.
13. You can always substantially change how much talent you have.
14. You can learn new things, but you cannot really change your basic level of talent.
15. No matter how much talent you have, you can always change it quite a bit.
16. You can change even your basic level of talent considerably.

(1F, 2F, 3G, 4F, 5G, 6F, 7G, 8G, 9F, 10F, 11G, 12F, 13G, 14F, 15G, 16G)

> **"Earlier in my career, I left McKinsey for an entrepreneurial job. It did not work out as we wanted and so I re-joined the Firm, but I had lost my confidence. I used to think everything was possible as long as you think big, but I learned the lesson that not everything always goes as planned or as you wish. The experience taught me a lot about implementation skills and the importance of experience. I felt really badly that I was not successful, but what I learned was that you can get strength out of this and learn from mistakes. Success is not about never making mistakes, but it is about how you deal with those mistakes and how you move on."**
>
> **Andres Cadena,** Senior Partner, McKinsey & Company, Bogotá, Colombia

> **"During difficult times at the hospital, I always try to remember to learn from situations; we all make mistakes, and in my profession that is even more so than in many other jobs, but then I need to learn from it and move on. Also, as a team, we need to learn from it – there is this saying amongst surgeons: "If you have never had complications, you have not done enough**

surgeries". In other words: it is impossible to never have complications; the question is, what have you learned from them?"

Jan J. Wever MD, PhD, Vascular Surgeon, Haga Hospital, The Hague, The Netherlands

"I have been leaning in continuously to fear. Let me tell you one of my seminal moments. I had a really difficult situation with a boss, 12-15 years ago. In hindsight, I am grateful to him. I did not have the courage to give him the feedback on a number of things I was struggling with, so I suffered for about two years with that. I am talking about a time early in my career. I was very nervous, and I did not give him the feedback. I kept suffering, kept getting upset, frustrated, gossiped, and felt that I was not able to tell him what I thought. I was afraid it would impact my career; I was afraid that I would be seen as incompetent – because if you cannot make things work, then you must be the problem. (If you can't handle a difficult boss everyone else seems to be handling, then the problem is me and I would be seen as a failure). Either way, I was the first woman in India who was a manager and I also felt that I could not afford to fail. I had to be perfect and had to show that I could work in any difficult situation with any difficult boss. So my initial solution for this situation was that I decided to quit. It was humiliating to me. I spoke with my husband about it and he told me to tell my boss the way I felt. I thought that I didn't have the courage. And so, I wrote a handwritten letter to him, saying exactly what I thought, providing different examples, how it impacted me and the team. And I thought it's fine, I am resigning, and it doesn't matter what he says. I thought about it long and hard, mailed it Friday evening and immediately felt so much better. It was so liberating. I had made up my mind and I was leaving. There was a huge burden off my shoulders. Monday morning, I got a call that he wanted to see me. When we met, he looked shattered as if he had not slept for 48 hours. He told me that he had no idea that he had this impact on me or on others and that I felt humiliated. The letter and the feedback had a profound impact on him. No one ever gave him this feedback. And then, after two years of working with him, getting into this situation, we had a very honest conversation and it was a big growing up moment for me. In my job as an HR Business Partner, I have to constantly give feedback to people who are powerful, and that particular

> **lesson with this boss really helped me move beyond my fears. I now face into fears about giving feedback to leaders easily, and I am open to receive feedback as well."**
>
> **Leena Nair,** former Chief Human Resources Officer (CHRO), Unilever; current CEO of Chanel

> **"I went from Managing Director of Avon Germany to being promoted to run all of Asia Pacific. Suddenly, I could not communicate because of the language(s) and so had to work through others rather than depend on myself. This was key to developing leaders and the leadership to run the Asia Pac markets. In my 20s, I had great success in business. In my 30s, the businesses fell apart. But it was not wasted – I learned from it."**
>
> **Rick Goings,** former CEO and Chairman Emeritus, Tupperware

> **"Our profession puts you out of your comfort zone. You have to reinvent yourself all the time, develop a new S-curve.[186] So, the system itself gets you out of your comfort zone. In this process, I have relearned the power of training and practicing. If I have a tough meeting, I go back to the basics and I practice. This is analogous to sports people. They practice all the time. Don't think you are too senior for this; it is a characteristic of professionals to practice and fine-tune all the time."**
>
> **Felipe Child,** Partner, McKinsey & Company, Bogotá, Colombia

> **I have moved to different companies a few times and that helps in learning how to be humble and be open about the fact that you don't know everything and need to learn. I learned to have the courage and humility to be wrong as well. I don't like to be in the comfort zone; I like to be challenged.**
>
> **Chet Kuchinad,** Chief People Officer, Save the Children International

186 S-curve here refers to a new phase in your career or a new role. Development often happens in an S-curve process, in that in the first phase it can be a bit challenging to get moving on a smooth path upwards. At a certain point, when one has mastered the new role or phase, development slows down (top of the 'S'). See Figure 45.

7.4.2 Self-compassion – always, and especially when things get really tough

Description of this tool	**What will this tool enable for you:**
This tool explains the basic principles of self-compassion, why it is an essential part of authentic confidence and how to practice it, even at work.	• It will give you the skills to practice self-compassion in your professional context, especially when things get tough.

Introduction

Being kind to yourself is not a luxury. Many of us have learned not to focus too much on ourselves but rather on our obligations in life. In our busy lives, many of us are always there for others but we forget to be kind to ourselves. We sometimes beat ourselves up when we make mistakes, consciously or otherwise, especially if we are perfectionistic by nature, and we often do so for no reason at all. This tool will help you to become aware of your own level of self-compassion and it includes a short exercise to help you do that. It is one of the most crucial tools in this book.

Life is full of challenges. Unfortunately, life sometimes involves suffering, too. We may be blessed with family, friends and great colleagues, but in the end we have to help ourselves through the challenges we face. If we are our own biggest enemy because of the way we talk to ourselves, consciously or unconsciously, we are not giving ourselves a fair chance. This exercise may come across as a bit strange at first but give it a try. You will experience its power and impact if you do.

One of the leading academic researchers in self-compassion is Dr Kristin Neff. Her research, and that of many others, has revealed that (practicing) self-compassion is positively related to psychological well-being and supports the process of becoming willing to accept challenging emotions and thoughts. For more information on the extensive research into self-compassion, please refer to: http://selfcompassion.org/.

Self-compassion tool

This tool has two parts. The first part is an awareness exercise to help you reflect on your level of self-compassion. The second part is about how to apply self-compassion in the workplace.

Part 1: Awareness exercise: how would you treat a friend?
Before we describe the 'self-compassion at work' tool, we will first explore what is at the heart of self-compassion with a first awareness exercise. Please take out a sheet of paper and answer the following questions.

First, think about times when a close friend feels really bad about her or himself or is really struggling in some way. How would you respond to your friend in this situation (especially when you are at your best)? Please write down what you typically do and what you say, and note the tone in which you typically talk to your friends.

Now, think about times when you feel bad about yourself or are struggling. How do you typically respond to yourself in these situations? Please write down what you typically do and what you say, and note the tone in which you talk to yourself.

Did you notice a difference? If so, ask yourself why. What factors or fears come into play that lead you to treat yourself and others so differently?

Please write down how you think things might change if you responded to yourself in the same way you typically respond to a close friend when you are suffering.

Why not try treating yourself like a good friend and see what happens?

Source: www.selfcompassion.org, reproduced with permission.

Part 2: Applying self-compassion in the workplace: identifying what we really want
Think about the ways that you use self-criticism as a motivator at work. Is there any personal trait that you criticise yourself for having (too stupid, too lazy, too impulsive, et cetera) because you think being hard on yourself will help you change? If so, first try to get in touch with the emotional pain that your self-criticism causes, giving yourself compassion for the experience of feeling so judged.

Next, see if you can think of a kinder, more caring way to motivate yourself to make a change if needed. What language would a wise and inspirational coach, mentor, boss or colleague use to gently point out how your behaviour is unproductive, while simultaneously encouraging you to do something different? What is the most supportive message you can think of that is in line with your underlying wish to be healthy and happy?

Every time you catch yourself being judgmental about your unwanted trait in the future, first notice the pain of your self-judgment and show yourself some compassion. Then try to reframe your inner dialogue so that it is more encouraging and supportive. Remember that if you really want to motivate yourself, love is more powerful than fear.

Source: adjusted from www.selfcompassion.org, reproduced with permission.

If you are interested in reading more about this topic and the research on the power of self-compassion, please refer to the work of Dr Kristin Neff at www.selfcompassion.org.

7.4.3 Your 'year of saying yes' to the career challenges you need

Description of this tool	**What will this tool enable for you:**
You will learn to reflect on your 'year of saying yes' to the challenges you need to face in order to grow and develop.	• Understanding of the concept and its importance. • Helps you to reflect what you could choose to say 'yes' to.

Introduction

As previously discussed, a well-known technique in psychology for treating fears is known as 'exposure'. Exposing yourself to the source can help to remove the fear. This is always done under the guidance of a professional psychologist. However, you can also explore exposing yourself to what you fear in the workplace, keeping in mind that things are never as bad as they seem. Shonda Rhimes, the lead writer and producer of the TV show *Grey's Anatomy* wrote a book about this called *Year of Yes*. A quote from her:

> **"A while ago, I tried an experiment. For one year, I would say 'yes' to all the things that scared me. Anything that made me nervous or took me out of my comfort zone, I'd say 'yes.' Public speaking? Yes. Acting? Yes. A crazy thing happened — the very act of doing the thing that scared me undid the fear."**
>
> **Shonda Rhimes**[187]

187 https://blog.ted.com/shonda-rhimes-tells-her-story-at-ted2016/

This is exactly what we aspire to with this particular tool: this could be your 'year of saying yes' to overcoming a critical fear that has been keeping your confidence low. A critical fear is one that is related to what is important to you (see Chapter 5 on purpose and values). Before we explore this a bit more, we will first discuss the concepts of 'comfort zone' versus 'learning zone' versus 'terror zone'. As learning and development professionals, we aim to design learning experiences that lead the participant into the learning zone and not into the terror zone. That would be counterproductive. During a training or coaching session, this is something the trainer and coach needs to manage.

In this exercise we propose that you find your own *outside-my-comfort-zone* experiences, while acknowledging the risk that you might become too enthusiastic and too ambitious all at once. We will explain in the tool how to find the learning zone and stay away from the terror zone. The terror zone is the area where you take on challenges that are just a step too far. For example, if you are afraid of making a presentation in front of a large audience but you do want to move out of your comfort zone and give it a try, a terror zone would be to immediately jump on stage to do a TEDx talk. This is usually a leap too far and you may end up making your fear even greater than it was to begin with. Your stress response may be so strong that you learn nothing (or you may even learn that you are more afraid of presentations than before). That is not helpful; you are taking a step back instead of forward. Please keep this in mind when working with the tool.

> **"I used to really struggle with a fear of heights. Even in relatively unthreatening situations I would become ill. On one occasion my two sons, brother-in-law and I decided to climb Mount Formosa, which is famous for its views of the bay. We were very close to the top but the last ten metres was a vertical climb where one slip could be fatal. I couldn't have found myself in a worse situation. My boys went ahead of me and got to the top. I said to myself there is no way I cannot get to the top too and join my boys; It took a huge effort to control my fear but I reached the top and I have never suffered from a fear of heights since."**
>
> **John Brand,** Consultant, Bowmans, South Africa

A tool to help you define your 'year of saying yes'
Your 'year of saying yes' is about identifying one or two activities or skills you want to learn in the coming year or period, and about saying 'yes' to the opportunities to practice them and seeking out those opportunities. It is important to reflect on the exercises you did in Chapter 5 on purpose and values in which you identified what is important to you and what you want to focus on at work. The activity, skill or behaviour you want to change - and for which you are prepared to move out of your comfort zone - should be related to something that is important to you. Of course, we all have lots of things that take us out of our comfort zone. But if we have not identified them as being important to us, why would we bother doing them at all? If you are afraid of heights, that does not mean you need to learn rock climbing just to move out of that particular comfort zone. If something is not important to whatever it is you want to achieve or if it doesn't bother you all that much, it is okay for you to leave it as it is.

Which steps do you need to take?

1. *Identify the skill you want to learn but that you are afraid of at this moment*
   Make sure this skill is related to what is important to you. Examples can be: speaking in front of a large audience, facilitating certain kinds of workshops, leading a project or writing a book.

2. *Identify your 'comfort zone' versus 'learning zone' for this particular skill*
   Reflect on moments where you are comfortable executing or practicing this particular skill and on when the situation changes and becomes challenging. For example, you enjoy making a speech in front of your family but you dread giving a speech or presentation in front of your colleagues or an audience of professionals. It is important to picture the learning zone setting in your mind and when that learning zone could potentially become a terror zone. As with all the tools in this book, if you are finding it hard to figure out how to use them, you can seek the help of a professional coach or mentor. But remember to be very careful not to enter the terror zone.

> **"I came from an industry where I was one of the best professionals in the world and I knew my subject matter. Then I moved to a completely different professional area, and I knew nothing**

> **about that space. I did not move from my comfort zone into my out-of-comfort zone; I moved into my terror zone!"**
>
> **Senior Executive,** anonymous contribution

3. *Find opportunities to practice your skills; integrate them into your operating model (we explain this tool in Chapter 10)*
   Once you have identified opportunities for practicing and developing a skill and building your courage, find moments where you can integrate these into your working schedule and operating model. When you are going through the experience try to open yourself up to uncomfortable feelings and emotions. Observe them, thank them and keep your focus on the activity (Acceptance in action, tool 7.4.5). Also, be kind to yourself when things go wrong along the way (Self-compassion, tool 7.4.2).

> **"When I joined a new company at mid-senior level I realised this was the start of a new S-curve. I had been used to doing things on auto pilot, but when I started there I felt that I had to learn everything all over again. This made me focus on actively looking for out-of-comfort zone opportunities. That kept me fresh and my personal learning curve was given an enormous new impulse. When my work became less challenging, I tried to find my challenges in extracurricular work, like being a chairman. And I learned that you sometimes have to perform on stage in that role. I remember when I had to appear on the TV show Jinek. I was very nervous. I pushed myself to get out of my comfort zone because I believe one always learns from that. For me, as a shy person by nature, it helped me to overcome my shyness."**
>
> **Ron van der Jagt,** Senior Executive

> **"I don't mind saying when I don't know something. There are many moments when no one knows everything and we just take the best info we have and work towards the best decision for that moment. I don't think there is anything that I am too scared to do; if I feel scared, I talk myself into doing it. I make myself do it and expose myself to the challenge, because my experience is: you always get through it."**
>
> **Abbe Luersman,** CHRO, EVP and Chief People Officer, Otis Elevator Co.

> **"The interesting thing is that I suffer from very little conscious anxiety at this stage of my career. But certainly in the early stages, I suffered from anxiety, particularly in relation to public speaking. I had a bad experience at school, and it knocked my confidence; then I got into my legal career, and it became necessary for me to speak publicly, which I found very stressful. I do a huge amount of public speaking now and suffer from no anxiety today; I managed to overcome it. The kind of coping mechanisms which I have for that and for other things is that I am an obsessive preparer – I really overprepare as a means of dealing with my anxiety, which impacts in other ways, too because you spend too much time preparing. More confident people just get on with it."**
>
> **John Brand,** Consultant, Bowmans, South Africa

7.4.4 Reframing through anxiety reappraisal pre-performance

Description of this tool	What will this tool enable for you:
You will gain an understanding of the concept and the neuroscientific explanation of anxiety reappraisal and how to execute it.	• It will help you to apply this concept in challenging situations and to create a positive experience out of a potentially negative one.

Introduction

In their research, Wolf and colleagues (2016) found that employees who reframed 'distress' as 'passion' were perceived as more competent than those who attributed it to emotion. In another study, this reframing led to a greater likelihood of being hired or being invited to join a team. Their advice is to find a way to reframe feelings of distress as passion in tense situations.

One of the authors of the study, Alisson Wood Brooks, explained that it is easier to turn anxiety into excitement than to turn anxiety into calmness because they are both arousal[188] emotions and have similar symptoms.[189] With both emotions, the heart beats faster, cortisol le-

188 'Arousal' means being in a state of high emotional energy. In this example this is either positive (excitement) or negative energy (anxious).

189 See also: http://www.theatlantic.com/health/archive/2016/03/can-three-words-turn-anxiety-into-success/474909/ and http://www.theatlantic.com/video/index/485297/turn-anxiety-into-excitement/

vels go up and the body gets ready for action. However, according to Wood Brooks, the difference between these emotions is that excitement is a positive emotion that is focused on all the things that could go well, while anxiety is a negative emotion that brings with it the fear that things could go wrong. In an experiment, participants were told to say either 'I am anxious' or 'I am excited'. Those who said they were excited outperformed those who said they were anxious. In another experiment, excited participants outperformed the ones who tried to remain calm during a maths test.

FIGURE 30: ANXIETY REAPPRAISAL

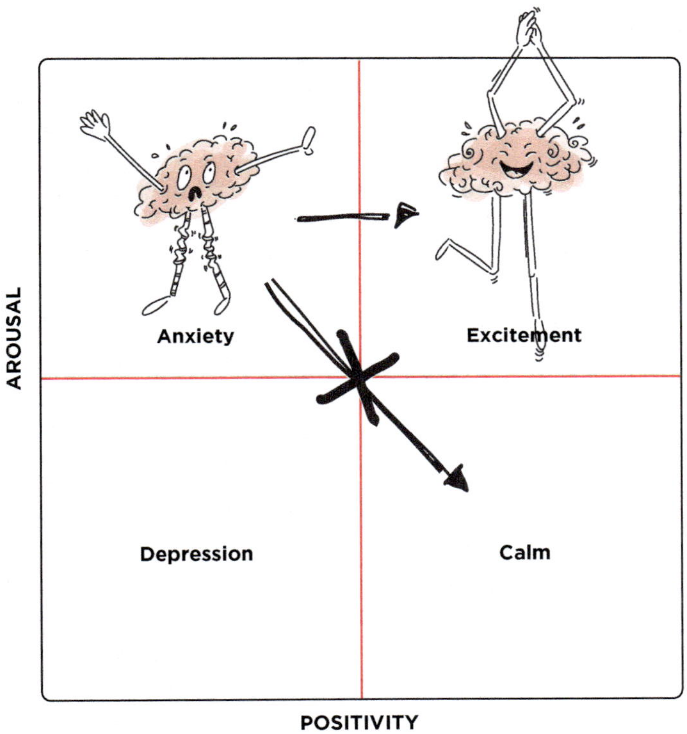

Source: Based on the research by Wolf and colleagues (2016).

The reframing did not make participants less anxious and neither did it lower their heart rate (because they are both arousal emotions). Instead the change can be found in the opportunity mindset that was created versus the threat mindset that you experience when you are anxious. This is not about ignoring what you feel but about fully engaging with the challenge. It is rewiring in action:

linking a new experience to an event that used to evoke negative emotions and creating a new positive perspective.

How do you 'reappraise' anxiety?
This tool is very straightforward. The next time you are facing a big challenge, say 'I am excited' out loud three times. Try to visualize the reasons why you feel excited and see what happens. Lean in fully to the challenge, one that is important to you. If you are in a work setting where you cannot say this out loud three times, try instead to say out loud how excited you are about going on stage. You can even say: 'Yes, I've got a few butterflies in my stomach' (accepting the feeling of distress) 'but I am very excited about the opportunity' (reframing).[190]

7.4.5 Acceptance in action: facing and embracing the challenge when your impact is at stake

Description of this tool	What will this tool enable for you:
Acceptance in action will help you understand how you can deal with difficult emotions in situations where you are 'on stage' and have to perform.	• This tool will help you to stay focused in tough times at work, when you feel challenging emotions and you would prefer to avoid the limelight.

Introduction
It is easier to talk about stress and insecurity when you are not confronted with a stressful situation yourself. However, when you are in a meeting or standing in front of a group and you feel your sense of insecurity rising, your mind can start to go crazy: you feel your emotional response becoming stronger and your physical response, too. What to do? Failing is NOT an option; your impact and your career are at stake here. Your first reaction is to suppress the feeling. The weird thing, however, is that when you push the uncomfortable feeling away it often just becomes worse. The key lesson to take from this tool is that it is more or less impossible to rid yourself of all your fears, but you can learn to live with them, as visualized in Figure 31.

190 Important to note though that this should not mean you are ignoring how you really feel. In the true spirit of ACT, whatever you feel is of course okay, as long as you acknowledge that with kindness. At the same time, exploring whether you can also reframe it as a positive emotion is what this tool is about.

FIGURE 31: MAKING FRIENDS WITH YOUR FEARS

Once again, this tool may sound a bit odd at first, especially if you have never tried this kind of stuff before. However, we encourage you to give it a try; no one needs to notice. See how it works for you.

Acceptance in action
When we feel anxious our inner critic shows up. If your inner critic tends to visit you often, why not give her or him a name?

> **"I have a few inner critics, but the one that visits me most (although less frequently these days) is the one that says, 'I'm not good enough'. I call this one my 'Chimp' or 'Fred' and the monkey in the photo [reprinted here as Figure 32] has been on my desk for many years now. It is a stress monkey, which I also use in workshops. When I have considered the inner critic's message to me, I thank it and offer it a seat in the room. As you can see, the symbol I chose, the chimp, has a smile on its face. Although it really is a cheeky monkey that gets me into trouble every now and then, it means well."**
>
> **Jacqueline Brassey,** McKinsey & Company, Luxembourg

FIGURE 32: EXAMPLE OF AN INNER CRITIC: THE 'I AM NOT GOOD ENOUGH' CHIMP

Source: Monkey, The Training Shop UK.

The next example combines a defusion technique[191] with the acceptance approach, but the emphasis when explaining this tool will be on acceptance. When you are in a situation where you have to perform and there is no way out, your stress level will begin to rise. Try to be aware of and observe what happens. Sometimes it all happens in less than a second. If you practice mindfulness on a regular basis, you will be more aware of what is happening. Do not judge what happens, just observe. Tell yourself 'I am having this thought that ...', or 'I feel that ...' (you can do this without saying it out loud, of course).

If you feel comfortable, thank your inner critic.[192] Remember, it is there because that is how we are built. It is normal to have an inner critic, even though we are not always happy with what it tells us. It is simply doing what it is supposed to do. Everyone has an inner critic and it behaves differently for everyone. You can observe it and be thankful (accepting) but if it is not helping you, you can 'park' it. After you have observed the inner critic's voice, you can also observe what you are feeling. Is it fear? Where do you feel it in your body? Observe the feeling, invite it in and open yourself up to the experience. When you locate it in your body, try to see what shape it has or draw an imaginary line around it in your mind. This may be very uncomfortable and scary, but give it a try.

191 We describe defusion in more detail in Chapter 8.

192 This approach is inspired by Harris, R. (2011). For more details on the book see the references.

Once you have invited the feeling in, observe it and let it be. And if this all happens while you are in the middle of work, try to do the above while at the same time keeping an eye on the objective of what you are doing or are about to do. Of course, this description takes longer to read than the time it actually takes for this to happen. Then, while paying (authentic) attention to what is happening to you in that moment, take a few deep breaths and focus on where you feel the emotion in your body. Park the thought in your mind (offer it a virtual place to sit so that it stays with you; do not push it away) and then lean in to the activity you were about to undertake and use your sense of curiosity to continue with it. In this way both processes can happen: the reality of dealing with your stress in the moment and also being present and participating in the task at hand. These steps are visualized in Figure 33.

FIGURE 33: ACCEPTANCE IN ACTION

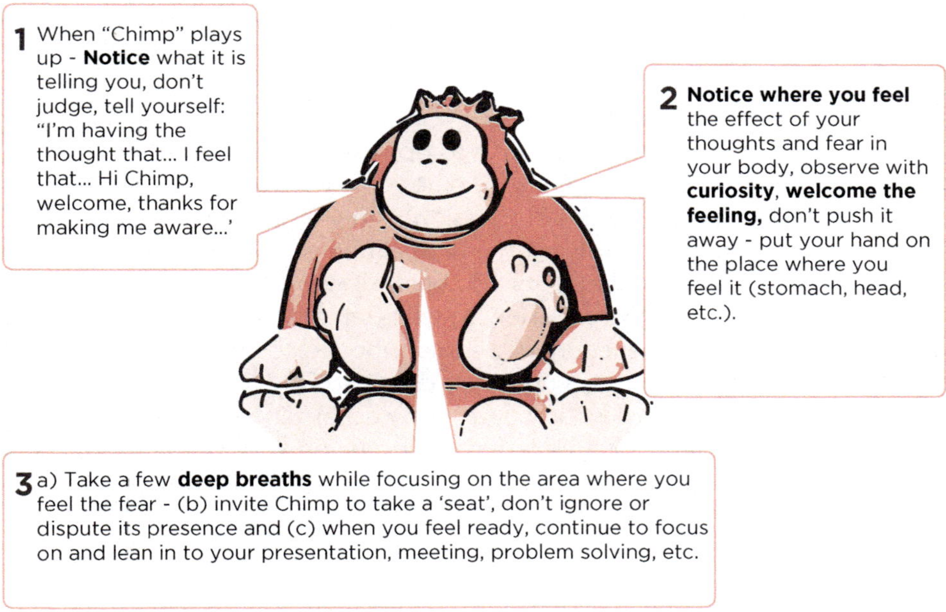

Source: Monkey: The Training Shop UK.

It is possible that many of you will find this exercise a bit idiotic, certainly in relation to the workplace. It takes a while for this to become second nature. However, there is a clear neuroscientific explanation for why it can be effective. In the spirit of the Acceptance and Commitment Theory, the purpose of this exercise is not to diminish the uncomfortable feeling or thought but rather to allow you to continue focusing on what is important to you (e.g., pursuing a meaningful career) and carry out related activities, while at the same time acknowledging uncomfortable feelings and experiences.

One common side effect of a willingness to accept an uncomfortable thought or emotion is that its impact tends to fall dramatically. This can also be explained from a neuroscientific perspective. First, when you engage with the situation and your feelings and emotions, you involve the prefrontal cortex in the process. As a result you add different options in terms of the possible outcomes when interpreting the situation, including a 'safe' outcome. This may be the reason why you and your body calm down when you use your curiosity to focus on exploration. When you engage openly with the thought, feeling and situation that you are afraid of, you often end up concluding that the actual situation is not as bad as your mind had made it out to be. In a way, you start rewiring your brain with regard to a particular situation, which can help you to remain calm (it may downregulate the stress response) and lean in whenever you encounter similar situations in the future. This builds authentic confidence.

The mix of mindfulness skills, knowing what is important for you at any given moment (leaning in as opposed to running away) and accepting difficult thoughts and emotions (acceptance) with kindness towards yourself (self-compassion) is a very powerful combination. When you start applying these qualities you will eventually find a way to use them that suits you best. However, the key to success is to be open to the experience, while at the same time leaning in. Sometimes we encounter people who are only willing to accept their fears when they know that doing so will diminish the negative feeling. This is not what we mean by acceptance, however, because you cannot accept a negative feeling when your primary goal is to curtail it.

CHAPTER 8

8. PRACTICE 4 – DEFUSION

you are one of those
that have no
other choice
than to climb
the rocky roads.
you would have slipped
on the smooth path.
|easy come.
easy go. |

the words
reach for me
the way
water reaches
the sand
and become the shore.
|becoming
and unbecoming. |

hurt has a memory
and if it is really deep
it will come back
again
and again and again
and again.
|memories are not
feelings. |

your life line
is carved
into your spine
and every time
you turn your back
on me
i see where you
come from
a little better.
|spinal
cords. |

Noor Intisar, former Campus Poet, University of Antwerp

> **"The most decisive event in your life is when you discover you are not your thoughts or emotions. Instead, you can be present as the awareness behind the thoughts and emotions."**
>
> **Eckhart Tolle**[193]

8.1 What do we mean by the practice of defusion?

Bomb and fuse is a good metaphor when it comes to explaining defusion in relation to emotions. In that context we call it cognitive defusion: when thoughts are separated from the person who is

193 You can find many inspirational videos related to this topic on Tolle's YouTube channel, including https://www.youtube.com/channel/UCj9fPezLH1HUh7mSo-tB1Mg

thinking them. You become, as it were, the observer of yourself.[194] As soon as you realise that your thoughts are just thoughts and not the truth, you can look at them and acknowledge them for what they are: just thoughts. When you don't identify with your thoughts they have less impact on what you do and feel. It's like the bomb that can no longer explode when it has been defused. If you learn to look at your thoughts in the knowledge that 'they are only thoughts' as opposed to thinking 'I am my thoughts', 'they determine who I am' or 'they are part of me', this can help you to stay focused in stressful situations. It will also help you to keep doing what is really important to you without allowing your thoughts to have an impact on what you are intending to do.

In this practice you will learn how to do this in the workplace. The techniques in this chapter can help you to create a distance between your thoughts and yourself so that your thoughts will have little or no impact on how you feel. This boosts your ability to perform at your best at any given moment and to be less distracted when negative thoughts suddenly pop up in your mind.

8.2 Why develop defusion skills?

The primary goal of this process is to learn how to reduce the impact of negative thoughts so that they do not distract us or take us away from what is truly important to us. For many of us, this would represent a big win. Our research shows that a considerable number of people fail to avail of opportunities or to lean in to challenges when they lack confidence. They do not dare to speak up in teams or in front of large audiences. Their fear prevents them from capitalising on the terrific opportunities that are presented to them.

At the decisive moment there may be a thought that holds you back (even unconsciously). One of the key words in the quote from Eckhart Tolle (at the beginning of this chapter) that resonates with us is the word 'decisive'. It is an excellent adjective in this particular context. When you learn defusion skills you become more decisive.

194 For more details on 'observer' and 'Integrated Awareness' see this McKinsey & Company article by Jacqueline Brassey and Michiel Kruyt: https://www.mckinsey.com/business-functions/people-and-organisational-performance/our-insights/how-to-demonstrate-calm-and-optimism-in-a-crisis

This enables you to lean in to the task at hand and steer the conversation in a team meeting or problem-solving session because the voice inside your head is no longer controlling how you feel and act.

Cognitive defusion is also known as 'detached observation'. Pittman and Karle (2015) describe what happens in the brain when you use techniques that help you to create a distance between you and your thoughts. Having a 'fused' reaction to your thoughts and emotions can lead to an emotional response (which happens, for example, when you identify with them and start judging yourself). Creating distance between you and your (unhelpful) thoughts rewires your brain. Pittman and Karle also describe it as 'changing the anxiety channel', like changing the channel on your TV. When you can continue to focus on what you are doing or you can change your focus without being impacted by your (unhelpful) thoughts, you create another connection between an event, the thoughts that come up in your mind and your reaction (or feeling). This facilitates the process of downregulating your (potential) stress response in the moment.

8.3 Defusion – 'From > To' behaviours and thoughts

Once you have learned how to apply defusion techniques effectively, you will immediately experience an increase in the amount of 'mental space' you have to think and reflect, as well as less 'mental drain' or loss of mental energy. The key to applying these tools and this technique – in line with ACT – is not to deny or ignore your thoughts. Instead, you learn to give them a seat at the table. Figure 34 shows a number of key behaviours and thoughts that you may experience when you apply defusion techniques.

FIGURE 34: DEFUSION 'FROM > TO' EXAMPLES

From	To
TYPES OF BEHAVIOUR	
Experiencing an immediate response to a trigger	Breathing, taking a step back
Thinking that my thoughts = me	Thinking that my thoughts are not me, I observe them
Experiencing critique and feedback as personal	Parking criticism and feedback, keeping them at a distance
TYPES OF THOUGHTS	
"I was criticised by that client, I'm stupid"	*"Interesting feedback - let me park it for now and focus"*
"I'm a failure, I should not do the presentation"	*"Thank you mind for your feedback! I've got this one, will come back to you later!"*

8.4 Tools for developing defusion skills

8.4.1 Observe your thoughts and let them go when you have to focus

Description of this tool	**What will this tool enable for you:**
Observing your thoughts is a key tool when creating distance between you and your thoughts. Learning to 'detach' helps you to continue to focus.	• You will learn that your thoughts are only thoughts, you can observe them, let them be and let them go, which is especially helpful when you need to focus in the moment.

Introduction

Your thoughts often get you into trouble when you are lacking in confidence. This happens when you have developed an unhelpful relationship with your thoughts. When you start to believe your thoughts, consciously or otherwise, you 'fuse' with those thoughts. For example, you make a mistake in an analysis report and during the subsequent meeting start thinking: 'Why did I not spot this? I am so sloppy, I am stupid, I'm not up to the job.' You end up fusing who you actually are with your thoughts and you believe those thoughts to be true. This can become problematic, particularly if you let the situation affect your performance. The thought now 'owns' you and may prevent you from reaching your full potential.

An example: You have to submit a report at work and the very thought of having to do so makes you feel terrible. In order to avoid that pain you come up with lots of excuses not to submit the report, even though it is essential to your work and you are keen to lead the project. So even though a thought may sound like great advice in the heat of the moment, we also know that our thoughts are often not true or helpful (see Chapter 3). With the following tool we hope you will learn to how to distance yourself from your thoughts, decide what to believe and what not, and to move towards what is most important to you.

> **"I have trained myself over the years to learn to observe my thoughts, becoming a detached observer. These are techniques I learned from meditation and I have not lost my temper in fifteen years!"**
>
> **Leena Nair,** former Chief Human Resources Officer (CHRO), Unilever; current CEO of Chanel

How to observe and let go of your thoughts
In Chapter 6 (Mindfulness) we examined how we observe our own thoughts. In the accompanying exercise we became aware of the huge amount of thoughts we have every day. Many just come and go without causing us any trouble; it's all part of how we are built. Sometimes, however, we have thoughts that really hold us back because of the way we end up talking to ourselves. If we say, 'I am stupid', or 'I will not be picked for this project because they think I am not good enough', there is a danger that we will start behaving in line with those thoughts. In other words, we start believing that we are not good enough or that we are stupid and this can result in us becoming quieter and quieter in meetings and problem-solving sessions. However, as explained earlier, we make so many connections between experiences in our brain that even understanding this may not immediately make those negative thoughts go away. When you are in the middle of an important team or board meeting you rarely have the time to explore what is going on at a deeper level in your mind. In the meantime your thoughts continue to distract you.

For moments like these there is a magic trick you can use to relieve the tension. This tool has three simple steps that you can go through in a matter of seconds, although they take much longer to describe in writing. The more you use the tool the easier it becomes, until it is almost second nature to you.

1. **Breathe** – Take a deep breath and become aware of 'you' in the meeting and your 'distracting thoughts'. What are you thinking right now?
2. **Observe** – Examine your thoughts, what are they saying? Then repeat in your mind: 'I am thinking that ...' followed by 'I notice that I am thinking that ...' and then let go.
3. **Re-focus** – Be curious and engage with what you are trying to do in the meeting or with the problem on the table. You can say to yourself: 'Okay, what are we actually trying to achieve in this meeting? Let's have a good look.'

Repeat this cycle whenever you are being distracted by negative thoughts. What happens when you do this? First of all, you calm yourself down by taking a deep breath. If you were feeling tense, the deep breath activates your parasympathetic nervous system (PNS). In the next step, when you start noticing your thoughts, you distance yourself from those thoughts and they immediately lose a lot of their impact on you. After all, if you take the fuse out of a bomb, it can no longer explode. If you had continued to entertain your unhelpful and distracting negative thoughts, you would have felt the effects in your body. Sometimes the effects can be so bad that you might have a stress response (or move towards one) during a meeting. Instead, by observing your thoughts you create some distance. You immerse yourself in the meeting again with curiosity and engage with the new content. You put the spotlight on what is happening in the room and no longer on your (unhelpful) thoughts and on how you identify with them. This can help curb your stress response. It is a very simple tool – easy to learn but very powerful.

If some of your thoughts (or inner critics) manage to persist, you can take this tool a step further, too. We will explain how to do this later on. But if you have never done anything like this before, we suggest you start with the above tool first. Try it out and observe how it works.

8.4.2 Naming your inner critic and offering it a seat at the table

Description of this tool	What will this tool enable for you:
Naming your inner critic helps you to create space for it, to acknowledge it and 'give it a place' so you can continue to lean in to your meeting or activity.	• You will learn a very helpful technique to enable you to continue and stay focused even when you feel distracted by your thoughts and inner critic.

Introduction

A very helpful reaction to your unhelpful inner thoughts, according to Tarah Mohr, author of *Playing Big*, is to simply respond by saying, 'Thank you, but I've got this one!'[195] Mohr acknowledges the inner voice, even thanks her,[196] and continues to focus on what she was planning to do. The words 'I've got this one' are essential here as they reflect a calm and intrinsic trust in your own core capabilities. Saying these words, while at the same time acknowledging your inner voice, can be very powerful and can help you to continue to lean in to what is important to you. The tool we describe next is a different variant but it uses a similar technique.

The giving your inner critic a seat at the table tool

In Chapter 7 we explained that giving your inner critic a name can be helpful. It puts some distance between you and the critic (defusion) and also helps you to deal with your worries in a lighter and more humorous manner. Naming your inner critic, or even a number of your key inner critics, is helpful in the process of recognising what you are experiencing at any given moment. If your inner critic is persistent, you may be visited by it frequently throughout your working day.

The chimp stands for the inner critic that shows up and says that you are not good enough. Many (if not most) of us have one or more of these inner critics and they often hinder us in our day-to-day performance. These critics are fine as long as they do not keep us from doing what is important to us. The moment they start preventing us from being at our best at work, we need to deal with them in a way

195 https://www.taramohr.com/the-playing-big-book/

196 We have chosen to refer to the inner voice as 'her' but wish to acknowledge that referring to it can be done in either the male or female form. This applies also to the references in this book where both forms could have been used but a choice was made to use only one form.

that allows us to keep leaning in and moving forward. The steps below are similar to the steps in the previous tool but they go a bit further.

1. **Breathe** - Take a deep belly breath and become aware of what is happening in your mind right now; be present in the moment.
2. **Observe** - Observe what your inner critic is telling you. Tell yourself 'I am thinking that ...', 'I notice that I am thinking that ...' or 'I notice that [inner critic name] is here to make me think that ...'
3. **Thank -** Thank your inner critic for her excellent advice and if that advice is helpful you can even visualize offering this inner critic a seat at the table: "Thank you [inner critic name]. That is very thoughtful of you but I've got this one. Take a seat. I'll come back to you later."
4. **Re-focus -** Re-focus on the meeting or the problem that you were trying to solve or focus on other challenges.

The difference between this tool and the acceptance tool (in the previous chapter) is not huge. And remember, no one in the room needs to know you are using the tool; it can all be done in a matter of seconds (with practice) and without anyone seeing that you are using the tool, so it is very safe. Through defusion we can distance ourselves from our thoughts and realise that we are not our thoughts, while through acceptance we can open ourselves up to uncomfortable feelings.

The two (defusion and acceptance) often go together. Once you become better at using these tools, applying a simple defusion technique can sometimes be enough when you want to continue performing in the moment instead of becoming bogged down in emotions. As we have already said, all of the practices are highly interactive and highly interconnected. And don't forget, practice makes perfect.

8.4.3 The bubble technique: create space and stay focused in tough situations at work

Description of this tool	**What will this tool enable for you:**
This is a defusion technique that helps you to keep external events, which may trigger thoughts and predictions that lead to a stress response, at a distance until you are 'ready' to deal with them. You are not ignoring them, you are just not getting caught up in them.	• Keep external events (that may trigger negative thoughts followed by stress) outside of your nervous system. • Stay focused on your tasks.

Introduction

There are different variations of the basic defusion techniques that we described above and we would like to share one that we learned from a senior partner at McKinsey & Company. He uses this technique to deal with any stress and anxiety he experiences in the moment and he explains just how powerfully it works for him. The technique can be used whenever and wherever you are working. No one needs to know you are using it and it can help you to prevent a potential stress response or stop low-grade stress from distracting you from what you need to focus on.

Bubble technique tool

The technique requires you to visualize a location outside of yourself where you can store unhelpful thoughts that could otherwise cause you stress and anxiety. These thoughts can arise in any situation at work: a boss giving you feedback in an unhelpful way, a comment from a colleague, a customer being unhappy about your work, etc. If you fuse with these messages, it is likely that you will immediately feel terrible. Examples of the kinds of thoughts that might pop up in your head are: 'I am stupid', 'I feel guilty about making that mistake', 'What if my boss thinks I can't do it? I will be demoted' and so on.

When that happens it means that the thought has got you in its clutches. You identify with the thought and this can lead to an emotional reaction and reduced performance, stress or another response that is unhelpful at that moment. So how can you keep your cool when you see this coming? As we mentioned before, mindfulness is an important basis for becoming good at identifying these situations. The steps are simple and although they look lengthy when written down, they can be performed in a matter of seconds:

1. **Breathe** - When you notice the trigger moment of stress, take a deep belly breath and become aware of what is happening in your mind right now; be present in the moment.
2. **Observe** - Observe the message that is coming towards you, observe the thoughts that this message is producing and repeat to yourself: 'I am observing this message ...', 'This message gives me the thought that...', and 'I notice that I am having the thought that...'
3. **Visualize** - Imagine opening up a soap bubble and putting your thought into the bubble; observe the thought when it has gone into the bubble; you can let the bubble become as big as you like.
4. **Re-focus** - With the message now at a safe distance, decide what you want to do at this moment. What do you need to do right now? If you need to re-focus on the task at hand, do that and revisit the bubble later. If you need to act right now, do so, keeping in mind that you have parked the message at a safe distance and that you can deal with it objectively. If you still feel emotions in your body, calmly observe them; do not push them away, just let them be where they are. If the emotions become very strong, you can also apply one of the techniques from Chapter 7 (e.g., tool 7.4.5).

What you basically do with this exercise is you keep your negative thoughts outside of your nervous system.[197] You don't ignore them, however. In fact, the opposite is true. You acknowledge them but you decide to keep them at a healthy distance for the moment. You realise these are just thoughts and you do not allow them to define or distract you. You are not fused with them. If you can do this, you can continue to concentrate on what you are doing (committed action, which we discuss later on in this book) in line with what is important to you at the current moment (present moment awareness or mindfulness).

It is crucial to remember that applying this technique does not mean you will not feel any stress or anxiety. This technique helps you to manage stress and anxiety so that you can continue to work towards what is important to you: your clients, your projects and so on. It means that stress and anxiety are no longer in the driver's seat. Instead, you take control and stay in charge of doing what is important to you.

197 What we mean by this is that the exercise reduces the emotional response, hence the phrase 'outside of your nervous system', figuratively speaking.

There are different ways of visualizing where you can put your unhelpful thoughts. Aside from the bubble, you could also store them in other places, like a cloud, a car, a drawer, on a leaf in a stream, etc. Experiment with what works best for you. The same processes are going on here as described in the previous exercise: you are basically downregulating a possible stress response. It has done miracles for many, so it is absolutely worth a try.

> **"I think all of us have anxieties and maybe stress. One of the techniques I use to reduce stress is by imagining soap bubbles in which I put the problems. Imagine yourself on a phone call, somebody walking into your office, somebody sending you an email. How many microseconds until you figure out trouble is coming? I would say, it takes less than a microsecond. You hear it from the way people breathe on the phone, you see it from the posture when they walk in, you see it from the first word in the subject comment from the email that trouble is coming. What I do when somebody comes with a tough message? I try to craft the message, and basically open a soap bubble in which the message is stored. For example: 'client angry, very angry, is really upset about our impact.' By the way, not upset with me, but they are upset with you. And it points a finger at me, so it gets bigger and bigger and the bubble blows up. But by putting it in the bubble, it doesn't get into my heart, it doesn't get into my nervous system and I can still objectivize what's going on in the bubble. I can look at the bubble and I can say what do I do now? I can listen, I can wait, I can go to the client, I can call the client. And when I call them, I can listen, I can talk, I can ask a question and what do I do. That is just an objective rational discussion; that just keeps me calmer on the issue. Now the good thing is that, at any given moment, I will have about twenty of those bubbles around me; you don't need to solve them all. Because basically over time some of these bubbles 'pop'. The client calls and says, 'I was very angry at your colleague. The reality is that I had a big problem and I got frustrated and I am sorry that I was so angry.' So one of the worst bubbles that could happen, 'client angry', can just pop. My sense is that about half of the bubbles pop by themselves, so I don't need to deal with them. And they didn't go through my heart and therefore they didn't give me a lot of pain. That is just one visualization technique that I use, and I think it helps me reduce stress and anxiety."**
>
> **Sven Smit,** Senior Partner, McKinsey & Company

8.4.4 Psychological halloweenism: step into someone else's shoes[198]

Description of this tool	What will this tool enable for you:
This tool inspires you to use your imagination and step into someone else's shoes when you need more creativity or 'distance' from a problem you are struggling with or are anxious about solving.	• This tool will offer you a creative way of looking at the same problem from different angles – creating a distance can prompt new answers and enable detached observations.

Introduction

A number of the tools in this book support the development of the ability to focus, which is an important driver of excellence and performance success. The tools that help to create focus include mindfulness and breathing exercises. We have also identified sleep and exercise as critical components of a healthy support system and essential to developing authentic confidence and relaxing the brain at the same time. The tool that we describe here includes a healthy variation of exercises and we show you how unfocusing helps to develop a flexible mind. Applying a mix of different tools to support focus as well as unfocus is important because the brain operates at its best when you can do both.

The tool that we discuss in this section is called psychological halloweenism (Pillay, 2017). It involves learning to unfocus by imagining yourself as someone else for a brief period of time. When you do that, a whole new world of creativity and ideas opens up. For a short while you can let go of the thoughts that make you feel trapped. It is fun to do and generates a lot of new insights. The exercise is about creating a conscious unfocus. We give ourselves a break from the kind of 'rat race' that we often experience in our brain. Our habit circuits and constant focus are switched off so that we can create a moment of freedom to let our minds wander into a new creative environment.

The psychological halloweenism tool

A study by Dumas and Dunbar (2016) showed that people who attempt to solve a problem while imagining they are eccentric poets are much more creative than those who imagine they are stiff libra-

198 This section includes special contributions from Dr Srini Pillay, Harvard-trained psychiatrist and brain researcher; Chief Medical Officer and Co-founder of Reulay and CEO of NeuroBusiness Group.

rians. When the groups changed identity and the eccentric poets became rigid librarians, their results immediately suffered. Adopting a stereotype can affect how we perform in various situations. So if you find that your mind is running in circles or that you suffer from feelings of anxiety or guilt when working on a project, try this exercise. Imagine you are a different persona for a while.[199] It will help you to create distance between you and the stress and anxiety you are feeling in relation to a task and to re-identify with the challenge by looking at the same problem from a different angle. And it is highly likely that you will have a lot of fun as well.

The steps for this exercise are as follows:
1. **Identify your problem** - Whether you are at work or thinking about work, clarify for yourself the problem you are trying to solve. Make sure you identify the real problem.
2. **Imagine** - Look at your problem: what are the different personalities, expertise areas or other creative angles you could use to look at the problem? Think, for example, of pop stars, medical professionals, famous athletes, political figures, renowned academics, animals or trees - be as creative as you like. Pick a few of these and step into their shoes for a while. This will give you new energy. *Be* them and then imagine how they would go about solving your problem. How would they interpret the problem? What solutions would they come up with?
3. **Capture** - Act out, write down, draw and Google everything that pops up in your mind. There are no right or wrong answers; just enjoy doing it all and being this new person.
4. **Revisit** - Revisit your initial problem. Which new insights has this journey of imagination brought you and how can they help solve your problem?
5. **Connect with yourself** - Breathe deeply: how do you feel right now? Was the exercise refreshing and did it result in new inspiration?

199 You can also try to include an exercise like this in a workshop with your team.

FIGURE 35: STEPPING INTO SOMEONE ELSE'S SHOES

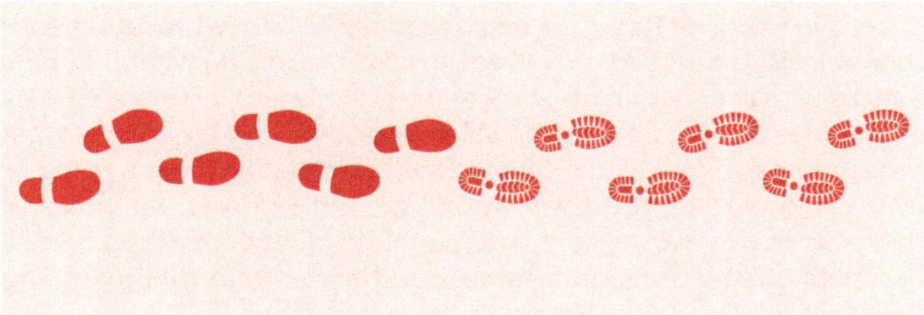

What happens when you do this exercise? If you feel you are stuck in a rut and are becoming more anxious by the minute, you will probably spend all of your time worrying about the potential consequences if you do not come up with the perfect solution to your problem. When you are stuck in the habit of being yourself, your brain comes up with the same old solutions (including similar thought processes that can drain your energy or frustrate you). If you want to escape the habit circuits in your brain, trying on a new identity can be a great help. This process requires imagination and simulation, both of which engage the brain's unfocus circuit - the default mode network. This allows you to think outside the habit circuits in your brain.

If you want to find out more about learning to unfocus, we gladly refer you to the work of Dr Srini Pillay and his latest book, *Tinker Dabble Doodle Try* (2017). You can find more information in our reference list.

8.4.5 For brave types (and not for in the office): special voice techniques for defusion

Description of this tool	What will this tool enable for you:
This tool helps you to rewire any relational frames you may have with certain unhelpful thoughts.	• You will learn how to reframe the relation you have with certain thoughts simply by repeating the thought using different voices.

Introduction

As already described, 'defusion' is a process that reduces the impact of certain words or thoughts on our actions. When we 'fuse' with our thoughts we often hold ourselves back from pursuing what is important to us. When we think we are not good enough we sometimes decide not to take on a particular role or task and try to avoid the pain that may come with it (avoidance). Our thoughts are a result of everything we see and hear around us and the way we interpret things at work - with a client, in a meeting or in the boardroom. How thoughts affect us depends largely on their emotional impact and their believability. Let's examine what this means.

A well-known study that is fundamental to the insights described above dates back to 1916. The British psychologist Edward B. Titchener used word repetition exercises in his studies. He found that repeating the word 'milk' for 45 seconds or more caused the word to lose its meaning. If you say a word out loud or even sing it in different voices or as a cartoon character, all of its associations, emotional impact and believability will eventually disappear (Snyder et al., 2011). This may sound very odd, but the exercise has been proven to be effective in many more studies since it was first developed. In 2004 Masuda and colleagues[200] found that this technique was more likely to reduce discomfort and believability than other similar approaches. Five years later, another study by Masuda and colleagues in 2009[201] found a reduction in the emotional impact of words after 3 to 10 seconds of word repetition, while their believability was reduced after 20 to 30 seconds of repetition. This effect was an indication that there are two aspects to this exercise and the impact of words: an emotional aspect and a believability aspect. The findings were also supported in other studies (see, e.g., Masuda et al., 2010). In this tool we will describe a version that can be applied within the context of work.

How to defuse using a voice technique

In 2018 a LinkedIn® post by Gordon Tredgold attracted our attention. In it he described how he struggled with feeling like an imposter all of the time:

> **"Imposter syndrome is something that I, along with many others, suffer from. It's a strange affliction because it affects confident people as well as insecure people, and it's not**

200 https://www.ncbi.nlm.nih.gov/pubmed/14998740

201 https://www.ncbi.nlm.nih.gov/pubmed/19028961

> **something that anyone but us notice about ourselves, and yet when I mention it to others, they tell me 'Yes. I suffer from that too'. Last month I was selected by Inc as one of their Top 100 Leadership Speakers for 2018, and yet still that does nothing to allay these feelings of being an imposter. This is the second time I made the list, and the first time I actually assumed they had mistaken me for someone else, even though I had dozens of amazing testimonials and had received standing ovations and rebookings from my talks."**
>
> **Gordon Tredgold,** CEO and Founder, Leadership Principles

As we mentioned earlier in this book, Gordon is certainly not alone in this. The idea that you are an imposter can seriously cripple you at work. It can impact how you lean in to your work, discuss things with a client and your willingness to speak at conferences. Thoughts like 'I am not good enough' often pop up in your head as well and they can eat up a lot of mental space and energy. If this happens regularly, you can feel emotionally drained at the end of the day. The following exercise is meant to help you create distance between you and your thoughts in a different, creative and effective manner. It is unlikely that you will want to do this in your open space office, but feel free to do so if you want. Alternatively, you can do this exercise in your car when driving to or from work or when you have time to think before or after your working day.

Let us use the example of Gordon Tredgold and the idea that he may be an impostor. The following steps can reduce the impact of that thought:

1. **Breathe** - Take a deep belly breath and become aware of what is happening in your mind right now; be present in the moment.
2. **Observe** - Observe what your inner critic (the chimp) is telling you. Tell yourself 'I am having the thought that I am an impostor', and 'I notice that I am having the thought that I am an impostor.'
3. **Reflect -** What springs to mind when you say the word 'impostor'? To you, being an impostor might cause you to think that 'they might find out I am not good at all' or that 'they made a mistake hiring me'.
4. **Repeat out loud -** Repeat the word 'impostor' out loud for one to two minutes, regardless of where you are. If you are in a brave or funny mood, you could also sing the word repeatedly to your favourite tune: 'impostor, impostor, impostor...'
5. **Notice -** Notice what this does to you. Is the sound of the word 'impostor' or the muscle movement in your face when you repeat

the word more prominent in your experience than the meaning or emotional impact of the word?

Doing the above exercise increases the likelihood that your distracting thought will have less impact on how you feel and how you act and diminish the believability and discomfort of that thought (Snyder et al., 2011).

If you are interested in reading more about these kinds of techniques, check out the references at the back of the book (e.g., Hayes et al., 2012).

CHAPTER 9

9. PRACTICE 5 – SELF-AS-CONTEXT

you are one of those
that have no
other choice
than to climb
the rocky roads.
you would have slipped
on the smooth path.
|easy come.
easy go. |

the words
reach for me
the way
water reaches
the sand
and become the shore.
|becoming
and unbecoming. |

hurt has a memory
and if it is really deep
it will come back
again
and again and again
and again.
|memories are not
feelings. |

your life line
is carved
into your spine
and every time
you turn your back
on me
i see where you
come from
a little better.
|spinal
cords. |

Noor Intisar, former Campus Poet, University of Antwerp

> **"If you change the way you look at things, the things you look at change."**
>
> **(exact source unknown)**[202]

This quote is both powerful and true. It is often used to explain what you create for yourself when you have a certain view on how the world works. For example, if you think that human nature is inherently egoistic and selfish, you will automatically distrust people before you can really understand their intentions. You dictate the way in which you interact with the world. When you distrust people before you even start interacting with them, you presume that the relationship you develop with these people will not be a positive one. You can also apply this way of thinking to the relationship you have with yourself and your surroundings. We will explore this in more detail in the following sections.

202 The quote has been attributed to Wayne Dyer.

9.1 What do we mean by the practice of self-as-context?

We would like to quote a classic ACT intervention from Hayes et al. (2012: 568) to explain the focus of this particular practice:

"It's as if there is a chessboard that extends infinitely in all directions. It's covered with different-coloured pieces, black pieces, and white pieces. They work together in teams, as in chess - the white pieces opposing the black pieces. You can think of your thoughts, feelings, and beliefs as these pieces; they sort of hang out together in teams too. For examples, 'bad' feelings (like anxiety, and bad memories). Same thing with the 'good' ones. So, it seems the way the game is played, is that we select which side we want to win. We put the 'good' pieces (like thoughts that are self-confident, feelings of being in control, etc.) on one side and the 'bad' pieces on the other. Then we get up on the back of the white queen and ride to battle, fighting to win the war against anxiety, depression, thoughts about using drugs, whatever. It's a war game. But there's a logical problem here, and it's that from this posture huge portions of yourself are your own enemy. In other words, if you need to be in this war, there is something wrong with you. And since it appears that you're on the same level as these pieces, they can be as big or even bigger than you are - even though it is not logical - the more you fight, the bigger they get. If it is true that 'if you are not willing to have it, you've got it,' then as you fight them, they get more central to your life, more habitual, more dominating, and more linked to every area of living. The logical idea is that you will knock enough of them off the board that you eventually dominate them - except your experience tells you that exactly the opposite happens. Apparently, the black pieces can't be deliberately knocked off the board! So, the battle goes on. You feel hopeless, you have a sense that you can't win, and you can't stop fighting. If you're on the back of that white horse, fighting is the only choice you have because the black pieces seem life-threatening. Yet, living in a war zone is no way to live."

You may have noticed that the different practices come together in the above description. In order to observe what is going on - on the chessboard of your life - you can use your mindfulness, defusion and acceptance practices. This allows you to observe 'what is' (instead of pushing things away). A practical part of the self-as-context practice is that you learn to observe yourself (as a whole human being) in whatever context you find yourself (situation, career, etc.).[203] Looking at yourself from a distance (we will explain the balcony perspective below) helps you to reconnect with your purpose and values and to be aware of what is happening to you, consciously and unconsciously, at any given moment. We will include some practical exercises in this toolkit to help you look at yourself within particular contexts and from a balcony perspective.

9.2 Why develop self-as-context skills?

Developing the skills required to look at yourself in a certain context will help you to apply all the other practices as well. The tools we will describe in this section of the toolkit can be used for reframing situations, distancing yourself from what is happening and focusing on looking at yourself and the challenging situation within the broader scheme of things. Learning to become reflective and distancing yourself from an event can prevent a stress response in the brain and body. This allows you, from a purely awareness perspective, to look at the situation and yourself within the particular context. In this practice you engage your sense of curiosity. This in turn changes the channel of what might be going on in your mind - e.g., from the anxiety channel that potentially leads to a stress response to a different channel that reframes what you experience (and adds to the possibilities of what could be true).

9.3 Self-as-context - 'From > To' behaviours and thoughts

When you develop this practice you will begin to understand what actually drives your current behaviour (without disputing it). You will learn how to deal with negative thoughts and to adopt more positive ones. This transformation can help you to move yourself from the 'dancefloor' to a spot on the 'balcony' that is more distant

203 For the sake of completeness, we wish to emphasise that we will include a few tools and reflections that may not strictly be part of the traditional ACT but are complementary and might help you to develop authentic confidence. We have gained experience with these additional tools in our own practice of leadership development and have found that they are very effective in supporting the development of emotional flexibility.

from the situation. Figure 36 shows a number of changes in behaviour and thoughts that can result from applying these tools.

FIGURE 36: SELF-AS-CONTEXT 'FROM > TO' EXAMPLES

From	To
TYPES OF BEHAVIOUR	
■ Trying to be 'perfectly' prepared	■ Preparing as well as possible and remaining flexible when things change
■ Zooming in on that one mistake you made and overemphasising it	■ Accepting yourself, viewing your performance from the perspective of who you are
■ Seeing yourself in isolation	■ Seeing yourself in context or from a distance
TYPES OF THOUGHTS	
"That board member is having a meeting with my SVP Marketing, they must be discussing my failure"	*"Interesting to see they are meeting. I should not jump to any conclusions about what they might say"*
"I messed that one up - man, I am so stupid!"	*"Let's take a step back, what is really going on here?"*

9.4 Tools to develop self-as-context

9.4.1 The wisdom of writing: journaling everywhere you go

Description of this tool	What will this tool enable for you:
This tool will describe how journaling can help you to understand yourself better and untangle your thoughts when you experience lots of stress.	• View things in perspective and put into words what you are experiencing and feeling - this will help you to clarify and process what is truly happening during stressful situations.

Introduction

Journaling has been proven to be an effective way of expressing emotions. Various studies have shown how it can positively impact one's overall well-being (see, e.g., Pennebaker, 1997).[204] It is in the context of emotional flexibility that we present the tool of journaling here, but it can also be used for all of the practices that require self-reflection. Writing down experiences and insights can feel uncomfortable at first, but give it a try and you will soon experience its positive benefits. Journaling helps you to put your feelings into words and to look at a situation that you are trying to comprehend from a distance. In the process of writing, many subconscious elements may become clear to you as well.

King (2001) found that writing about achieving future goals and dreams can make people happier and healthier. The most important outcome in terms of building authentic confidence is that it helps you to engage with, become aware of and learn to understand your experiences and the challenges you are struggling with. By writing them down, you give structure and clarity to your thoughts, which helps you to remain calm and achieve a better understanding of where the real problems lie. Another benefit is that you can let your thoughts go when you put them down on paper.

Journaling tool

There are many ways you can keep a personal journal. You just need to find the one that works best for you. You can choose to carry a small journal with you wherever you go and use it for personal reflections on the fly. Or you could keep one on your bedside table and write down your thoughts at the end of the day. There are also journal apps available if you prefer to keep notes digitally. And if you think it would help to use reflection questions every day, you could use a journal that has questions already pre-printed. To help kickstart your authentic confidence journaling process, try using the following questions (some questions can be used for morning reflections, others for evening reflections):

- What am I experiencing right now and why (what do I feel, think, smell, hear)?
- What I appreciate about myself is ...
- Today I am grateful for ...
- If I were the CEO of my company, I would ...
- Today my biggest 'aha' moment was ...
- I would like today to go like this: ...
- Over the next few days I will integrate these challenges into my work to learn and grow: ...

204 http://www.gruberpeplab.com/teaching/psych3131_summer2015/documents/14.2_Pennebaker1997_Writingemotionalexperiences.pdf

- If I were not scared of conflict, the honest feedback that I would give to my colleague would be ...
- The things that are going well for me at work at the moment are ...
- One area I would like to make a change in my day-to-day work is ...
- The biggest challenge I experienced today at work was ...

These are just a few examples. You can add, remove and change whatever you like.

9.4.2 Understanding your iceberg to change your behaviour

Description of this tool	What will this tool enable for you:
This tool will help you understand current behaviour that you want to change. It will help you to evolve your 'From' > 'To' behaviour.	• Understand what drives current behaviour. • Understand how to change and take a first step.

Introduction

Sigmund Freud was one of the first psychologists to write about the role of the unconscious mind. Later, in 1973, Harvard professor David McClelland wrote an impactful paper called 'Testing for competence rather than intelligence'.[205] He suggested finding a different way of looking at how to predict future success and to replace pure intelligence testing with competence testing. Like Freud, in his work he referred to the fact that there is much more to human behaviour than what we can see and observe.

A well-known metaphor that is used nowadays is the 'iceberg' of human behaviour. The behaviour we can observe is no more than the tip of the iceberg. We all know that the part of an iceberg that is under the surface of the water is much larger than what we can actually see. Similarly, many of the things that drive our behaviour are invisible too. They have to do with our mindset, the different layers of what we think and feel, our values and beliefs, and ultimately, deep below the surface, our needs and fears. The figure below visualizes the iceberg model used by Aberkyn – McKinsey & Company.

205 https://www.therapiebreve.be/documents/mcclelland-1973.pdf

FIGURE 37: THE ICEBERG MODEL

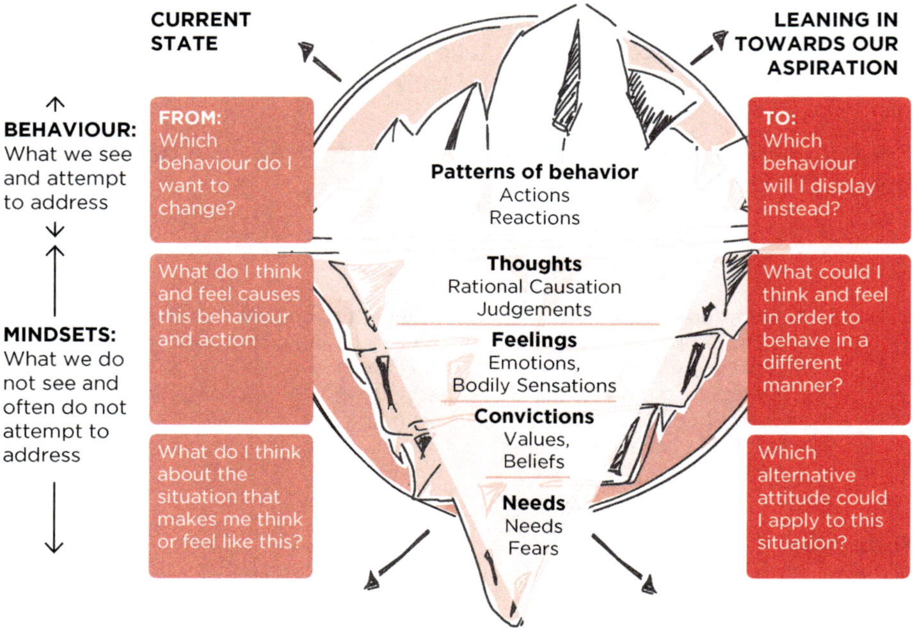

Source: Aberkyn – McKinsey & Company

The iceberg tool[206]

Changing your behaviour is difficult enough, but even more so when you do not understand what drives that behaviour. The iceberg tool can help you to develop an understanding of a particular behaviour that you would like to change. To illustrate how this tool can help, let's take Jack as an example.[207] Jack's problem is that he tends to overprepare for meetings. He spends an enormous amount of time making sure the documents he is preparing as input for a meeting are absolutely perfect. He checks them multiple times, far more often than is necessary. Also, he invests a lot of time in preparing answers for all of the questions he could possibly be asked during the meeting. Most of those questions go way beyond the scope of the document and the decisions that need to be made. Jack also prepares for questions on peripheral topics that might arise. He basical-

206 For the sake of completeness, in this particular example we don't deep-dive into the bodily sensations, an important element of Lisa Feldman Barrett's Theory of Constructed Emotion.

207 The name is fictitious. This example is a version of a real story that we hear frequently.

ly wants to have an adequate answer to every possible question. The result is that he often works very long hours. He feels that if he does not prepare well, he will not be able to participate fully in the meeting or call.

Fortunately, Jack has realised that his behaviour is not very effective. He wants to change his behaviour from 'overpreparing but ready for all eventualities' to 'preparing well and willing to accept what happens in the moment'. Jack would like to develop the courage to think on his feet and just go with the flow in the meeting. However, making this kind of 'from>to' switch is not easy and won't happen just because he wants to change. If he tries to change his behaviour without understanding the hidden layers of his iceberg, the old behaviour will just return again. To make a real and permanent change he must first understand what actually drives his current behaviour (his mindset) and then figure out what he can change in order to stimulate the desired behaviour. This change is shown in Figure 38. We will use the iceberg worksheet reproduced in Figure 39 to illustrate how this change in mindset and behaviour is achieved.

FIGURE 38: FICTITIOUS EXAMPLE OF AN ICEBERG

	FROM	TO
Behaviour	• Over preparing, not speaking up, etc.	• Preparing well **and** going with the flow
Thoughts **Feelings**	• I haven't thought this through so I can't contribute • Feeling guilty about not having done enough to prepare • Stupid, not worthy	• I have done my best. If I make mistakes, I have an opportunity to learn and grow • I feel relieved and self-empowered
Convictions	• Excellence and high standards are what count	• Giving it the best I can, that's all that counts
Beliefs	"I am not good enough"	"I am good the way I am"
Needs	• Appreciation • Acceptance • Inclusion	• (Self) appreciation • (Self) acceptance • (Self) inclusion

FIGURE 39: ICEBERG COACHING WORKSHEET

1. Your biggest improvement goal: Fill in using the Iceberg coaching questions

2. Behaviour	3. Thinking/feeling	4. Values/beliefs	5. Needs/fears	6. Climbing the iceberg	7. Climbing the iceberg
A. What behaviors do you find yourself doing/not doing that get in your way?	A. What are your feelings in this situation?	A. Which important values is this behaviour in conflict with? (if you don't know, think about your top 3 values)	A. Which need are you trying to fulfil with this (your current) behavior?	A. How is this mindset (4) serving you?	A. Which behaviours, feelings and thoughts would become possible with your new mindset?
				B. How is this mindset not serving you?	
B. If these behaviours continue, what might be the outcome?	B. What are your immediate thoughts/self-talk when they are triggered?	B. Which underlying beliefs or assumptions are driving this behaviour? (What meaning do you assign to them?)	B. What are you afraid will happen if you stop behaving the way you do?	C. How would your work/life be different without this mindset?	B. What are you willing to let go of? And what are you willing to commit to?
C. Why is this improvement goal important to you?			C. What is the worst thing that could happen?	D. What is a more powerful mindset you could choose?	C. Which small experiments could you carry out to test this new mindset?

Source: Aberkyn, McKinsey & Company.

For Jack's case we will use the same numbering for the questions that are used in the worksheet in Figure 39. The biggest improvement goal here is (1): Jack wants to go from 'overpreparing or otherwise not speaking up' to 'preparing well and accepting whatever happens'. Next, question 2A: which behaviour is getting in Jack's way? Clearly, as described above, Jack tends to overprepare for meetings, which results in long working hours and very little free time. Also, because you can never prepare perfectly, Jack's behaviour prevents him from participating fully in a meeting, thereby running the risk that he will not be seen and fail to fulfil his potential. Question 2B: if these behaviours continue, what will be the outcome? Not only would Jack eventually become exhausted by all this overpreparing, but his talent would also remain unacknowledged because of his tendency to hold back. This relates also to question 2C: why is this improvement goal important to Jack? For him it is important because he wants to be able to lean in during meetings and participate fully. Also, he feels he is spending too much time preparing, which always forces him to choose between private time or additional work time. So, if he could change this behaviour, he would have more free time and participate more fully in meetings, which would make him feel better about himself.

The next question, 3A: what are Jack's feelings in this situation? This question addresses the unwanted aspects of the situation. Jack feels stupid and unworthy. His immediate thoughts (if during a meeting he finds he cannot answer a particular question) are: 'I can't contribute, I have not thought this through well enough' and 'I feel guilty about not having prepared well enough.' When he reflects on his values, this is in conflict with 4A: Jack realises that he has jeopardised a number of his values. Firstly, by overworking he cannot spend time enough with his family, who are very important to him. Secondly, he has less time to go running, which he loves doing a few times a week. Thirdly, he values his own freedom and space, but because of his manner of working he feels restricted and imprisoned. Finally, he really wants to be authentic and to contribute fully during meetings, but because he tends to hold back he is not living by that value.

Underlying this behaviour is the belief that only the best is good enough (question 4B), and Jack often believes that he is not good enough. Jack has a need to be appreciated, accepted and included (5A) and fears that if he is not good enough, none of that will happen (5B). In his opinion, being 'good enough' means that he needs to have an answer to everything and therefore to be perfectly prepared. This is a one-way ticket to failure. The worst thing that could happen (5C) is that the management will fail to appreciate his contribution and that he might be passed over for future work or roles. Jack's current mindset gives him a false sense of security (6A). He thinks he is doing himself a favour behaving as he does because he is avoiding the perceived risks. The paradox, however, is that this mindset is not serving him well at all (6B) but is actually doing the opposite of what he wants to achieve. By overpreparing and holding back, he is not really doing himself justice and the management are unable to see what he has to offer. His life would be so much better without this mindset (6C). He would have much more time and space to rest and refuel. And he would be less troubled by the stuff that goes through his mind at meetings.

In his exploration of his iceberg, Jack realises that he is lacking in self-appreciation. He is too hard on himself all of the time. So a good start in terms of behavioural change would be to build his sense of self-appreciation, acceptance and inclusion. A more powerful mindset (6D) would be one that would tell him that he is good enough the way he is. Giving the best he can is all that matters and a value worth embracing. If he can do so, and (7A) if the triggering situation occurs again, he could choose to reflect and say to himself, 'I have done my best. If I make mistakes it means I have an opportunity to learn and grow.' As a result, he would feel relieved, self-empowered and less anxious. His behaviour would change into preparing well and simultaneously accepting what emerges in the meeting and going with the flow (recognising that it is impossible to prepare perfectly and predict how a meeting will go).

In order to make that happen, he needs to reflect on what he is willing to let go (7B). In our example, he decides to let go of the need for perfectionism and the feeling he cannot perform well enough (or rather, perfectly) if he doesn't work until well past midnight. He also needs to let go of his fear of making mistakes and be prepared to take a risk every now and then. Not easy, of course, but he can make life less difficult by committing to the value that we can learn from our mistakes (7B). By thinking of small experiments (7C) – for example, using the upcoming team meetings to consciously practice leaning in – and using other tools in this toolkit, he may be able to take the first steps on the road to real change.

Figure 39 (Iceberg coaching worksheet) has all of the questions you will need to guide you through your own reflections on what is going on in your iceberg. Use it when you want to change a behaviour that is not helping you into one that will. You can use this series of questions for self-reflection or you can find a peer coach to help you if you believe that would work better for you. Questions 1 to 5 help to clarify the left-hand side of your iceberg and questions 6 and 7 help you to clarify the right-hand side and identify a more helpful mindset that will support your behavioural change. If you enjoy this exercise, you can find more in-depth and advanced approaches in the book *Deliberate Calm, how to learn and lead in a volatile world* by Brassey, De Smet and Kruyt (2022).[208] For more information we refer you to the reference list in this book.

9.4.3 Ambidexterity during the project: zooming in and zooming out

Description of this tool	**What will this tool enable for you:**
This tool will help you to learn to focus on switching between being deeply engaged in the details at work and looking at situations from a distance - becoming more ambidextrous.	• The tool will help you to become more aware of the importance of alternating between focusing on the details at work and adopting a more distant perspective.

Introduction

An important skill in terms of personal and professional growth and effectiveness is the ability to function at different levels at work: at the level of detail and at the level of the bigger picture. Harvard professor Ron Heifetz uses the analogy of the 'balcony and the dance' to explain this.[209] He uses the phrase 'being in the dance' to refer to the day-to-day activities at work, which is the part that does not allow much time or space for reflection. This is the time when you have to deal with the never-ending stream of emails, conversations, meetings, discussions, sudden business crises and negotiations. In order to be able to make value-driven decisions at work, it is important to master the skill of 'being on the balcony' as well. This is when you get to reflect on your purpose and values and also on your commitment to your actions and your operating model (see Chapter 10, sub-section 10.4.2). Being on the balcony means that you are able to stand back, reflect and see the bigger picture at any given moment. You look at the whole system and the patterns of behaviour in those moments that present a challenge for you - i.e., when your confidence is challenged the most. This tool includes a brief reflection

208 https://www.harpercollins.com/products/deliberate-calm-jacqueline-brasseyaaron-de-smetmichiel-kruyt?variant=40244138344482

209 https://hbr.org/2002/06/a-survival-guide-for-leaders

exercise that shows the difference between the balcony and the dance for you at work. It will help you to reflect and see things in perspective (self-as-context) while working towards what is important to you.

> **"In a difficult situation where I had to take the lead, being mindful and reflecting on how to impact in such a way so as not to be labelled as the 'bad guy' in the process is important. There was a possibility of losing credibility because of driving a process that was not sensitive to the surroundings. So looking at the bigger picture helped me to think things through."**
>
> **Michelle Roborg-Sondergaard,** Senior HR Executive

Balcony versus dance

Being aligned with your feelings and self-confidence requires reflective action. In particular, if you are in a position of leadership, you need to be able to manage the complexity and pace of day-to-day activities while also being conscious of the bigger picture and emerging patterns. This state of witness consciousness — being present in the moment *and* at the same time detached from that moment — is the state athletes refer to as being 'in the zone'. A world-class footballer or basketball player is both present in the moment of receiving a pass *and* aware of the whole playing field, as if they are watching the game from the commentator's box. They are simultaneously up on the balcony and down on the dancefloor.

People who lead adaptive change most successfully have a diagnostic mindset with regard to themselves and the situation. They continually strive to understand what is going below the surface, how they themselves change over time and how they, as a system, interact with their organisation as a system. Whenever you are trying to lead a group or organisation through an adaptive change you may experience conflicts between your various loyalties. This is because you are a system (an individual) within a system (your organisation). Within yourself as a system, your interests, fears and loyalties all affect your behaviours and decisions. To become more aware of this and be better able to stand on the balcony, take the time to reflect regularly on questions like:

- What are the complex forces influencing my behaviour and choices?
- What role do I play in this larger organisation?
- What purpose do I seek to serve?
- What values do I want to adhere to?
- What changes do I need to make myself to lead more effectively?

Like everyone else, you have your own default settings: your ways of interpreting and responding to events around you. To gain greater latitude and freedom to respond in a more useful way, it is essential to know what those default settings are, particularly the ones that are in line with your own values. You can reflect on the dance and balcony questions when you are at work. If you have developed a state of mindfulness that allows you to do this, creating space for balcony reflections can be done in the moment. If you need more distance from a situation, you can use your short breaks or lunch break, for example, to create the space you need.

> **"I had to give a presentation to our top 400 leaders in a foreign language (Dutch). So, I had to connect with the people in the room and have, of course, good content as well. For me the concept of 'being on the balcony and in the dance' is very powerful, and helped me while leading this presentation. I was zooming in to focus on the moment and being present with the audience and being on stage. Zooming out meant making things relevant and managing the context: thinking of the total journey that we had been through so far and where we would go next, connecting that to the detail (dance). I feel it made me more effective and helped me to keep things in perspective, giving me confidence. I am aware of this concept and use it a lot in my day-to-day life as an HR leader. In a way, you are always working on something in the moment while building on a longer-term story. The storyline is not always known, but by zooming in and out it becomes clear along the way, helping you to see things and yourself in the context of something bigger, connecting with your purpose and values, and those of the larger team and organisation."**
>
> **Nicholas Brassey,** Global HR Executive

9.4.4 Taking a flexible perspective

Description of this tool	**What will this tool enable for you:**
This tool will help you to look at situations that you are experiencing as challenging or anxiety -provoking through a different lens: you take a flexible perspective.	• You will learn to can look at the same situation from another angle and have a different experience by adopting a flexible perspective.

Introduction

Human beings are very quick to jump to conclusions, especially when we feel emotionally sensitive or are lacking in confidence. Thinking back to the neuroscience of fear, our worries and lack of confidence can be triggered by a prediction of an external event and the worrying process related to this. If we continue to ruminate about something that triggered our worrying, we may even create a stress response in our brain and body. This will not help us in our performance and do our well-being no good either. To disentangle ourselves from worry, we can challenge ourselves to look at things from a different perspective. In particular, when we do not know all the facts it can help to focus on what we know and what is important to us, because jumping to conclusions can get you into trouble. A technique that can help is reframing or adopting a flexible perspective. We will now introduce an ACT-consistent variation on Rational Emotive Behaviour Therapy (REBT)[210] in which perspective, values and committed action are combined.

How to take a flexible perspective

Figure 40 visualizes how we can 'think' ourselves into a stressful situation and trigger an emotional reaction very easily by the predictions we make – for example, when we are working at our desk and someone enters the room.

210 http://albertellis.org/rebt-cbt-therapy/

FIGURE 40: FLEXIBLE PERSPECTIVE TAKING (EXAMPLE A, MID-MANAGER LEVEL)

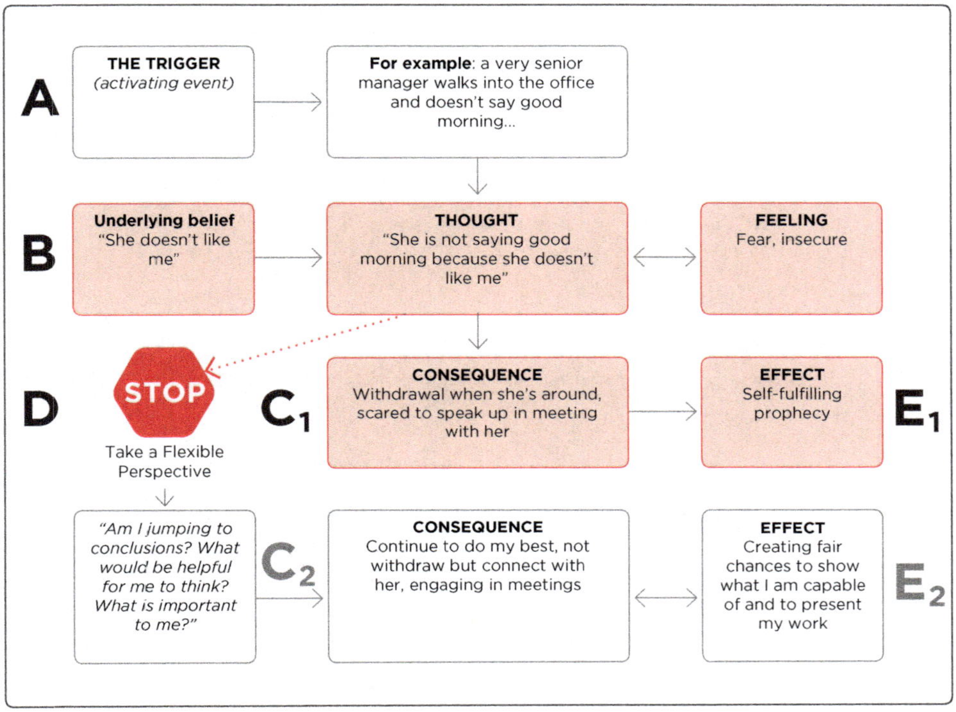

Source: Our own ACT-consistent interpretation of Rational Emotive Behaviour Therapy (REBT) reframing, using the approach of taking a flexible perspective instead of 'disputing' the thought.

The example in Figure 40 describes a situation that many of us may have experienced, especially earlier on in our careers. However, this situation also occurs at all executive levels. The following example is an anonymous but true story from a board member at a large multi-national enterprise.

FIGURE 41: FLEXIBLE PERSPECTIVE TAKING (EXAMPLE B, BOARD LEVEL)

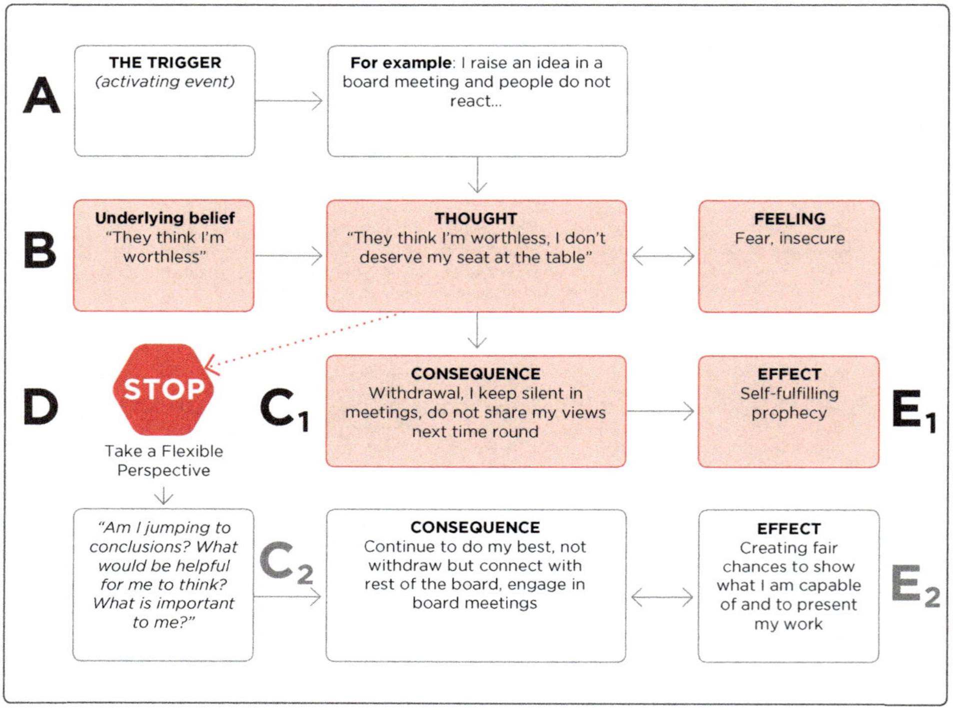

Source: see Figure 40.

Reacting from a flexible perspective

These five steps can help you to react flexibly and adequately to a situation:

1. If you become aware that you are suddenly having negative thoughts, try to think what could have triggered this (IDENTIFY TRIGGER).[211]
2. Explore how the thought makes you feel and what is happening to you in this moment. Take a deep breath (IDENTIFY THOUGHTS AND FEELINGS).
3. Take a pause. Change the place where you are standing right now or turn your chair around; just move to a different position (if physically possible) and try to take a flexible perspective (PUSH PAUSE BUTTON AND REFLECT ON PERSPECTIVE).

211 For pragmatic reasons we have decided to keep the description in this exercise very simple – understanding the underlying process of the 'trigger' is slightly more complicated, as described in Chapter 2.

4. Ask yourself: 'Am I jumping to conclusions? What would be helpful for me to think? What matters to me right now? What is important? By doing this you help your brain to predict different possible outcomes and you can connect with what matters to you in the moment (TAKING PERSPECTIVE AND CONNECTING WITH WHAT MATTERS).
5. Then decide for yourself, irrespective of the disturbing thoughts that you may have (you can apply defusion and/or acceptance techniques here as well if the thoughts are bothering you a lot), if you can move on towards what is important to you (COMMITTED AND VALUED ACTION).

> **"I had to make some challenging decisions about my voluntary organisation. It was emotional, but I was able to look at the topic from a distance; uncoupling the emotional from the rational aspects was very helpful for me, putting things in perspective and analysing the issue in a rational way. What is still possible, what is not, and asking myself honestly: what do I want?"**
>
> **Josette Dijkhuizen,** Honorary Professor in Entrepreneurship Development and Entrepreneur

> **"So, imagining the worst-case scenario is something I have done in a lot of situations when I lack confidence. It is very easy to jump from worst case to knowing it's probably not going as badly as I fear and so there is a chance to come in with a more realistic expectation of it going just fine. As a psychologist, the thing that I am struck about is that when we lack confidence, we tend to focus only on the things that could go wrong and forget that there may also be things that could go right. So, after envisioning the worst-case scenario, I think the possible benefits of doing this are that I can then adjust what I am about to do."**
>
> **Adam Grant,** Professor of Management and Psychology, The Wharton School, University of Pennsylvania, USA

> **"It is very important to put things in perspective as well; in the end, we (at Unilever) are (only) selling soup and soap."**
>
> **Jan Zijderveld,** referring to his role as EVP Europe and Member of the Executive Board at Unilever

> **"I went through my last big crisis a few years ago. One morning, I was waking up and I was in a bad place and remember calling my wife crying saying, 'I am totally messed up - I don't know what to do anymore.' In this situation (and many more before), my wife has been a tremendous help and support, and challenges me well. I felt out of control at work, in private life, thinking I don't know where I stand with the Firm; here I am, it is 6AM in the morning and I am experiencing a lot of anxiety. My wife asked me: 'What is the worst thing that can happen to you?' She really helped me to put things in perspective and go through the whole story. This helped me to really get it very clear what is important to me. In the end, nothing is that bad, and even the bad things that can happen are things that can be survived. So really picturing what is important and finding my inner values and purpose helped me through this."**
>
> **Beltrán Simó,** Partner, McKinsey & Company, Bogotá, Colombia

CHAPTER 10

10. PRACTICE 6 – COMMITTED ACTION

i put my life
on the line
and you play
jump rope.
still
you have
no idea
what keeps me
balanced.
|word
for word. |

how powerful
is that emotion
that makes one believe
the world would be a lesser
place without adding to it.
|invisible
is the one thing
that makes me see everything
clearer. |

when your heart
starts throbbing
in your throat
let it speak.
|pushing it forward.
let your voice be heard. |

i planted
my seeds
in infertile soils
and grew
with envy
at the sight
of weeds
grown in the wild.
|time taught me
patience is not always
a virtue.
get going. |

Noor Intisar, former Campus Poet, University of Antwerp

> **"But reflection without action is ultimately as unproductive as action without reflection."**
>
> **Kegan and Lahey,** 2009: 411

10.1 What do we mean by the practice of committed action?

> **"Vision without action is merely a dream. Action without vision just passes the time. Vision with action can change the world."**
>
> **Joel A. Barker**[212]

212 https://www.brainyquote.com/quotes/joel_a_barker_158200

If you really want to change a certain behaviour, you have to commit to yourself to doing so. In fact, if you are not committed, there's not much point in even trying. What we mean here is that you need to consciously think and act on what is important to you in the context of building your authentic confidence. For instance, if you are afraid to speak up in meetings, you will have to commit yourself to learning how to speak more confidently.

In this chapter you will discover how to design your own learning journey so that you can build the skills you need and develop the courage required to create out-of-your-comfort-zone experiments that matter to you. You have already explored what matters to you in the chapter on purpose and values. At a pragmatic level, applying that to your current role and the role you want to play a few years from now[213] will help you to reflect on the experience and skills you need to develop in order to be able to play that particular role in the future. You will identify the gaps so that you can start planning actions. Committed action means dedicating yourself to working on those issues that are important until you have mastered them. You can do this by integrating the relevant actions into your personal operating model, which is one of the tools we offer.

10.2 Why develop committed action skills?

We often fail to link our new learnings to concrete actions. We follow a training programme, read a fantastic book, become inspired by someone or something and then ... nothing; we fail to change our behaviour or our actions. And nothing changes in terms of how we feel, either. If we really want to move forward and change, we have to take action. This is most effective when we link committed action to our learning needs and what is important to us and when we do it in such a way that it can be easily integrated into our own operating model.

The best advice is to insert a number of concrete micro-level activities or habits into your operating model that are feasible for you and

213 In the context of the life you want to lead, holistically speaking, a role is only one aspect of all you do and does not define who you want to be. So when we talk about a 'role' we recommend that you view it in the context of the bigger picture, your purpose and what you see for yourself further down the line.

will help you on your development or transformation journey. These will serve as the lead indicators for the change you want to achieve. For example, if you want to become fitter, you might want to insert a commitment to eating two vegan meals and one 'normal' meal a day into your operating model. And you could also commit to going for a 30-minute run twice a week. This kind of commitment means no compromise. When you stick to your commitments and do what you said you would, at some point you will develop a new habit that will support your ultimate objective: becoming fitter.

An essential part of building authentic confidence is being aware of the concrete changes you must integrate into your work schedule and committing yourself to those changes. Developing habits (even small ones) can make a huge contribution to your efforts to achieve behavioural change (see Chapter 3).

10.3 Committed Action – 'From > To' behaviours and thoughts

Creating the focus and presence of mind required to determine where you should direct your attention during your busy work week is vital to: (a) staying connected to what is important to you; and (b) developing your authentic confidence. This particular practice links your purpose, values and strengths to what you do and promotes continuous practicing. Identify a number of areas you wish to address and then identify the practical and concrete micro-level actions they require. Over time, you may want to change certain activities or add new activities that are important to you on your learning journey. Figure 42 contains a few examples of behaviours and thoughts that are related to these kinds of 'from > to' changes.

FIGURE 42: COMMITTED ACTION 'FROM > TO' EXAMPLES

From	To
TYPES OF BEHAVIOUR	
Leaning back	Leaning in
Working harder	Working smarter and taking care of myself
Not giving things a try	Having a clear operating model with clearly defined micro-actions
THOUGHTS	
"I hope the Board cancels the meeting so I don't need to do a presentation"	*"I'm excited about the meeting with the Board - I will lean in and learn!"*
"I will not put my hand up to lead that workshop"	*"I will take the opportunity to lead that workshop and ask for help"*

10.4 Committed action tools

10.4.1 Matrix for advancing authentic confidence

Description of this tool	**What will this tool enable for you:**
The awareness framework brings together the key aspects of all dimensions of emotional flexibility so you can make choices on committed action.	• An insight into bringing together what is important to you and how your thoughts and actions help you to move towards or away from what is important to you.

Introduction

As mentioned in the previous chapter, by creating balcony moments you can reflect on where you are heading, whether that be in the right or the wrong direction. In this section we will introduce a simple but powerful matrix based on the work of Polk and colleagues (see Polk et al., 2016).[214] This tool will help you to reflect on what is

214 http://www.theactmatrixacademy.com/.

important to you in the professional context and whether you are (or are not) acting in line with what matters to you.

This tool helps you to become aware of how important it is to be grateful for those areas where you are actually acting in line with what is important to you. You can also use it to identify opportunities for committed action. We also provide a few workplace examples to guide you through the exercises.

The authentic confidence matrix tool
The matrix is visualized below.

FIGURE 43: AUTHENTIC CONFIDENCE MATRIX

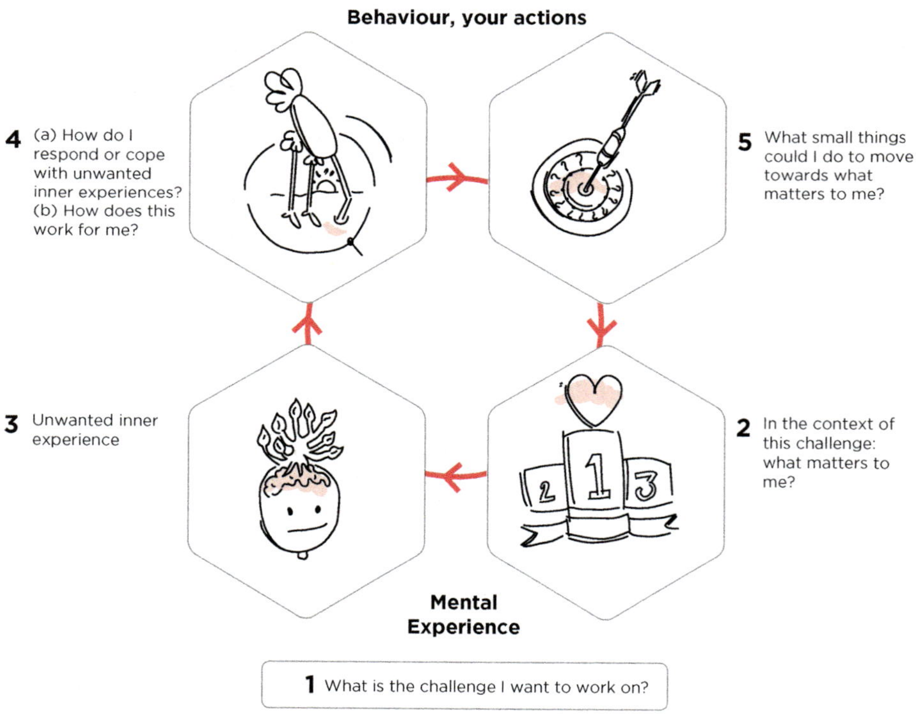

Source: Own adaptation, based on the work of Polk et al. (2016)

Reflection questions

1. **What is the challenge you want to work on?**

- What are you not doing at this moment due to your lack of confidence, but that you want to start doing?

Examples: speaking in front of an audience; taking on a particular financial management role at work; speaking up in meetings; participating in problem-solving sessions; giving feedback to seniors.

2. In the context of this challenge: what is important to you?

- Why does tackling this challenge matter to you? Which of your values are related to the challenge?
- Which principles are important to you in life in this context?
- Reflect on how this challenge fits into your career: does it concern an important skill you need to learn or will need in the future?
- Is this *really* important to you or is it something you think you have to do because it is expected of you by others?

Examples: I want to learn to speak in front of an audience because it is important for my career; I want to take on that particular financial role at work because I need the experience for the future; I want to speak up in meetings and contribute actively because I have a lot to offer and I enjoy contributing; I want to express my version of the truth.

3. Unwanted inner experience: what hurts?

- When you start moving towards what is important to you (for example, if you are thinking about doing a presentation or speaking up in meetings) which thoughts or emotions do you have?
- Which thoughts do you have when you think about rising to the challenge?
- Write down everything that comes to mind.

Examples: I am not good enough to speak in front of an audience; I will tremble; I will say something stupid; I will feel my heart beating and start sweating; if I say something stupid, it will impact my career; if I give unfavourable feedback to my seniors, it will impact my performance review.

4. a) How do you respond to or cope with unwanted experiences?

- Reflect on how you act upon or cope with the thoughts you just wrote down in response to question 3. How do you usually cope with these thoughts and emotions in the context of this particular challenge?
- Think about what is important to you and the thoughts you have when you think about rising to the challenge. Reflect on how you usually react or on how the things you are doing at this moment

may be taking you away from what is important to you. When you are not living up to your values and principles, what do you do instead?

Examples: I avoid doing the presentation (and miss out on a learning opportunity); I ask if someone else can take on the project (and miss out on a learning opportunity); I keep quiet during meetings and problem-solving sessions (and fail not only to contribute but also to grasp the opportunity to be seen by others as a team member who is willing to make a contribution); I do not give honest feedback (potentially making the relationship worse because the problem does not get solved).

b) How does this work for you?

- Reflect on the examples you have written down. How do they work for you? Do they bring you closer to what is important to you or move you away?

  Examples: Thinking and reflecting on this only moves me further away from what is important to me.

5. a) Which small things could I do to move towards what is important to me?

- Reflect on a few small actions you could take to move you towards what is important to you. They may feel slightly outside your comfort zone but they will help you move towards what you value.
- Also, reflect on how the tools from chapters 6 (Mindfulness), 7 (Acceptance), 8 (Defusion) and 9 (Self-as-context) can support you in moving towards what is important to you.
- Start thinking of small behaviours or actions that you could take to move towards your objective, accepting the uncomfortable thoughts you might have along the way but that also move you closer to what matters to you.
- What can you do to minimize the risk of negative thoughts becoming reality? What can you do to accept the outcome, whatever that outcome may be?
- If you can connect in a genuine way with your purpose and values, can you also accept that every outcome of your action is a good outcome? Or do you need to revisit and reassess your purpose and values?

  Examples: I could start practicing speaking in front of audiences in smaller and 'safe' environments; I could start practicing feedback skills with a coach; I could ask the help of a trusted friend and practice in front of her/him and get feedback.

b) Which of these small actions can I integrate into my operating model (tool 10.4.2)?

- If you have identified small actions that you plan to work on, find opportunities to practice your skills. Integrate them into your operating model so that you can really start acting upon them.

10.4.2 An operating model that leads to authentic confidence

Description of this tool	What will this tool enable for you:
This tool helps you to incorporate concrete elements into your way of working in support of your committed actions. A good operating model will serve as a compass to bring you closer to your goals.	• Understand and make explicit at a very concrete level how you want to plan your way of working to support what is important to you.

Introduction

The term 'operating model' is usually used in the context of organisations. How an organisation operates and is organised is summed up in its operating model or way of working. However, we can also apply this concept to ourselves as individuals. If we have thought through what is important to us (purpose and values) and where we feel we should lean in more to learn, grow and build confidence (for example, with the help of the Iceberg tool in Chapter 9 or the matrix for advancing authentic confidence in this chapter), we can define a set of concrete actions we would like to build into our daily life. It is important that these actions involve commitments at the micro-level. Committing ourselves to something vague that is not concrete enough will not facilitate change. For example, sometimes we hear people say that they should lean in a bit more and speak up in meetings. This is an excellent intention, but what does it mean? Does it mean you will speak up once in every meeting? Does it mean you will actively lead a discussion in your next meeting? Or does it mean you will look for five concrete opportunities this year to lead a discussion in your team meeting from beginning to end and that you will make plans to do so immediately? Does it mean you will commit yourself to ten minutes of meditation practice every morning? Does it mean you will commit to two 45-minute cardio sessions per week? Will you start practicing with acceptance techniques? And if so, what opportunities are available to you? Will you stop eating refined sugar to help balance out your energy levels?

This is what it means to describe your goals in the most concrete terms possible: what will you *actually* do differently to help develop your emotional flexibility? The authentic confidence development tool brings together all of the key aspects: your priorities and values and how they relate to the work you do. Aisling and Trish Leonard-Curtin also describe this beautifully in their book *The Power of Small: Making Tiny But Powerful Changes When Everything Feels Too Much* (2018). They explain how small, powerful changes can transform your life and help you to move towards what is important to you. In addition to the tools in this chapter, we also recommend that you explore their work.

When you have established what is important to you, the trick is to know where you can find the fuel that will enable you to grow, to develop your authentic confidence and to continue moving forward. We will elaborate on this in the next section.

Authentic confidence 'way of working' development tool

The tool is presented visually in Figure 44. Go through the questions so that you can translate all that you have learned from the different tools into a concrete plan of action. Even if you have not applied all of the other tools yet, you can still use this tool to achieve clarity on how you want to live your life. You can use your journal to record the information you want to keep and revisit it in the future.

FIGURE 44: OPERATING MODEL TO DEVELOP AUTHENTIC CONFIDENCE

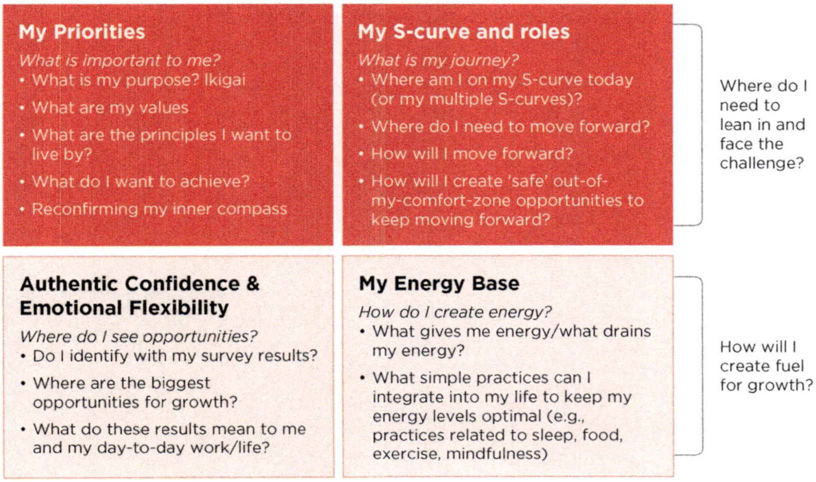

We will go through all of the questions with a bit more explanation to help you clarify your own operating model and committed actions.

Quadrant 1: my priorities

Using the tools presented in Chapter 5, you can identify what is important to you, which values you consider to be important and the principles you wish to live by. What do you want to achieve in life? Who do you want to be? What is important to you in the different areas of your life: as a professional, an individual, a parent, a husband, a brother or sister and as a friend? What is your true inner compass?

Quadrant 2: my S-curve and roles

An S-curve is a helpful framework for enabling your learning and development over time and especially for understanding when your confidence is most likely to be challenged. The S-curve is visualized in Figure 45 (Matrix for advancing Authentic Confidence).

FIGURE 45: S-CURVES AND PERSONAL GROWTH

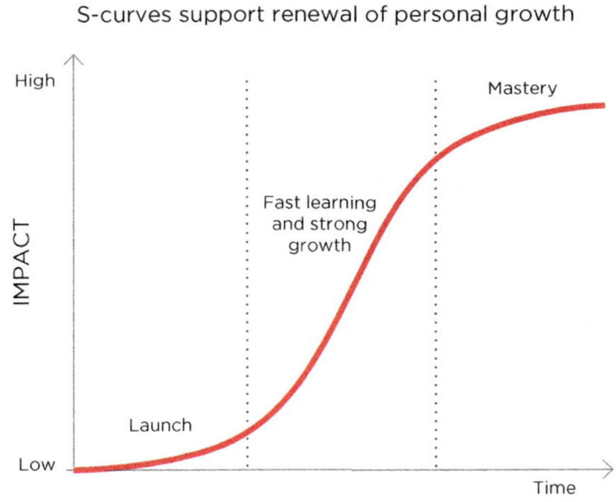

You can examine the professional roles you play along an S-curve. For example, when you start something new it is highly likely that you will first need to learn the how and what of your new role or project. Over time, you will develop your skills and an understanding of your expectations and your confidence will grow gradually as well. You will move upwards along the S-curve until you reach a point where you feel you are learning less and the added value begins to flatten out.

This is when you should think about launching a new S-curve. At any given point in time, you may be going through multiple S-curves: the S-curve of your main job, an S-curve as a volunteer or as a supervisory board member, the S-curve of a new training programme, etc. Mapping out where you are on the different S-curves of your professional (and personal) life can help you to gain an insight into where your external challenges come from and also how to pro-actively plan for extra support in difficult times. Additionally, knowing that you can expect a lot of challenges when you start multiple new things at the same time and planning strategically for the array of new projects will help you to build a strong confidence base.[215]

215 More about the S-curve can be found in this article by Brassey et al. (2018) https://www.mckinsey.com/business-functions/people-and-organizational-performance/our-insights/shaping-individual-development-along-the-s-curve

If you take the first quadrant to a more concrete level, what would that mean for you in the next five years? What do you want to create in your professional life? What kind of work do you want to do? What are the steps you need to take to achieve that? And reflecting on where you are today, what is the one key 'From > To' behaviour that you would like to change to make your vision a reality? Which experiences do you need to create, both inside and outside your comfort zone, to be able to move towards the vision you have for your next S-curve?

Quadrant 3: authentic confidence and emotional flexibility
With regard to the two quadrants above, what do they say about where you are today in terms of your level of authentic confidence? Looking at your assessment results, how do they resonate in the context of what is important to you and what you want to achieve in the next five years? Where do you see the biggest opportunities to practice and grow? And what would that mean in concrete terms for your day-to-day activities? For example, you could ask yourself: where are the biggest opportunities for growth and continued progress in my professional and personal life? Which activities do I need to lean in to during the coming year and how can I move out of my comfort zone to grow towards the vision that I have for myself? What does 'courage' mean to me in this context and how can I ensure that I integrate my concrete experiences into my operating model so that I can support my authentic confidence journey?

Quadrant 4: my energy base
How can I keep my energy levels high so that I can achieve my vision? What is important to me and what will facilitate the emotional flexibility I need to stay authentically confident? If I reflect on my regular working week, what gives me energy? What drains my energy? What does that mean? How can I add activities to my programme that fuel my overall emotional flexibility (for example, regular mindfulness, sufficient sleep and exercise)? What things should I not lose sight of and what do I need to integrate into my way of working so that I continue to pay attention to those things (e.g., quality time with family)? How can I engage in honest conversations (Chapter 11) to make sure I stand for the things that are important to me? And what can I do to make sure I approach my life and career as a marathon (in a sustainable way) and not as a sprint?

> **"I know when I am not balanced, I feel like I am in a sprint, experiencing too much stress, which creates worries, too many**

> **small things on my mind. I know then I have to take a closer look at my operating model again and make a change."**
>
> **Andres Cadena,** Senior Partner, McKinsey & Company, Bogotá, Colombia

> **"Another important reflection to manage your stress and anxiety when you become a senior leader is to understand on a practical level how you will lead others. I am not talking about all the management books and leadership, I am referring to the operational skill of being a day-to-day leader. I learned this from Sandy Ogg, who was my HR business partner in the past at Unilever. You have to reflect on how you will lead others. You can be in the middle of a group, leading the work as a spider in the web. The consequence is that you will be involved in every detail and lead everything yourself. And hence you can only focus on one big project. Once you get more responsibilities, you have to learn how you can lead from the side of the group or in between groups. You don't need to do all the work, but you work with one or a few members of the group that subsequently lead the work. You make connections between them and make clear agreements about responsibilities. Once you get even more senior, you have to lead perhaps a dozen of these groups or more, and you have to reflect clearly on what style you apply with each group. The skill and art of indirect leadership becomes super important. You have to manage in a different way. You learn this through dedicated practice. I often use the analogy from rugby called TCUP (Thinking Correctly Under Pressure). You learn that from dedicated practice. Dare to try, understand how to 'pass the monkey', get extra challenge and out-of-the-comfort-zone experience, not into your terror zone but just enough challenge. This mechanism is important. Understand what you like and what you are good at. The way of leadership and pass the monkey, not solving all the problems in the world."**
>
> **Jan Zijderveld,** former CEO Avon Inc. and President of Unilever Europe

> **"Rhythm and routine are also very important, I am a strong believer in that. An operating model to guide what is important to me and how I need to prepare for important meetings or presentations. I am also a true lifelong learner. My iPad and iPhone are completely full of ideas and important topics I am**

> **reflecting on for my role – from politics to leadership, and information to support my narratives. This way of working helps me be organised, makes me feel secure and prepared."**
>
> **Jan Zijderveld,** former CEO Avon Inc. and President of Unilever Europe

> **"I ran six days a week until ten years ago when I started to have problems. Now I cycle. I say to my wife that I am very happy on a Saturday and Sunday because I cycle. It has helped my depression and it also was apparent when I was training for Comrades, which is a 90k run. I did ten of those. In the law practice, we have to fill out time sheets. I found that contrary to what you would expect. When I was training hardest, sometimes two hours per day, you would think it would negatively impact productivity, but during that time I had the most work productivity."**
>
> **John Brand,** Consultant, Bowmans, South Africa

> **"I have a few things that are very clear in my operating model. Certain habits that I have. I take a lot of exercise and I don't work at the weekend."**
>
> **Fernando Ferrari,** Senior Partner, McKinsey & Company

10.4.3 Mitigating excuses for success

Description of this tool	**What will this tool enable for you:**
This tool will help you think about your conscious and unconscious 'excuses' for not achieving your goals, and mitigates the risk of these excuses becoming reality.	• An insight into how your current behaviour is driving you away from what is important to you (excuses). • An insight into how you can mitigate that risk.

Introduction

> **"The dog ate my homework."**
>
> **Unknown**

Human beings are extraordinarily good at finding excuses for not doing something. Generally speaking, we have two choices in such situations: we either admit to ourselves that we are making excuses and focus on finding solutions or we get bogged down in those excuses and end up moving away from what is important to us. If you would like to take ownership of your journey and take responsibility for your life, then read on. One way to ensure you keep leaning in to what is important to you is to think about the challenges you might have to face and then apply some proactive risk management.

For example, if you want to eat healthily but you know you have to board a long-haul flight where they only serve unhealthy food, you could try to think of a solution. Take some fruit and nuts with you in your bag. Eat before you board. Drink lots of water. Stay clear of the food on the plane as much as possible and find something nutritious to eat when you reach the other side. You simply have to put your mind to it to make it happen. Often, we do not plan ahead and find ourselves tucking into the inflight food before we know it. The same applies to this exercise and the challenges you want to face: if you want to be serious about them, think about the excuses you might create to avoid the challenges (and miss the learning opportunities). Then mitigate those excuses so that the probability that you will continue to learn can rise to a maximum.

How to mitigate excuses

This tool is quite simple. List all of the commitments you are planning to fulfil. Check your personal operating model to make sure you've got them all. Then, for each commitment:

- List 5 to 10 excuses you would use not to follow up on your committed action.
- For each excuse, think of how you could mitigate this excuse so that it will no longer work.
- Do whatever you need to do to mitigate the excuse so that you can increase the probability of success.

10.4.4 Set up a personal board of advisors as your support system

Description of this tool	**What will this tool enable for you:**
This tool will help you reflect on which key stakeholders could become part of your personal board of advisors to help you achieve your goals - and how to bring them on board.	• Identify key stakeholders who could be your personal board of advisors for your objectives. • Make a plan and act to get them on board.

Introduction

Growth and development have many sources. One very effective source is a group of mentors that can monitor your committed actions and provide inspiration. Such a group of mentors can help you to build your confidence by integrating your committed actions, while at the same time offering you support in terms of your plans for your career.

In the work context this is often referred to as your personal mini-board. Many successful leaders have a formal or informal mini-board. This mini-board can consist of a group of professionals who are not your direct colleagues but with whom you may have worked in the past and who may be able to provide peer coaching. You could also choose to include a few senior leaders in your mini-board - professionals who are on a career track that you admire and could help you with your next steps. This mini-board can also be mutually supportive and reinforcing.

How to set up a personal board of advisors

So how do you go about selecting the right kind of people for your mini-board? Should it involve an official process or do you want to keep it more informal? Below we have included a few reflection questions to help you make the right choices and take the first steps.

A. Selecting: the right members and the right number

The first thing you need to do here is to go back to your purpose and values (Chapter 5). What do you want to achieve? What is important to you and what are your goals for the next couple of years? In other words, in what areas do you need mentors? This is important not only in terms of selecting the people with the right profiles for your mini-board, but also in terms of identifying what you require from each prospective member of your mini-board.

Once you are clear about the above, you can think about the kinds of profiles that will provide the support you need. Generally speaking, you will benefit more from selecting a very diverse group of mini-board members who can help you with different aspects of your questions. For example, you could select someone who can help you with your more substantive questions in relation to your profession or the area you wish to learn more about. One important consideration is whether this person should be a more senior person or a peer coach with a lot of expertise.

You should also consider selecting someone who can give you advice on the next steps in your journey. If you are required to make decisions about follow-up processes and new roles, a more senior person could help you make the right choices and help you to decide which out-of-your-comfort-zone activities you need to carry out in order to get to that next level. You may also decide to select a few members who have similar profiles but are from different industries. You could choose people you admire because they have certain skills and fulfil the kinds of roles you aspire to. Other criteria for selecting the right mini-board members include: field of expertise, knowledge of new skills, career advice, network access, opportunities for collaborating on work or research and the ability to provide coaching in specific behaviours and skills.

There is no simple answer to the question of how many people you should invite to join your mini-board. It depends primarily on how much time you can put into it and the possible benefits of having a larger mini-board. If your career is a complex one with multiple roles, you may need a larger board. Remember, however, that the more members you invite, the more time it takes to create and maintain valuable relationships. It may help to think in terms of different 'circles of engagement', with a small number of excellent mentors in your 'inner circle' with which you will engage on a weekly or fortnightly basis. This circle has to be kept small, of course, otherwise it will take up too much of your time. It can also be very helpful to have easy access to your mentors when you are faced with challenging questions. This is easier to achieve when you maintain close relationships with them on a regular basis.

B. Undertaking a commitment

When adding a new member to your mini-board, it is always a good idea to explain your intentions and what you expect from her or him. Be specific about what you are looking for and what that might mean in terms of the amount of time or type of engagement required from both sides. You will have to enter into a kind of negotiation and you can make that as formal or as informal as you like. But in order to gain the most benefit, you must not be afraid to ask a potential mini-board member to give you a firm commitment. It is better to find out quickly whether someone is willing to commit themselves or not so that you can look for an alternative mini-board member if needs be. You will have to reach agreement on things like how often and where you will meet (virtual or non-virtual) and what the focus of your conversations will be. Also, think of how you can create a win-win situation in which your mini-board relationship can be of mutual benefit. For example, you could work together on presentations, seminars and research if that would be helpful and relevant. This is also a way of learning from each other and entering into a peer mentoring relationship.

C. Sustaining and renewing

It is important that you take the relationships you maintain with your mini-board members very seriously. This means focusing on sustaining those relationships and knowing when to assign a mini-board member a less active role when there is no obvious benefit to the relationship anymore. There will also be moments when you need to think about replacing a certain member because your development needs have changed. This is perfectly fine and it is something you can also discuss with a new mini-board member when you first approach them. As with the board of advisors in any organisation, renewal is a crucial part of managing your mini-board and so you might need to replace certain board members over time.

> **"When I was an SVP thinking about my next step in my career, I set up a personal board for my own development. I selected who would be on that board carefully and it helped me tremendously to learn and grow. At some point in my career, I also interviewed a number of CEOs to learn from their world and what they would need from an HR professional at that level."**
>
> **Abbe Luersman,** CHRO, EVP and Chief People Officer, Otis Elevator Co

> **"Make sure you do not become too dependent on one person. Build your network of mentors in the organisation."**
>
> **Jan Zijderveld,** former CEO, Avon Inc. and President of Unilever Europe

10.4.5 Employing a professional coach (and how to select one)

The lead author of this sub-section is Dr Brodie Riordan[216]

Description of this tool	**What will this tool enable for you:**
This tool will help you to reflect on whether you would like to work with a coach to help you further in particular areas towards your goals. The tool offers reflections on how to select the right coach for your needs.	• Decide if working with a professional coach is the right choice for you. • Select a coach who is a good fit for you, based on your goals and preferences.

Introduction

Coaches, mentors and sponsors[217] can play a critical role in navigating your way through your career, working through challenging situations and achieving your goals. For certain goals and challenges a professional coach is sometimes a better fit. Professional coaches are trained to use tools such as listening carefully, asking powerful questions and holding up a mirror to their clients in order to provide them with a fresh perspective. Coaches tend to be non-directive and bring an objective view. They don't tell you what to do but are there to help you work through challenges and take ownership of the solutions and your path forward.

Working with a coach is a structured, highly-personalised and time-bound way to create self-awareness, clarity and direction in your personal or career goals. It can also help you to gain confidence, establish a clearer sense of what you want and why and develop stronger problem-solving skills. If you require a more intense level of emotional and psychological support, working with a therapist or some other mental health professional may be more appropriate.

216 Dr Brodie Riordan is an I/O Psychologist, ICF-certified coach and author of the book *Feedback Fundamentals and Evidence-Based Best Practices.*

217 Coaches, mentors and sponsors can be thought of as a continuum from least to most 'involved' in your career. A coach supports you in solving challenges. S/he is non-directive and not there to provide wisdom and advice. A mentor provides wisdom, guidance and advice. A sponsor actively helps you navigate your career and may remove obstacles and/or advocate for you.

> **"I wish I had found someone I could bounce things off and share my concerns with sooner - a professional coach."**
>
> **Michelle Roborg-Sondergaard,** Senior HR Executive

A tool for finding the right coach

Choosing the right coach is essential if you want the experience to be both satisfying and effective. Coaches have a wide variety of backgrounds, training and credentials, all of which can vary greatly depending on where you are in the world. However, no matter where you are or what you are looking for, coaching always involves a close personal relationship between two people.

Below is a list of aspects worth considering when selecting the right coach for you:

- **Demographics**. Gender, age, culture and nationality all play a role. Think about the kind of relationship you want to have. Does gender matter to you? Do you want to work with a coach your age or one who is older/younger? Do you want a coach with a specific cultural background? Ultimately, it all depends on your personal needs and preferences.
- **Background**. Some coaches are trained psychologists, but many have other industry/sectoral backgrounds: attorneys, accountants, teachers, scientists and business leaders. Some have been coaches for decades, whereas others are newer to the profession. A coach's background will influence her or his experiences and perspectives, but not necessarily their capabilities. Think about whether or not certain backgrounds or perspectives will enrich your experience.
- **Qualifications**. Training, certification and credentials vary across the globe. The International Coach Federation (ICF) is a large credentialing body that ensures a minimum level of education, experience and competence for coaches. You might want to look for a credentialed coach or a coach trained in specific techniques, based on your own needs and interests. For example, coaches with somatic training are specially trained to use the body in their practice and help their clients to be aware of their bodies and the connection between thoughts, feelings and the physical body. In any event, make sure the coach of your choice has been professionally trained and certified.
- **Tools and method**. While dialogue is the backbone of all coaching, some coaches incorporate other tools and methods into their practice. For instance, many coaches use assessments or questionnaires to help their clients get feedback and develop self-awareness. Some coaches may be more or less directive in

their practice (e.g., offering advice and direction versus leaving all direction to the client) while others may use tools like meditation or physical exercise. Think about the kind of experience you are looking for and ask prospective coaches to tell you about their approach to coaching.

- **Meeting format**. Technology has created a great deal of flexibility in terms of when, where and how coaching can be given. Traditionally, coaching sessions were carried out face to face, which limited the pool of coaches available and required you to work with someone local or incur the costs of travel. In recent years, virtual coaching (by telephone, video chat, etc.) has grown significantly in popularity. Virtual coaching can open up a larger pool of coaches because geography no longer matters. Virtual coaching can also be more cost-effective and less time-bound. Some people prefer face-to-face contact, whereas others prefer the telephone or video chat. Only you can decide which format is best for you, depending on your lifestyle (do you travel a lot?), budget and personality (do you get distracted when you are on the phone and can you focus better in face-to-face situations?).
- **Who is paying for the coach**. Many organisations will pay for their employees to work with a coach. If you are in that position, be sure to get clarity about the level of accountability your coach has to your organisation and how they are expected to report your progress. In some organisations, what goes on between a coach and an employee is completely confidential and coaches are only expected to report on how often they meet or how many sessions are scheduled, based on the contract. In other organisations, some HR, talent or business leaders may expect coaches to focus on the employee's specific goals or development needs and to report periodically on progress. You always have the option, of course, to employ a coach completely independently without your organisation being involved. This may be more expensive for you personally but it will ensure that you have complete ownership of your work with the coach and complete confidentiality.

Preparing to work with your coach

Working with a coach can be an exciting and potentially life-changing experience. Many people gain tremendous clarity about what they want, what is important to them and what they want to pursue next in their life or career. Most coaching relationships last for a few months (usually 3 to 12) and involve weekly sessions. The timeline and frequency of your sessions will depend on what you are trying to achieve and in which timeframe. Some issues have a shorter and tighter timeline, such as making an immediate career switch or addressing critical and time-sensitive developmental feedback. Others require a longer period to be truly effective - e.g., figuring out what to do with your life, engaging in deep self-reflection or intensive leadership development.

In order to get the most out of your time with a coach, it can help to have a rough idea of what you want to address before you start working together. Your coach will also talk this through with you in your first coaching sessions to help you identify what you want to focus on, what you want to achieve and what success would look like. Most coaches will ask you to set the agenda for each coaching session, starting off each one by asking you what you want to focus on for that hour and what you want to achieve by the end of the hour. You may need to spend a few minutes thinking about that before each session.

If you are interested in finding a coach who uses the Acceptance and Commitment Therapy approach, you can contact the Association for Contextual Science via https://contextualscience.org. They have networks around the world with coaches that can help you further. Of course, you can also do a Google search for an ACT coach in your own country.

> **"The way I dealt with my anxiety and difficult times is that I hired a coach, one that I already knew and trusted. It helped me tremendously in becoming more conscious of myself and finding ways to cope."**
>
> **Michelle Roborg-Sondergaard,** Senior HR Executive

> **"I found a coach myself, and in order to help expedite my learning I am also doing an executive MBA."**
>
> **Senior Executive,** anonymous contribution

CHAPTER 11

11. PRACTICAL SKILLS TO SUPPORT AUTHENTIC CONFIDENCE

We discovered in our work on authentic confidence that there were a number of recurring themes that people 'fear' the most or where they lack confidence. Apart from leaning in, these were: (1) speaking up in meetings or problem-solving sessions; (2) giving feedback or having difficult conversations, especially with seniors; and (3) giving a presentation in front of a large audience. These fears were partly fuelled by inner voices and insecurity, and partly, or perhaps mainly, by the fact that they did not know how to do these things well. Building authentic confidence is, of course, also driven by developing the skills or acquiring experience in the areas that are regarded as important. Often, when you do something for the first time, you feel way more uncomfortable than when you have done the same thing a few times already. This applies to all of the skills we have introduced: once you master them you will find it much easier to use them. In this final chapter we will take a deep dive into these common triggers of fear and will begin with the skill of learning to learn. When you master the skill of self-directed learning you will empower yourself for lifelong learning and relevance in the workplace.

The following quote from Rick Goings, former CEO and Chairman Emeritus of Tupperware, is relevant here. We asked him whether he still has insecurities or anxieties as a CEO and how he deals with those as a leader and role model.

> **"Sure ... but the cumulative effect of experience and years of continued success has supported growing levels of confidence in these areas. I think of it as adding to my carrying strap of skills, experiences and successes. I love the story of Leonardo da Vinci trying to get a job with the Prince of Milan (he was originally from Florence). When he put together his CV, he described his experience in architectural design, military weapon design, having a good understanding of event and theatrical production ... and, also, I can paint. It's about continuing to become the best version of yourself."**
>
> **Rick Goings,** CEO, Tupperware

11.1 Learn how to learn: lifelong learning

Description of this tool	What will this tool enable for you:
Lifelong learning is a philosophy of life. In this tool we will explain the lifelong learning mindsets that will help you to continuously grow and develop while remaining aligned to what is important to you.	• Understand the seven mindsets of lifelong learning and understand how to stay relevant in the workplace.

> **"Many people think that in order to be successful in life you have to be successful in business. I am completely convinced it is the other way around: in order to be successful in business you have to be successful in life. Business skills and competencies are important, but life skills and life competences are more important to become successful as a leader."**
>
> **Tex Gunning,** CEO, Leaseplan

Welcome to the digital age. This era, marked by constant technological breakthroughs that repeatedly disrupt the business world, has been dubbed the Fourth Industrial Revolution by Klaus Schwab of the World Economic Forum. It is an era in which only the nimblest companies are said to survive and in which only the workers who constantly reskill and upskill themselves will continue to find jobs. Two broad trends are shaping the digital age: (1) an acceleration of the rate at which new technologies are adopted, and (2) the ongoing disruption that these new technologies are causing to businesses, economies and societies, as well as the people working in these communities of change.

Let us look at the acceleration first. It took radio 38 years to reach 50 million users globally. Television achieved that in 13 years, internet in 3 years, Facebook 1 year, Twitter 9 months, Angry Birds 35 days and Pokémon Go 19 days. However, it is not just games, devices and platforms that are adopted rapidly. What is more important – and more disruptive – is that innovations such as mobile computers, cloud technology and big data are changing the way business is done and how democracies work. In all likelihood, even greater upheavals will occur when robotics, artificial intelligence, autonomous transport and the internet of things become fully incorporated into our daily lives. Automation will also transform business even further.[218] All of these technological innovations will have a profound impact on the economy and in some cases this is already the case.

FIGURE 46: TIME REQUIRED TO IMPLEMENT CHANGES PRE-COVID ESTIMATE VERSUS ACTUAL DURING THE PANDEMIC[219]

Digital Transformation Initiative	Estimate Pre-Covid	Actual
Remote working at scale	1-2 years	11 days
Moving critical assets to the cloud	1-2 years	3 weeks
Using more advanced technologies in operations	2 years	1 month

Source: McKinsey & Company (October 2021). How COVID-19 has pushed companies over the technology tipping point—and transformed business forever (see https://www.mckinsey.com/business-functions/strategy-and-corporate-finance/our-insights/how-covid-19-has-pushed-companies-over-the-technology-tipping-point-and-transformed-business-forever).

In his book *Creative Destruction* (2001), Yale professor Richard Foster took Joseph Schumpeter's famous theory and applied his logic to prestigious companies on the Standard & Poor Top 500 list. He noticed that their lifespans had dramatically declined from 90 years in 1935 to 30 years in 1975. Anthony et al. (2018) found that the lifespan of an S&P company in 2017 had fallen to 24 years and the prognosis is that this lifespan will be as short as 12 years by 2027.

There is also an important non-technological factor that is set to contribute to the drastic reshaping of tomorrow's workforce: the fact that people are living much longer now than they have in the past. Data suggests that humans—at least those in developed nations—have seen a three-month increase in life expectancy every year since 1840. And as they live longer, they will be working longer, well into their seventies or eighties. Businesses and societies must deal with both digital-technological and demographic-non-technological disruptive trends simultaneously (next to and on top of the challenge of climate change and environmental exhaustion). Taken together and sticking to this book's subject matter, these trends im-

218 Harnessing automation for a future that works https://www.mckinsey.com/featured-insights/digital-disruption/harnessing-automation-for-a-future-that-works?cid=eml-web

219 https://www.mckinsey.com/business-functions/strategy-and-corporate-finance/our-insights/how-covid-19-has-pushed-companies-over-the-technology-tipping-point-and-transformed-business-forever

ply that workers can no longer expect to be employed at a limited number of companies for their entire careers using skills they mastered in their twenties. Institutions of higher education must be prepared to deliver the skills and experiences that will ensure that tomorrow's workers are employable for as long as they want to hold jobs.

Becoming lifelong learners
Digital and AI technologies are transforming the world of work and today's workforce will need to learn new skills and continually adapt as new occupations emerge. Research by the McKinsey Global Institute has looked at the kinds of jobs that will be lost, as well as those that will be created as automation, AI and robotics take hold. And it has identified the type of high-level skills that will become increasingly important as a result. The need for manual and physical skills, as well as basic cognitive ones, will decline, but demand for technological, social, emotional and higher cognitive skills will grow.

The following illustration shows 56 foundational skills in which higher proficiency is already associated with a higher likelihood of employment, higher income and greater job satisfaction.

FIGURE 47: SKILLS THAT WILL HELP CITIZENS THRIVE IN THE FUTURE OF WORK

COGNITIVE

CRITICAL THINKING
- Structured problem solving
- Logical reasoning
- Understanding biases
- Seeking relevant information

PLANNING AND WAYS OF WORKING
- Work-plan development
- Time management and prioritization
- Agile thinking

COMMUNICATION
- Storytelling and public speaking
- Asking the right questions
- Synthesizing messages
- Active listening

MENTAL FLEXIBILITY
- Creativity and imagination
- Translating knowledge to different contexts
- Adopting a different perspective
- Adaptability
- Ability to learn

INTERPERSONAL

MOBILIZING SYSTEMS
- Role modelling
- Win-win negotiations
- Crafting an inspiring vision
- Organizational awareness

DEVELOPING RELATIONSHIPS
- Empathy
- Inspiring trust
- Humility
- Sociability

TEAMWORK EFFECTIVENESS
- Fostering inclusiveness
- Motivating different personalities
- Resolving conflicts
- Collaboration
- Coaching
- Empowering

SELF-LEADERSHIP

SELF-AWARENESS AND SELF-MANAGEMENT
- Understanding own emotions and triggers
- Self-control and regulation
- Understanding own strengths
- Integrity
- Self-motivation and wellness
- Self-confidence

ENTREPRENEURSHIP
- Courage and risk-taking
- Driving change and innovation
- Energy, passion, and optimism
- Breaking orthodoxies

GOALS ACHIEVEMENT
- Ownership and decisiveness
- Achievement orientation
- Grit and persistence
- Coping with uncertainty
- Self-development

DIGITAL

DIGITAL FLUENCY AND CITIZENSHIP
- Digital literacy
- Digital learning
- Digital collaboration
- Digital ethics

SOFTWARE USE AND DEVELOPMENT
- Programming literacy
- Data analysis and statistics
- Computational and algorithmic thinking

UNDERSTANDING DIGITAL SYSTEMS
- Data literacy
- Smart systems
- Cybersecurity literacy
- Tech translation and enablement

Source: McKinsey & Company (June 2021). Defining the skills citizens will need in the future of work (see https://www.mckinsey.com/industries/public-and-social-sector/our-insights/defining-the-skills-citizens-will-need-in-the-future-world-of-work).

While 21st century workers will need to master new hard skills to keep up with advances in technology, they will also have to develop softer practical skills because tomorrow's jobs will require workers who can create content or judge the relevance of information. More than one third of all future jobs will require workers who can solve complex problems. About one in five jobs will need workers with social skills such as emotional intelligence, a service orientation and the ability to negotiate and collaborate with others. In addition, about 15 per cent of jobs will require cognitive skills such as creativity and mathematical reasoning. In fact, creativity will become one of the most important skills for the workforce with regard to inventing new business models, products and services, ways of working and customer experiences. Creativity will also contribute to solving problems in fresh new ways. Finally, the Fourth Industrial Revolution will require a workforce with a wide range of deep knowledge and easily transferrable skills. The World Economic Forum estimates that 65 per cent of today's elementary school students may end up working in jobs that do not exist today.[220]

We simply do not know what future jobs will look like. The foundations for adaptability and lifelong learning need to be laid early on in life and should become integrated in education along the way. A recent UNESCO report called for more holistic and individually tailored learning throughout childhood, which would also support the development of lifelong learning skills.[221]

While educational systems are now catching up, it is also essential that tomorrow's workers not only have a broad range of skills but also that they understand how to gain new ones and upskill themselves. They must become adept at lifelong learning. At the heart of learning how to learn and becoming a lifelong learner lies the need to develop authentic confidence. We will see that the art and skill of becoming a lifelong learner has quite a bit of overlap with building authentic confidence. Even though we are discussing this topic here from a different angle, we trust it will be complementary to what we have discussed in the previous chapters. Developing the skills associated with learning how to learn will also support your confidence in navigating your S-curve(s) and career.

In some countries, lifelong learning is already a priority. The European Union has developed an indicator for measuring lifelong learning, defined as the percentage of the population aged 25 to 64 who participate in education and training.[222] The best-performing European countries are Denmark, Sweden and Finland. Denmark's score may be so high because it allocates funding for two weeks of certified training every year to all adults, in addition to emphasising the im-

220 http://reports.weforum.org/future-of-jobs-2016/chapter-1-the-future-of-jobs-and-skills/

221 https://vu.nl/en/news/2022/professor-nienke-van-atteveldt-supervises-unesco-education-report

222 https://ec.europa.eu/eurostat/statistics-explained/index.php/Glossary:Lifelong_learning

portance of on-the-job training. It is these lifelong learners who will continue to be employable in an economy characterised by disruptive technologies and evolving job requirements. But how do people become lifelong learners? Looking at a broad array of research, we learn that they tend to employ seven distinctive practices or mindsets that aid them throughout their careers. We will explore this set of seven practices below.

Practices or mindsets for lifelong learners
Van Dam and Brassey (2017) argue that there are seven practices or mindsets that will help tomorrow's workers to become lifelong learners. This set of seven is visualized in Figure 48.

FIGURE 48: SEVEN MINDSETS FOR LIFELONG LEARNING

Source: Van Dam (2016)

1. Focus on growth
As already described in sub-section 7.4.1, Stanford psychologist Carol Dweck, who has studied learners intensively, concluded that a person's mindset has a significant impact on how that person learns. In her 2006 book *Mindset* she differentiates between people with

fixed mindsets and those with growth mindsets. These two models predict how much effort learners will expend, how much risk they will take, how they will perceive criticism and whether they will be willing to accept and learn from failures. People with fixed mindsets believe their potential is finite and is based on their genes, heritage, socio-economic background and/or opportunities. They are inclined to say 'I'm bad at public speaking, so I should avoid it' or 'I'm not a good learner, so I shouldn't take the courses offered by my company.' In contrast, people with a growth mindset believe their true potential is unknown because they cannot foresee what they might achieve if they approach something with passion, effort and practice. They regard challenges as opportunities for personal growth.

Other studies also suggest that intelligence is not fixed at birth but can be developed over time. Many studies have confirmed that it is not just intelligence that creates expertise but also effort and practice - hard work, in other words.[223] The most successful people devote long hours to deliberate practice, tackling tasks beyond their current level of competence and comfort, observing the results and adjusting. Studies have shown that intelligence can be developed and that there are fewer limitations on what we can learn throughout our lives than is conventionally assumed. Indeed, the brain is like a muscle that gets stronger with use and learning prompts neurons in the brain to make new connections.[224]

One fascinating study that illustrates plasticity (and that a person's IQ is not fixed) began in 1932 when the entire population of Scotland's 11-year-olds—all 87,498 of them—took IQ tests.[225] Sixty years later the test was repeated, with five hundred of the original individuals participating. The results showed a .66 positive correlation between the ones that were top of the pack at the age of 11 and again at the age of 80. A strong correlation but by no means 100%! Some participants' IQ fell over time, while that of others improved. 'On average, people's individual (or absolute) scores on the test taken again at age 80 was much higher (over one standard deviation) than their scores had been at age 11, even though the rank ordering among

223 Geoffrey Colvin, "What it takes to be great", *Fortune*, October 19, 2006, fortune.com.

224 Jesper Mogensen, "Cognitive recovery and rehabilitation after brain injury: Mechanisms, challenges and support", *Brain Injury: Functional Aspects, Rehabilitation and Prevention*, Croatia: InTech, March 2, 2012, pp. 121–50, doi.org/10.5772/28242.

225 https://www.huffpost.com/entry/intelligence-is-still-not_b_1078112

people stayed roughly the same.'[226] Even though relative ranking fluctuates less, scores within individuals can fluctuate quite a bit. A completely different perspective on IQ was introduced in 2008 when researchers administered tests to the ten best chess players in the world and discovered that three had below-average IQs (Mackintosh, 1998). The most successful people practice for long hours to push themselves beyond their current levels of competence and comfort (and also to build their authentic confidence). They also are lifelong learners who are committed to a growth mindset and believe they have an endless capacity to learn. It is this attitude that makes them valuable workers, the kind who can constantly master the new skills they need in an ever-changing jobs market.

2. Serial masters

To stay employable, workers will need to develop deep expertise in multiple areas over the lifespan of their careers. In her book *The Shift* (2011), London Business School professor Lynda Gratton argues that we have seen the end of the 'shallow generalist' who knows a little about a lot of different topics. In a world of Wikipedia and instantly accessible information, surface-level knowledge is almost useless. Workers in the 21st century will have to depend on their intellectual capital to bring value. For a long time people have followed a T-shaped profile of knowledge mastery, developing deep expertise in one discipline early in their careers and supplementing this with broad competencies gained on the job. But this model is no longer sustainable; today's workers have to develop M-shaped profiles of knowledge.

More specifically, as relevant skills become the currency of business and people stay in the workforce longer, workers will need to develop deep expertise in a number of different areas over the course of their careers. They will have to combine that deep expertise with the broader knowledge they acquire on the job. For instance, a journalist might enter the workforce with a bachelor's degree in journalism. Then, after deciding to specialise in business reporting, she might pursue a master's degree in business economics. As economics becomes more complex over the next decade, she might enrol in classes on related topics, such as digitization. She will need to constantly evaluate the sell-by date of her current skills and add new ones that might be more useful. This is the only way she - and workers like her - can continue to create value and stay employed.

226 https://www.huffpost.com/entry/intelligence-is-still-not_b_1078112

In the past, a manager might have developed a T-shaped profile of knowledge – a broad business understanding complemented by deep expertise in one subject. But tomorrow's workers will need to develop M-shaped knowledge profiles by supplementing their general knowledge with a series of deeper skill sets, as visualized in Figure 49.

FIGURE 49: M-PROFILE OF A SERIAL MASTER

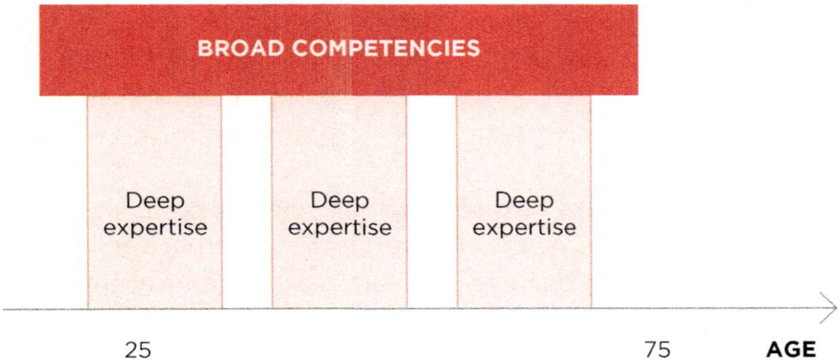

Source: Van Dam (2016)

3. Ownership of development

Because tomorrow's workers are unlikely to stay in one job for their entire career, they can no longer expect a single employer to direct them along their career development paths. Furthermore, as the century wears on, more and more workers will be self-employed. In 2016 it was estimated that roughly 20 to 30 % of all workers engage in some form of independent work.[227] There are approximately 19.2 million self-employed people working in the European Union (as of 2020).[228]

Many employers in the United States have indicated that they plan to increase their numbers of contingent or part-time workers in the coming years. In 2012, sociologist Richard Greenwald emphasised the growing and important role of freelancers in modern society.[229]. A development highlighted in research by McKinsey & Company shows a trend where employees are taking the lead in claiming flexi-

227 https://www.mckinsey.com/featured-insights/employment-and-growth/independent-work-choice-necessity-and-the-gig-economy

228 https://www.statista.com/statistics/946989/self-employed-persons-in-eu/

229 https://www.theatlantic.com/business/archive/2012/11/a-freelance-economy-can-be-good-for-workers-lets-make-it-better/265345/

bility and independence: many are leaving to take on very different roles or are choosing to leave the workforce entirely.[230]

This means that both company employees and contract workers will need to make their own investments in their development and education. To do so they need to take the following steps:

- **Create and execute learning goals**. Workers should ask themselves, 'How can I ensure that I'm more valuable at the end of the year than I was at the beginning?' They should assess their competency gaps and focus relentlessly on their most important learning objectives, writes strategy consultant Dorie in Harvard Business Review.[231] As she notes, too many people focus only on achieving quick wins instead of on gaining a long-term competitive advantage.
- **Work with mentors and seek feedback**. Workers should look inside and outside of their companies to find mentors who can offer guidance and be a role model for positive behaviour. They should also make it clear to various stakeholders - supervisors, peers, direct reports and clients - that they are open to feedback that will help them improve their performance.
- **Measure progress**. Workers should use learning journals or logs to track the things they have learned that have been particularly valuable and to assess the progress they have made.
- **Make personal investments of time and money**. In their book *Immunity to Change* (2009), Robert Kegan and Lisa Lahey suggest that people who take ownership of their development will be able to answer the question, 'What is the one thing you are working on that will require that you grow to accomplish it?' They will also be able to explain how they are working on this, who else knows and cares about it and why this competency matters to them.

4. Stretch

Many researchers, including Andy Molinsky (2017) of Brandeis International Business School, have suggested that learning only takes place when people move beyond their comfort zones where they acquire new knowledge and practice new skills.[232] After they

230 https://www.mckinsey.com/business-functions/people-and-organizational-performance/our-insights/gone-for-now-or-gone-for-good-how-to-play-the-new-talent-game-and-win-back-workers

231 https://hbr.org/2016/12/dont-set-too-many-goals-for-yourself.

232 See also: Andy Molinsky, "If you're not outside your comfort zone, you won't learn anything", July 29, 2016, in *Harvard Business Review*.

develop proficiency in these new areas, their new learning becomes part of their comfort zone and they can then stretch themselves. When people are engaged in tasks outside of their comfort zone they may find that they are exposed to risk and stress. Harvard psychologists Robert Yerkes and John Dodson have put forward the Yerkes-Dodson Law,[233] which proposes a strong relationship between an increase in stress and the enhancement of performance, but only up to a point. Beyond a certain level an increase in stress can cause too much anxiety and have a negative impact on performance. Therefore, it is important for people to expand their comfort zones with the right new tasks and at the right pace, which varies per individual.

One tool that facilitates reflection on the above is the S-curve model of growth and development, which we presented as part of the operating model tool in Chapter 10. In business terms, the S-curve explains how ideas and products spread through society: slowly, at first, until the adoption rate reaches a tipping point and then progressing with mounting swiftness only to slow down later. The S-curve business model was developed in the 1960s, but in a *Harvard Business Review* article on September 3, 2012, Whitney Johnson and Juan Carlos Méndez-García[234] examined how human learning follows a similar pattern. Whenever people start new jobs or take on new responsibilities, they launch their own S-curves. In the beginning – as they learn about colleagues, stakeholders, processes, information systems and organisational cultures – progress is slow, implying that they have limited impact in their jobs. Then they reach an inflection point, gaining competence and confidence in their new roles, quickly accelerating their abilities and having a progressively greater impact on the business. After they have been in their roles for a certain period of time, they reach the upper flat part of the S-curve, thereby losing the sense of excitement in the role, stalling in their personal development and reducing their impact.

At the management consulting firm McKinsey & Company, for example, the S-curve model is used to support the learning and development agenda, as well as the career progression of consultants and partners globally. It illustrates that if people continue to stay in roles where they are no longer emotionally charged and motivated, they may start to perform poorly and their performance will stall. It also helps to identify the number of barriers that might prevent workers

233 https://en.wikipedia.org/wiki/Yerkes%E2%80%93Dodson_law

234 https://hbr.org/2012/09/throw-your-life-a-curve

from stretching, thereby denying them the opportunity to unlock their full potential. For instance, a low level of self-confidence can have a hugely negative impact on a person's ability to grow and learn. Reflecting on where you are on the S-curve can help you to design support mechanisms to continue your learning and growth process.[235]

5. Personal brands and networks

We all create our own personal brands that differentiate us from co-workers and competitors. Key elements of a personal brand include a clear value proposition, a personal story, authenticity, expertise, consistency, visibility and connections. Smallwood and Ulrich[236] describe a number of steps people should take to shape their personal brand: determine the results they want to achieve in the next year, decide what they wish to be known for, define their identities, construct and test their personal brand statements, and make their brand identities real. In the future, people will need to rebrand themselves multiple times during their careers as they develop different skill sets and play new professional roles. Many will earn additional credentials from online vendors such as Coursera, edX, Linda.com and Udemy, all of which offer digital badges that individuals can post on their social media sites. These badges become part of each individual's brand and social networks become a way for workers to extend their brand reach.

Social networks can also be useful when workers are looking for jobs. In an article on August 21, 2015 in the *Financial Times*[237], John Gurskey of Melbourne Business School suggested that hiring managers often reach out to their professional networks before they even advertise a job opening, asking if anyone knows of someone who would be a good fit for the position. In addition, INSEAD's Herminia Ibarra[238] says that social networks are valuable because they help individuals stay informed, make them more innovative, encourage them to learn new things and act as sounding boards. The most useful networks, according to Karie Willyerd and Barbara Mistick in the book *Stretch* (2016), are diverse ones with people who can provide different connections, insights and career opportunities.

235 See, e.g., https://www.mckinsey.com/business-functions/people-and-organizational-performance/our-insights/shaping-individual-development-along-the-s-curve

236 https://hbr.org/2007/07/building-a-leadership-brand

237 https://www.ft.com/content/06e55a1a-0554-11e5-8612-00144feabdc0

238 https://hbr.org/2016/04/5-misconceptions-about-networking

6. Doing what you love

Apple visionary Steve Jobs once said, 'Your time is limited, so don't waste it living someone else's life ... Don't let the noise of others' opinions drown out your own inner voice. And most important, have the courage to follow your heart and intuition.' People will spend eight or more hours a day at work for the 40 or 50 years of their careers. It is essential that they do what they love, because work has such a huge impact on their health and well-being.

In his book *What Makes Life Worth Living?* (1996), Gordon Mathews of the Chinese University of Hong Kong describes the Japanese concept of *ikigai*, which translates as 'a reason for being' or 'a life worth living'. It encompasses all elements of life, including work, hobbies, relationships and spiritual beliefs. Mathews believes that when people discover their ikigai they find satisfaction and meaning in life. But ikigai can be even more powerful. In a 2008 article in *Psychosomatic Medicine*, Toshimasa Sone and his co-authors studied more than 43,000 Japanese adults and found that the risk from all-cause mortality was significantly higher among those who did not enjoy a sense of ikigai.[239] The Japanese believe that people can achieve ikigai by answering four questions, which can be found in the book *Ikigai* by Héctor García and Francesc Miralles (2017): (1) What do you love? (2) What does the world need? (3) What can you be paid for? and (4) What are you good at? Individuals will identify their ikigai at the intersection of these insights. Figure 50 visualizes the ikigai concept.

239 Toshimasa Sone et al., "Sense of life worth living (ikigai) and mortality in Japan: Ohsaki study", *Psychosomatic Medicine*, August 2008, Volume 70, Number 6, pp. 709–15, doi.org/10.1097/PSY.0b013e31817e7e64.

FIGURE 50: IKIGAI

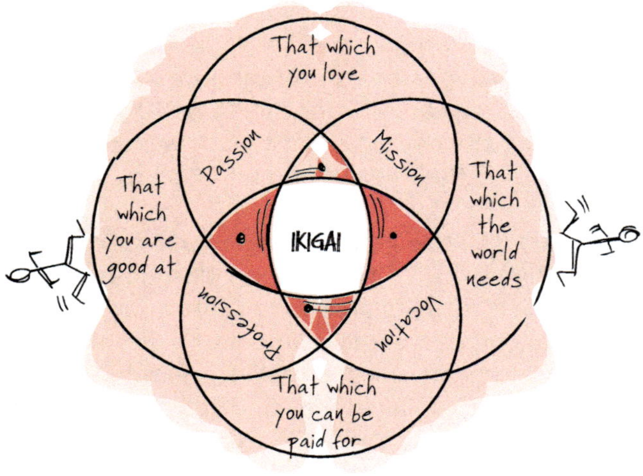

Source: Based on Garcia and Miralles (2017:9).

You will recognise this illustration from Chapter 5. Not everyone will find ikigai at the workplace. For instance, one person might see work simply as a job: s/he is motivated by financial rewards and has the goal of buying material objects. A second person is seeking a career: s/he is motivated by the desire for success and her/his objective is to achieve tangible milestones. But the person who considers work a calling will find it brings her/him ikigai. This person is motivated by the work itself because it serves a cause s/he believes in or brings her/him deep personal satisfaction. Although organisations have a great responsibility to provide a context for meaning, those who want to be satisfied in their jobs need to take steps to create a calling for themselves.[240] Lifelong learners will constantly refine their skills as they look for new ways to stay engaged in and passionate about their work.

7. Stay vital

Finally, the most successful individuals will be those who make it a priority to stay vital by paying attention to their body, their mind and their purpose & meaning, as shown in the following illustration.

240 See, e.g., also: https://hbr.org/2022/05/designing-work-that-people-love

FIGURE 51: HEALTH, WELL-BEING AND HAPPINESS

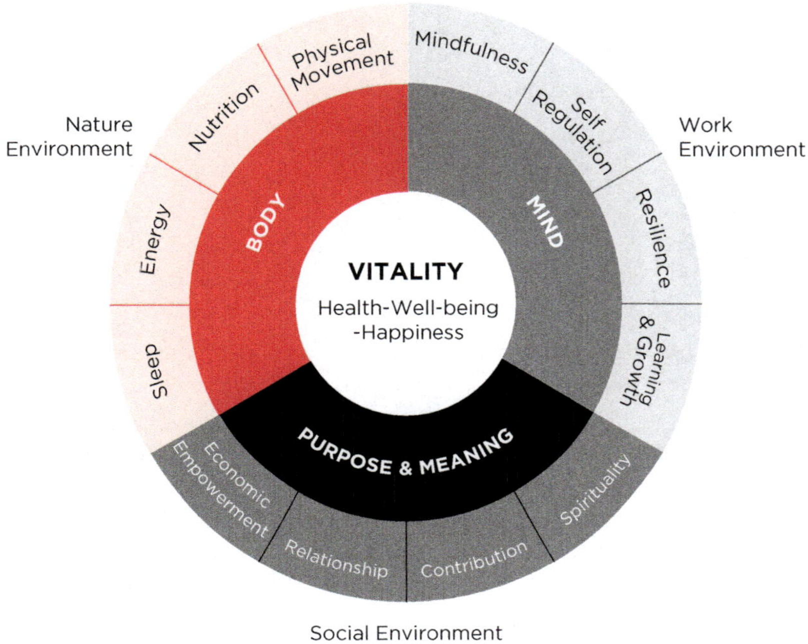

Source: Vitality Model (2020), Dr Noémie Le Pertel and Dr Nick van Dam.

An alternative (interactive) view on health is presented by the McKinsey Health Institute[241] in their launch paper.[242] Health and vitality is multifaceted and the details are beyond the scope of this chapter, but we will highlight one particular aspect: when it comes to learning and development, sleep is a foundational element and one that matters more than many people realise.[243] It has a huge impact on our ability to acquire and retain knowledge and it can also affect attention, concentration, creativity, development of insight, pattern recognition, decision-making, emotional reactivity, socio-emotional processing and the ability to develop relationships built on trust. All of these abilities are necessary for workers who want to succeed in tomorrow's workforce.

241 https://www.mckinsey.com/mhi/overview

242 https://www.mckinsey.com/mhi/our-insights/adding-years-to-life-and-life-to-years

243 Nick van Dam and Els van der Helm, "The organisational cost of insufficient sleep", *McKinsey Quarterly*, February 2016, McKinsey.com.

Are you a lifelong learner?
You can assess your own openness to learning at:
www.reachingyourpotential.org

Or via the QR code below:

11.2 The art of giving feedback and conducting an honest conversation[244]

Description of this tool	What will this tool enable for you:
This tool will explain the elements of great feedback and how to lead a courageous conversation. Having the skill is half the work!	• This tool will give you the key elements and a model to help you to conduct a difficult conversation and provide feedback in a skilful way.

Introduction

> **"Courage is what it takes to stand up and speak; courage is also what it takes to sit down and listen."**
>
> **Sir Winston Churchill**

Feedback, including 'saying no', is an incredibly valuable source of information. When you provide feedback to others you can help them gain more self-awareness, grow and develop and acquire insights into things they are doing well and can do more of or areas where they can do things differently to become even better. When we receive feedback we are better able to gauge the distance between where we are and where we want to be (our goals). However, both giving and receiving feedback can be very intimidating. When someone says, 'Let me give you some feedback' we are likely to feel

244 This section includes special contributions from Dr Brodie Riordan, ICF certified coach and Manager of Partner Learning and Development at McKinsey & Company, and Aberkyn Change Facilitators: www.aberkyn.com.

anxious and fearful of what will follow.[245] The prospect of critical feedback can activate fears and anxieties of being insufficient, incompetent, not meeting others' expectations and feeling like a fraud. Giving feedback to others can be just as daunting, but usually because we fear how the other person will react. Will they be defensive or become angry? Will this further escalate what might already be a challenging situation? Will they retaliate?

The truth is that if you let a conflict linger on, it can become worse than it was to start with. The model in Figure 52 illustrates this dynamic very clearly. You might start with a feeling of discomfort. Your gut feeling says something is wrong. If you do not take action, the feeling may develop into tension and eventually spark a crisis. You could have prevented this from happening by addressing the challenges at an earlier stage.

245 See, e.g., Chapter 15 titled 'Maximizing the impact of feedback for learning and behavior change' by Jacqueline Brassey and Brodie Riordan in the book *Elevating Learning and Development* (2018).

FIGURE 52: CONFLICT CURVE

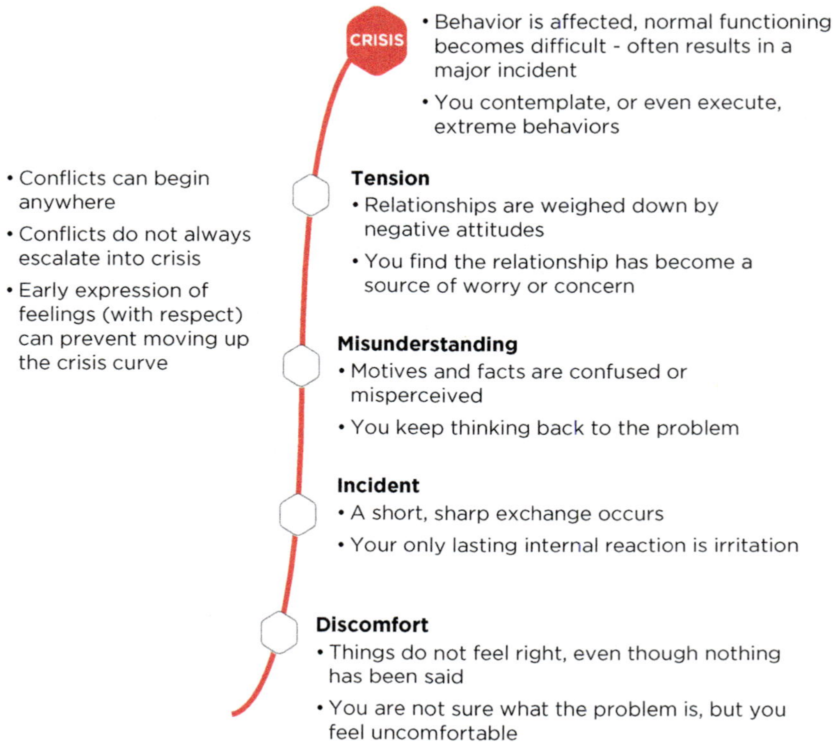

Source: ©The Conflict Resolution Network. Reproduced by kind permission.

Courageous conversations tool

There are three best practices that can make the act of giving or receiving feedback a little easier. We will guide you through these practices in the tool.

1. **Always focus on behaviour, not the person**. It is much easier to change your behaviour than who you are as a person. Feedback that focuses on someone's behaviour – things they did, do or have done – is more likely to be evidence-based, easier to act on and less likely to make the other person defensive. This pertains to both positive (praise) and developmental feedback. It is tempting to praise a person for who s/he is ('You are so smart') but your feedback will be much more useful and meaningful if you praise specific actions, ('Your empathy when assisting us as a team to resolve our tensions really helped').
2. **Make your feedback forward-looking**. It is also much easier to change your future behaviour than your past behaviour (unless

you have a time machine). One of the greatest challenges of feedback is that it focuses on past events, but we give it in order to inform future behaviour. Next time you provide feedback, offer a forward-looking suggestion, like 'Next time it would be great if you could do X instead' or let the other person decide by asking a question: 'Next time we are in that situation, what will you do differently?'

3. **Be specific**. The more specific your feedback is, the easier it is for the other person to recall exactly what happened, when and why. Specific and concrete feedback is also much more actionable than general and vague feedback. Ensuring that feedback is evidence-based and includes examples also increases the likelihood that the other person will accept and use your feedback. Feedback that consists of general opinions or sweeping generalisations is much more likely to make someone defensive and uninterested in your feedback. To really maximize the specificity of your feedback, you can structure it using the Situation-Behaviour-Impact framework: you refer to the situation where the behaviour occurred (e.g., a person's presentation in yesterday's team meeting), exactly what the behaviour was (e.g., they read directly from their notes and never looked up) and the impact of their behaviour (e.g., as a result, I could not always hear what you were saying and did not feel like there was an opportunity to ask questions). You can also follow this with a desired future behaviour, such as what you would like to see them do differently next time ('In future, can you make eye contact every now and then during your presentation?').

These three best practices can be woven into the next practical exercise on providing feedback to others. This practice is called 'courageous conversation' because giving feedback to others often requires courage, especially when the message is potentially tough to hear. This is also the reason why we tend to avoid this kind of conversation when we lack confidence. We do not want to hurt others, be disliked by them or even run the risk that our feedback might lead to unwanted consequences.

However, if the objective that we want to achieve is important to us, we sometimes have no option but to engage in this kind of conversation. Luckily, having a courageous conversation does not only require confidence and courage. A large part of its effectiveness is determined by the art and skill of conducting a conversation. The term 'courageous conversation' fits well. 'Courageous' stems from the French word *coeur*, which means heart. Courageous conversations are also called heart-to-heart conversations. You will probably find that you tend to have these conversations with the people you care about.

A key and often forgotten characteristic of such conversations is that they are not about winning, nor are they about 'out-arguing' the other person. It is about understanding what happened and learning about each other's feelings and perspectives. Great courageous conversations often end up taking a relationship to the next level. Learning how to conduct a conversation well demands practice and an understanding of the underlying mechanics. The model and questions in Figures 53, 54 and 55 will help you with the mechanics and how to prepare for your feedback or courageous conversation. As you will see, it is based on the Iceberg model that we discussed in Chapter 9 (tool 9.4.2). Please read through the example and reflect on the kind of conversation you would like to have. Then use the templates that follow to answer the questions.

FIGURE 53: MODEL TO PREPARE FOR COURAGEOUS CONVERSATIONS

Any challenging conversation gets easier when you prepare. Internal preparation helps you transform negative emotions into positive intention. Instead of "unloading" on the other, blaming and judging, you own and share your experience, express your interests, while staying respectful

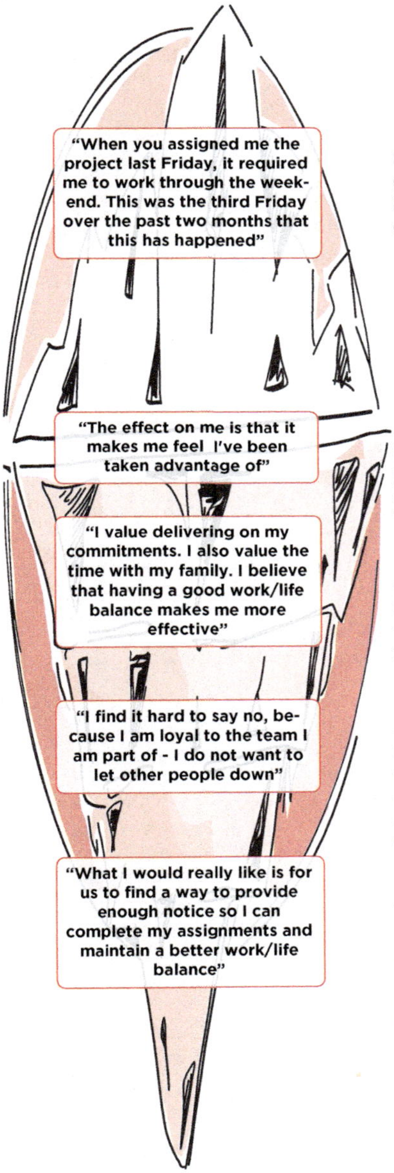

When I observe ...	Share the story of what you observed (see, hear, remember) without interpretation, judgment, assessment, or evaluation.
I feel/felt ...	Share how you felt. Be specific and personal — don't talk about the effect on others, talk about the effect on you. Talk about emotions than thoughts.
Because I need/ value ...	Identify what is underneath the feeling — what you need or value that causes your feelings, why it matters to you.
My part in this is ...	Identify what your part is. Reflect on what is driving your behaviour from within your own iceberg. Take ownership of your part in creating this tension.
What I would like to create, have happen ...	Engage in a solution-focused dialogue. Describe what the ideal situation looks like. Emphasise the benefits and consider how you could move towards them. Remain open to new outcomes.

Source: Aberkyn Change Facilitators - part of McKinsey & Company

FIGURE 54: PREPARATION – PART 1

Person's name

What is the context - what has happened between us?

What are the costs of not having this conversation?

What is the importance of this relationship?

Source: Aberkyn Change Facilitators – McKinsey & Company.

FIGURE 55: PREPARATION - PART 2

What is the intention of this conversation in terms of my relationship with this person?

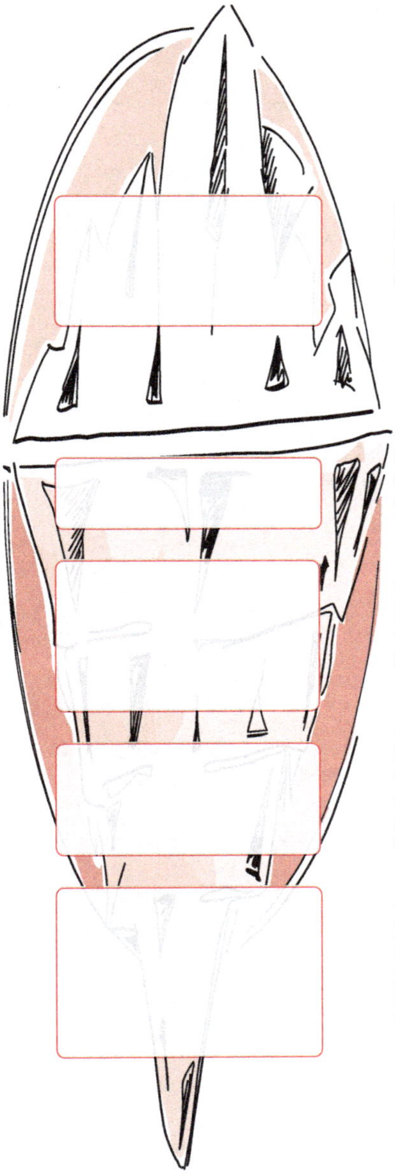

When I observe ...	Share the story of what you observed (see, hear, remember) without interpretation, judgment, assessment, or evaluation.
I feel/felt ...	Share how you felt. Be specific and personal — don't talk about the effect on others, talk about the effect on you. Talk about emotions than thoughts.
Because I need/ value ...	Identify what is underneath the feeling — what you need or value that causes your feelings, why it matters to you.
My part in this is ...	Identify what your part is. Reflect on what is driving your behaviour from within your own iceberg. Take ownership of your part in creating this tension.
What I would like to create, have happen ...	Engage in a solution-focused dialogue. Describe what the ideal looks like. Emphasis the benefits and consider how you could move towards them. Remain open to new outcomes.

Source: Aberkyn Change Facilitators - McKinsey & Company.

After you have written down your reflections, start planning your conversation. Below you will find a few tips on how to initiate and participate in the conversation.

TIPS FOR EFFECTIVE CONVERSATIONS

initiating the conversation
- Be very specific when sharing your observation. No generalisations or judgements
- Be brief when sharing your observation and its impact on you (60 sec is enough). Do not download all your frustration or try building your case
- Pause. Allow time and space for the other to respond
- Look for a win-win solution without being attached to a specific outcome
- Reach agreement, if possible, and achieve real closure by having the other repeat what was agreed

Participating in the conversation
- Listen without judging
- Try to understand what the other person feels, not only what (s)he says
- Ask clarifying questions, explain your iceberg: how did you feel, what did you need
- Engage in a win-win solution dialogue without being attached to specific outcome
- Reach agreement, if possible, summarise what you have agreed to and would both do differently next time.

Source: Aberkyn Change Facilitators - McKinsey & Company.

Once you have engaged in this conversation, use the reflection questions listed in Figure 56 to generate your personal insights and continue to learn on the journey.

FIGURE 56: INSIGHTS FROM COURAGEOUS CONVERSATIONS EXERCISE

What insights have you gained from your courageous conversation?

____

____

____

____

____

____

What are the benefits of having had this courageous conversation?

____

____

____

____

____

____

Source: Aberkyn Change Facilitators - McKinsey & Company

As with many behavioural skills, practice makes perfect. Most people experience courageous conversations as liberating and feel relieved after they have expressed their thoughts and feelings. It usually leads to a closer relationship with the other person and a better understanding of how you can work or live together.

To close this section, let us give you one more tip for success based on our own experience. The key moment in a courageous conversation, where you can feel the energy shifting and the negative charge diminishing, is when one or both of the parties share how they have contributed and what they have learned. And when an apology is merited, it is crucial that it is both offered and accepted in a genuine manner.

> **"There is evidence that when you get criticized it activates a physiological pain response because it signals you may be excluded or rejected from the group, or it might be a crushing blow to your ego, and nobody wants to experience that. But I once had a conversation with a business leader who has an almost simultaneous pain/pleasure reaction. When he got serious negative feedback in the past, he eventually learned something very valuable from it; he believes it's a big part of his success. And so, he has this two-step reaction like 'oh that feels bad', and every time I had feedback like this in the last few years it has led me to take better decisions, so that feels good."**
>
> **Adam Grant,** Professor of Management and Psychology, The Wharton School, University of Pennsylvania

> **"Once in my career I had to relay a very uncomfortable message to a chairman. He got angry with me and it was then that I learned I had to figure out how to build my narrative in a way that is grounded in data but at the same time not personal. Learning that skill later on helped me in my confidence to speak up. I have done this many times since. I connect with the facts, connect with my values and am always okay with the outcome, what ever it may be."**
>
> **Chet Kuchinad,** Chief People Officer, Save the Children International

11.3 How to speak up in meetings

Description of this tool	**What will this tool enable for you:**
This tool describes the skill and art of leaning in and speaking up in meetings and group settings.	• You will learn how to stay calm and focused when you find it scary to speak up in meetings and group settings.

Introduction

Research by McClean and colleagues (2018)[246] suggests that speaking up and sharing ideas and opinions can have different effects. They found that there can be negative side effects to the way you

246 https://journals.aom.org/doi/abs/10.5465/amj.2016.0148

speak up (prohibitive voice as opposed to a promotive voice), but they also revealed a gender impact.

Speaking using a promotive voice is related to gaining status among one's peers but also to being seen as a potential leader. When someone speaks with a promotive voice they are generally providing ideas for improving the group. However, this effect was not found among those participants who spoke with a prohibitive voice and focused on pointing out problems or issues. They were seen as potentially harmful to the team and needed to be stopped (Martin et al., 2017). Martin and colleagues also identified a relationship with increased status and leader emergence for men but not for women, thereby implying a gender effect. The message is clear: there is an art and skill to speaking up that you can make great use of when you have built up the confidence to do so, but the effect is different for men and women.

Adam Grant also offers important ideas on how to speak up effectively in his book *Originals* (2016, chapters 3 and 5 in particular). When we spoke with him about this topic he said:

> **"When I consider all the research about speaking up effectively, a few things come to mind. One is with the very steps that people need to take to marshal the confidence to speak up at all. And this can be the foundation for speaking up less effectively.**
> **When do we speak up? We speak up when we feel such strong emotions that we overcome whatever anxieties or hesitations we have. Those emotions can really cloud our thinking on how to present our ideas clearly and effectively. So, for example, people speak up when they are angry or feel attacked. Some speak up when they are extremely passionate and although that can be contagious, it can also suggest a blindness to the weakness of their idea. When I studied, I found that leveraging the emotional skills as part of EQ is really key. You need to experience enough emotion to want to speak up, but also know how to channel it so that it is appealing and convincing.**
> **A few additional ideas that I have found interesting, are the following. Systematically, people make the mistake, when they speak up, of only highlighting the strength of their idea and not acknowledging that their idea may have limitations. The research on that has a very interesting explanation of why you want to acknowledge the downside of your idea and not just the upside. I think part of it speaks to credibility. If I can say,**

"Hey, I have this idea and I am really very excited about this for the following reasons, and I am aware there are a few obstacles or a few imperfections", this increases credibility. The more I am candid about what's wrong with the idea, the more people can believe me when I say there is also something right about the idea. It changes the conversation from me selling to you into sort of an exercise of collaborative problem-solving.

Whenever you are trying to convince others of an idea or a suggestion, there is a risk that they immediately start to put up their defense mechanism. They don't want to be told that their opinion is wrong or that their decision or strategy is not going to work. I think of speaking up a little bit as an act of creative destruction in the sense of you having to advance your vision and you having to dismantle someone else's vision. So obviously, this can be very threatening. I think what happens when you say "Hey, I have this idea and here are the flaws", is that you activate kind of a fun feature in the availability heuristic. So normally when you give a bunch of reasons why people should accept your idea, they are going to start looking for reasons to reject your idea and if you don't match any problems to your idea, you have given them five reasons to reject. If you put on the table "Hey, I think this idea has three big flaws", they may have to work harder to come up with their own objections. The harder they work to come up with the sort of things that they think are problematic, the less they think is wrong with that idea. And so, I think we were all taught to do this when we were growing up in debate class; you were supposed to acknowledge the limitations of your argument and address counterarguments out loud. We forget to do this when we make suggestions and present ideas because we think they are fragile and we may shoot ourselves in our foot. Of course, there are very ineffective ways to do this: you don't want to say "Hey, I have this idea and I am pretty sure it's terrible so please don't take this too seriously." We have all seen people sort of self-limit in that way, but I think it is actually incredibly confidence signaling to say "Hey, I am really excited about this idea, here is why I think it's worth considering and you know like all ideas it needs some further development and I would love to talk through how to address these couple of challenges I notice with it." I think that is signaling that you have enough confidence in the strengths of the idea that you are not afraid

> **to have the conversation about its weaknesses. That for me is a pretty big take away for speaking up."**
>
> **Adam Grant,** Professor of Management and Psychology, The Wharton School, University of Pennsylvania

In the following tool we will provide you with some tips on the art of speaking up in meetings and also make the link to your reasons for speaking up.

How to speak up effectively
Creating the conditions for yourself to speak up successfully in meetings and calls.

A. *Before you start (let your voice be heard in the room or call from the outset)*
   - Let your voice be heard - say good morning out loud, ask questions, engage in some small talk with others in the room, etc.

B. *Be clear about your true intent and what is important to you*
   Feel your intent and connect with your body, mind and heart - this can be done in seconds once you become experienced at it.
   - Breathe deeply.
   - Explore what you feel, where you are in the moment.
   - What is your intent for this meeting or call?
   - Try to let go of the idea that there is one truth. Speaking up does not mean you have to proclaim the truth. This sets the bar too high. Instead, think of what you can contribute by adding to the existing insights, bringing a different perspective to the table and enriching the conversation.

C. *Your message (promotive versus prohibitive)*
   - Reconfirm what we want to achieve as a team and voice your intent.
   - Say 'yes and' as opposed to 'yes but'.
   - Say 'Can I build on this?' as opposed to 'I have a better idea'.
   - Emphasise why you think this is a great idea and point out possible weak points in your proposal. Propose a solution or a new perspective for each challenge or make it explicit that you do not have the answer yet and would like to work together to find one.

D. Physical aspects of how you speak (voice, body language and breathing)
- Talk from your stomach. Your voice will sound slightly lower than what you are perhaps used to; it is more grounded.
- Shoulders back, chest out.
- Breathe from your stomach (diaphragm).
- Does your voice go up or down at the end of a sentence? Just take notice.

E. Explore how you could activate 'support champions' before the meeting
- If you will be addressing a sensitive topic at the meeting, you can take some heat out of the conversation by doing some networking beforehand. Find out where your colleagues stand on the topic and get some of them to buy in by asking them to support you in the meeting.
- Reflect before the meeting on where everyone stands on each key topic you want to discuss and think of the potential arguments or input you can use when they speak.

In this section we introduced the book *Originals: How non-conformists move the world* by Adam Grant. If you are interested in finding out more about his work, please refer to the reference list for more details.

11.4 Effective presentation – tips and techniques

Lead author of this section is Anneke Brouwer, Systemic Dialogic Speaker Coach, Executive Voice Expert at the House of Silence.[247]

Description of this tool	**What will this tool enable for you:**
Building your presentation skills helps you to improve the way you present yourself and your topic. It increases your credibility, authority and therefore your confidence.	• This tool will enable you to find your own authentic style in public speaking, in a way that will help build your confidence.

Introduction

Great public speakers do not just speak, they perform. They have confidence in their story, find their own style and use intimacy, not intimidation. It is all about sharing, not speaking. Most of the execu-

247 https://annekebrouwer.nl/?lang=en

tives we work with want to feel more confident and relaxed about the way they deliver their message. By improving their presentation skills they can switch more easily on the spot between themselves, their content and their audience instead of feeling trapped in themselves and the content. Mastering these skills is a tremendous boost for them and the process is often a real eye-opener.

There are lots of great speakers but there is no single style that works for everyone. If you want to feel more self-confident when it comes to speaking in public, it is important that you find your own spark and modus operandi instead of trying to imitate someone else's style. Whatever the type of speaking engagement you are facing, be it in a meeting, at a social event or for personal entertainment, you should focus on finding your own style. We play all kinds of roles in life day in, day out, but we perform at our best when we are authentic and genuine. This starts by knowing and finding your own voice and daring to be 100% present when you speak in front of an audience. It is through your presence that you convince your audience, which brings us back to the topic of authentic confidence: this means being fully present, complete with all your emotions and fears. If you want an example of very powerful public speaking, have a look at the talk given by Susan David: 'The gift and power of emotional courage.'[248]

Next, we will take you through the key ingredients of a great presentation and describe a few key steps that will help on your journey towards the perfect delivery.

You can prepare for all of these elements in advance and once you start mastering them they will boost your confidence because you will develop your 'unconsciously skilled' muscle, which means you will have less to worry about the more often you give a presentation. The key ingredients of a great presentation are: (1) structure - how you organise your talk; (2) content - what you say; (3) delivery - how you say it; (4) the importance of rehearsing; (5) finalising details on the day of your presentation; and (6) how to handle the crucial first few minutes. We will close this section with a few reminders.

1. Structure: How to organise your story

Know your 'why' and your purpose

Take a few deep breaths and reflect on the following questions:

248 https://www.ted.com/talks/susan_david_the_gift_and_power_of_emotional_courage

- What is the magic I want to make happen in the room when I speak?
- How do I want to touch my audience?
- What are the key messages I want them to walk out of the room with when I am done?
- How does this relate to what is important to me?
- Why am I speaking to this audience?

Even when you are preparing for a small group or a 'safe' speaking environment, make sure you practice your speaking skills and always reflect on your 'why' and the purpose of your speaking engagement. This is the moment when you connect with your values and what is important to you, and it will also be a key source of confidence. Once you have answered the above questions, you can add the information to your talk to make your purpose come alive.

The core structure

Every good speech contains three basic elements: a beginning (hook), middle (meat) and an end (pay-off). They cement the key elements of your story together. The transition between these elements is important and you can ensure a good core structure by addressing the following questions:

- How do I build my story? Where do I start? What do I follow up with and how do I end? Connect this to your purpose.
- What will be your top-down message? An audience reacts best when you outline early on what you plan to tell them and offer them signposts for along the way. And you can write down the structure for yourself on a memory card if you are not using slides to support your story.
- Tell the audience at the outset how you plan to arrange your talk and outline your main points ('Today I'm going to talk to you about three key things ...'). Spend roughly the same amount of time on each part of your story and use verbal cues to let your audience know where you are in the talk ('That was the first point. The second point I would like to share with you is ...'). It is also very important to conclude with an easy-to-follow summary of what you have said and to issue a call to action to your audience.

Beginning (hook)

In the first 30 seconds of your speech your listeners should discover that you really have something interesting to say so that they can connect with you and your performance. Use your opening lines as a hook to immediately engage your audience. They will then be much more inclined to give you their undivided attention. Here are a few examples of how you can start a presentation in a powerful way: tell a captivating story; ask a rhetorical, thought-provoking question; use a powerful quote; make a statement; state a shocking statistic or headline; share a personal anecdote or experience; kick-off with a humorous anecdote; provide a testimony or success story; show a short video or a gripping photo; and so on.

Middle (meat)
The middle part of your speech is where you engage your audience with the content. They will be best able to follow your story if you organise it into a few bite-sized and logical pieces – for example, 'the three things you need to know about our new brand positioning are ...' – that follow a clear timeline. Or you can choose to shuttle back and forth between the current situation and what you envisage for tomorrow. In other words, offer your audience tasty bits of information.[249]

End (pay-off)
Plan, script and rehearse how you will close your story. Never assume you can improvise the end on the spot. Close your presentation with words that support your message so that you can maximize its impact. Avoid using cliches like 'It seems I've run out of time' and 'Thank you so much for coming'. A few examples of what you can do to end your presentation on a high note: ask a rhetorical question, review your points of wisdom, challenge your audience, issue a call to action, revisit your opening lines or use words in your closing lines that will linger long in the memory.

Time management
When someone asks you to give a 30-minute talk, prepare something that will take about 20 minutes to deliver. Time management is very important for a number of reasons. Firstly, most conferences end up running late, so if you are asked to shorten your presentation, it will still fit the timeline and you won't need to rush your story. You will still be able to make your point and come across as authentic, confident and someone worth listening to. Secondly, it helps you to make your message clear and boosts your credibility because you need less words to get the message across. And thirdly, staying within the time limit is a subtle way of showing your respect for your audience. You respect their valuable time and the opportunity they have given you to connect with them. Good time

249 Nancy Duarte: https://www.ted.com/talks/nancy_duarte_the_secret_structure_of_great_talks

management will result in a more relaxed and conversational kind of talk.

Q&A

Some of you will be familiar with the saying *'C'est le ton qui fait la musique'* (in English: 'It is the tone that makes the music'). When you are giving a talk, it is not only the words you use that matter but also your tone of voice. If we apply this to the Q&A section of a presentation, for example, you should think about the potentially difficult questions you might be asked so that you can have your answer ready (where possible) and avoid coming across as defensive, nervous or frazzled. You can make life easier for yourself during the Q&A section by using some of the examples shown below:[250]

- *"Let me be sure I understand which information you're looking for ..."*
- *"Based on what we know today, my thoughts are ..."*
- *"That's a timely question, because I'm currently gathering XYZ information ..."*
- *"I can answer that in part, but would like to consider it further and get back to you ..."*
- *"Great question. I'm just not familiar enough with XYZ to hazard a guess. Let me connect you with ..."*

Handling your Q&A with style, expertise, patience and perhaps a bit of self-deprecating humour can help to make this part of the talk much more relaxed. This in turn can help to boost your credibility and authority on the topic and build your confidence.

2. Content: what you say

How you organise your content will make the difference between a clear and a muddy message. It will determine whether your listeners see you as someone worth listening to or not. In the end it's all about credibility and authority. In this section we will explore a few important points concerning the content of your story.

Ensure that you have a point to make, but never more than three

How many times have you heard someone give a talk only to find yourself wondering afterwards, 'What was that all about?' It is a mistake that is commonly made by a lot of executives. What you say must make sense. Your listeners are giving you their valuable time,

250 These questions are quoted verbatim from: https://www.forbes.com/consent/?toURL=https://www.forbes.com/sites/work-in-progress/2014/08/08/five-alternatives-to-saying-i-dont-know/

so you must respect them by having at least one main point. Having too many messages, on the other hand, creates the same problem as when you have none. We recommend that you have at least one and no more than three main messages. Simple and to the point is always the best way to get your message(s) across.

Use poetry

There is a difference between words that are spoken and words that are written. They are basically different animals. Some things look funny on paper and work well orally too. However, other things that seem smart on paper can fall flat when spoken out loud. Winston Churchill once said, 'Every speech is a rhymeless, meterless verse.' He believed that a speech was written for the ear and should therefore sound like poetry. Your prose can become poetry simply by changing the layout of your speech and writing it down in such way that each new thought and phrase begins on a new line. Try to avoid jargon, too, and use shorter sentences and fewer words. Reading the final draft out loud will show you the amazing effect this can have. It breaks your speech into more manageable pieces.

Tell a story

Whether you are giving a speech in a business or social context, your listeners must be able to become emotionally involved with what you say. Graphics, data and technical terms do not touch an audience and are often extremely boring to listen to (if not presented effectively). Captivating stories, in contrast, do catch and hold the attention. There are many excellent examples of this, like the speech Steve Jobs gave in 2005 at Stanford.[251] This was a masterful speech organised around three stories: how taking calligraphy courses later impacted the MacBook (this is a clear example of a speech in which the speaker connects the dots in the story he tells), being fired from and returning to Apple (he uses a story about love and loss) and what he learned the first time he was diagnosed with pancreatic cancer (a story about death). Another great example from Steve Jobs is the speech where he introduces the iPhone in 2007.[252]

A good story touches people, potentially enabling them to visualize and feel what took place and recall the story later on. It is therefore strange that in business it is still not common to tell good stories. A captivating story has three ingredients: (1) a main character (e.g., CEO, company or product); (2) an incident (a hero's journey); and (3)

251 https://youtu.be/UF8uR6Z6KLc
252 https://youtube/9hUIxyE2Ns8

a conflict (climax followed by a solution). Try using a story structure the next time you give a speech and discover the effect it can have.

Connect and interact with your listeners

Your audience is the reason why you get up to speak. If there were no audience, there would be no need for you to do so. It is important that you focus on your relationship with your audience so that you can activate and interest your listeners. This will give you the confidence you need and enable you to deliver your message more effectively. Make the audience the focal point of your speech. Remember, minutes can seem like hours when you are stuck listening to a boring speaker.

Think of a speech as a two-way conversation. Every good speaker cares more about the audience than they do about her or himself. It means you need two things: confidence in your message and a respectful understanding of your audience. Being a good presenter is not so much about what you say but rather about how you listen to the needs of your audience. You interpret the content of your speech for your audience and the audience will relate to your content because you have told them why it should matter to them. Do not talk down to them, but translate your words instead into a language they are comfortable with. Give your speech a more conversational tone by asking questions from the beginning - real questions, but also rhetorical questions. And last but not least, make eye contact with your audience so that you can stay connected.

3. Delivery: how you say what you have to say

In business meetings the focus is usually on *what* a person has to say. But if you really want to persuade your listeners, you must also focus on *how* you say what you have to say. It is the ideal combination of content and delivery that makes a speech work and it is essential that you concentrate on these two areas. This will keep your listeners engaged and help you to speak with more clarity and credibility. And that is how you successfully inform and persuade your listeners.

Vocal variety

Your voice is your most flexible and effective communication tool when it comes to how you say what you have to say. It creates confidence and has a relaxing effect. To speak effectively, you need to vary the sound of your voice. It can make the difference between being heard or not. If you think you are vocally limited, try working with a voice coach to unlock your voice skills so that you can deliver your message successfully to your listeners.

If you want your listeners to stay tuned and to understand the things you say, you need to become familiar with and regularly practice these persuasive, effective and important voice skills:

- **Energy**. A presentation must vary in terms of energy so that the audience can become emotionally involved. Make sure every sentence you speak is confident and clear. Nothing turns listeners off more than a speaker who makes them work very hard and still cannot bridge the distance between speaker and audience. Ensure that your voice retains its energy until the end of each and every sentence.
- **Emphasis**. If you want your audience to understand something, it is important that you emphasise certain key words so that you are easier to listen to. Stress your most important ideas by lengthening the vowels of key words.
- **Pitch**. Speaking without any variation in your voice quickly becomes monotonous. Varying or inflecting your pitch adds colour and energy to what you say and keeps your audience engaged.
- **Rhythm and pace**. Audiences need a varied pace and rhythm to stay interested. If you realise you are rushing, take a moment to pause and breathe. Then continue and keep a steady pace by addressing one thought at a time. If you notice that you are rushing again, repeat the above. It is the variation in the pace that really works.
- **The power of silence**. Silence is one of the most powerful tools in public speaking. What you do just before you start your presentation is extremely important. Stay in the moment. Be aware of yourself in the room as if you own the space. Take a few belly breaths and express your thoughts one at a time. Pause before moving on to your next idea so that you can give your listeners the time to take in what you have just said. Pausing every now and then helps you to relax and will give you confidence. So make your pauses just as important as what you say. Use short sentences, separated by a pause. When you are not afraid to use silence and pauses your listeners will regard you as someone who trusts her or himself and who feels confident. And that will boost your credibility.
- **Voice quality**. Voice quality relates to aspects like tone, richness, pleasantness and emotional connection – the things that make human speech dynamic, authentic and unique. You can vary your tone of voice by choosing a different emotion while speaking.

Practicing this will make your presentation more colourful and your message will come across more easily.

- **Speaking mindfully**. Speaking mindfully means speaking with precision and energy by being aware of your pronunciation. Also, remember to drop your voice at the end of each sentence to avoid 'up-speaking' or making a statement sound like a question. Up-speaking (when your pitch rises at the end of a sentence) gives the impression that you are not sure either of yourself or your message. So drop your voice at the end of a sentence and only use an up-speaking tone when you are asking a question.
- **Body language**. Your body is a powerful natural tool of communication. People are more impressed when your body language also communicates what your voice is communicating. It can be very frustrating for an audience when your body language and your words are not in sync. You need to give physical expression to the things you are saying and this will help your audience to remember your message. Whatever you do physically, you will also do vocally. So you should plan beforehand and polish your 'dance' through practice. Hand movements and other gestures are important for effective presentation. And you should always stand if you have a choice. If you are using a lectern, come out from behind it from time to time. Use gestures to emphasise the points you are making. Use the stage effectively, moving to a different spot for each main point. Reduce the distance between you and your audience, as if they are your friends and you feel very comfortable speaking with them. Make real eye contact and maintain it during your pauses. Smile at your audience. Make sure you have a speaking and listening face that is warm and interested.

4. The importance of rehearsing

The fine-tuned version of your talk is ready. You have a clear message. You know your audience. You know your why and your purpose. You have a strong beginning (Hook), a middle (Meat) and a powerful end (Pay-off). Now you are going to rehearse in order to sharpen your purpose and increase your confidence. Below are a few useful tips:

- **Record yourself on your smartphone**. It helps to record yourself doing your talk out loud so that you can check things like timing and emphasis and sharpen the purpose of your message as well. When you play the recording back, watch out for repetitive phrases and fillers like 'uhm'. Record yourself again until you are speaking smoothly, dynamically and confidently.
- **Make easy-to-read notes**. Put your key notes on a card using a large typeface. As you speak, you will be able to follow your 'road map' with quick glances.

- **Keep track of time. Rehearse with a timer**. Keep track of the time so you can speed up or slow down, and cut or add material so that you finish on time.
- **Rehearse your talk in front of one or two trusted friends**. For timing, clarity and impact, rehearse your talk in front of one or two friends. When you do so, ask them for constructive feedback and not just praise. Did they understand the points you made? Was there a lack of logic or continuity? Do they think you spoke too quickly or too slowly? Use their feedback to give your presentation the final polish.
- **Rehearse standing in the room**. Rehearse 'live' but not in front of the mirror. You will only be distracted by yourself. Use the chairs or cushions in your room as an imaginary audience.
- **Visualize your best performance ever**. Starting a few weeks before your presentation, visualize the best speech you have ever given.

> **"In 2016, I was elected Full Professor at Nyenrode Business University. It is a custom in The Netherlands that newly appointed professors give an inaugural lecture for the rector, colleague professors, students, business relationships, members of the press, and invited family and friends. Although I have given many presentations during my career, I realised that this was a big deal. How to give a lecture that would be perceived as very interesting and inspirational for such different audiences. I decided to engage a speech consultant[253] to provide me with feedback. I practiced my first speech for her – standing behind a lectern and reading a 45-minute story, which is the customary presentation format for an inaugural lecture in The Netherlands. The speech coach was completely unimpressed by my performance. It was boring, not inspirational and it didn't feature 'the best Nick'. She coached me to change a number of things: walk around during my lecture, use gestures, memorize and tell a story versus reading a speech, watch and change the sound of my voice during the speech, use fewer PowerPoint slides and, finally, practice, practice and practice. As a consequence, the speech was perceived by everyone as very inspirational and it turned out to be very different from what people are used to. It showed the best Nick."**
>
> **Nick van Dam,** former Partner and Global Chief Learning Officer, McKinsey & Company, Professor of Learning and Development and Member of the Board of Directors at IE University, Spain. You can watch Nick's inaugural lecture here: https://www.youtube.com/watch?v=Py8vfmOWYNA&t=2005s

253 https://annekebrouwer.nl/?lang=en

5. Final touches on the day of your presentation

By now we hope you are feeling relaxed and confident about your message and delivery. However, there are still a few final touches that need to be made on the day of your presentation. Do not overlook these pre-presentation strategies. Without them you run the risk of derailing your relaxed mode, your confidence and your presentation. These are the most important final touches:

- **Check in early**. You need to give yourself time to feel comfortable in the room. So arrive early and check out the logistics of the space in which you will be speaking. Is there a stage? Where is it located? Where will you be standing or sitting? Are your listeners close enough to where you will be speaking to build intimacy?
- **Make friends with the stage**. When the room is empty walk on stage and plan where you are going to stand and when you are going to move during your speech. You do not want to distract the audience with unnecessary movements. Go through the main points of your talk. Imagine getting an enthusiastic response. The more time you spend getting comfortable on stage, the more you can relax and focus on the audience. This is what actors call 'making friends with the stage'.
- **Set up a clock**. Make sure you have a way to keep track of time. If you are including a Q&A session, make sure the presentation has a 'must-end-by' time. Scheduling this adds to your professionalism.
- **Make a sound with your voice**. Every room will have a different effect on the sound of your voice. Say something out loud and listen to your voice and how it sounds in the room. What effect does varying the pitch, loudness and pace have? Check that you can be heard in all parts of the room. Familiarise yourself with the microphone. Keep it at chin level. Just before you go on stage, use it as a tool to find your mindful voice and to calm and sooth your state of mind.
- **Double check your audio-visual aids**. If you are using a PowerPoint presentation, make sure the equipment is working properly.
- **Connect with the organiser.** Find out who will be introducing you and where you will be during their introduction.
- **Connect with some of the audience before you start**. A brief chat with a few of your listeners before you start your speech will make it easier to lend your presentation a more conversational tone.

How to handle the crucial first few minutes

You can be your own worst enemy and end up tearing down rather than building up your confidence as a speaker. In general, you can trust that the audience wants you to be successful. The simple fact that you are standing there on stage will usually get them on your side, even if they are 'critical' listeners. Remember the following six points during the crucial first few minutes. They will help you to feel that you are doing well and delivering a great speech:

1. Remind yourself that you have prepared well. If your speech is well structured and you have worked on your delivery and thought about your time management, you can feel confident that you have made all the necessary preparations. You have also rehearsed your speech a number of times out loud. For some, it also helps if you have visualized yourself succeeding on stage. For this you can also use tool 5.4.4 for aspiring to be your best self.
2. The important role of your attitude and mindset. It is crucial that you reflect on what you 'feel' for your audience, because they will experience that too. Instead of thinking that you want to get your speech over and done with as quickly as possible so that you can become anonymous again, try to embrace your audience and feel the kind of love you need to engage with them. They are genuinely interested in what you want to tell them. See them as your friends and try to feel grateful about being able to talk with them about your 'why'.
3. The audience wants you to succeed and will only feel terrible if you fail. Understand what they are looking for in you and see them as your partners. Make your speech conversational. Make real eye contact. Focus on interaction. If your inner voice tells you that you 'have to succeed', notice these thoughts and then use the defusion technique: 'I have the thought that I have to succeed'. Take a deep breath and try to reframe this into 'I would love the audience to understand that [fill in the blanks]'. This will change the focus from you (and your need to succeed) to the audience (and what you are about to bring them). This will help you to reduce any stress you may be feeling and to feel comfortable enough to share your thoughts and ideas. Do not try to be excellent; be a human being.
4. Remember how to use your body to become more comfortable on stage and feel authentically confident. There are three key ingredients: breathing, grounding and moving. Remind yourself to breathe more deeply and slowly (see also tool 6.4.2). As explained in Chapter 6, the skill of diaphragmatic breathing (or a physiological sigh) will immediately activate the parasympathetic nervous system and help you to calm down if you are feeling stressed. Once you have trained yourself, diaphragmatic breathing (or a physiological sigh) is the easiest and most comfortable way to

calm yourself down wherever you are, even in front of a large audience.

5. The result is that your voice will be warm, calm and relaxed, and that you will be more able to support or carry your voice. Furthermore, remember to stand up straight, with your shoulders tilted slightly back and with both feet on the floor. Imagine there are two magnets on your shoes and a sheet of iron under the floor, too, which are holding your feet firmly on the ground. You can also visualize that you are a tree whose roots are going through the soles of your shoes and into the ground. If you do this, you will stand tall and feel grounded. This is important for that moment just before you start: breathe, visualize yourself as grounded and then start talking - and moving.
6. Moving around during your presentation is very important. You can alternate your movement with moments when you feel grounded, and remember to breathe deeply when you pause. When you move, you release energy. So remember to move calmly and focused on and connected with the audience. When you turn your attention to a different topic, use the moment to change your position on stage. For example, if you are addressing two contrasting points of view, you could start on the left-hand side of the stage for one viewpoint and then move to the other side when addressing the other. This also helps to keep your audience engaged. The only thing that is left now is to practice as much as you can and remember to maintain a growth mindset (tool 7.4.1).

> **"A little technique someone mentioned at an early stage: focus on one person in the audience and speak to that person rather than to the abstract big audience. I found that with time my confidence built. I feel a little bit of anxiety or just a bit tense and that is a good thing. I would not overprepare anymore."**
>
> **John Brand,** Consultant, Bowmans, South Africa

> **"Recently I worked with a great CEO. As a person she is warm, engaging, clear-thinking. When she stepped up on stage, something happened. She became stilted, wooden. And it was a vicious circle because a lack of engagement from audiences had dented her trust in her voice. The big mis-conception for her, as for so many, is that speaking well in the spotlight is a gift - you either have it or you don't. This is utterly wrong. The most relaxed conversational speakers have put the thinking and the rehearsal in - sometimes over many years. When you**

> **understand that it unlocks a growth mindset, we can all be good speakers, in our own way, if we practice. My client recently spoke at an event where a new member of the leadership team was present. He turned to the HR director and said "Wow, she's impressive." Belief and practice, with some focused support at the right moments, are all you need to help you find the trajectory from wooden to 'wow'.**
> **And the absolute key is to learn from performers. It's the scientifically proven way to overcome stage fright. If you can get past the dread and rehearse your words aloud, allowing yourself to have what actors call the initial 'stumble through', you will ultimately be so much more confident in your performance. The performer's rule is that the first run through is usually bad, and that's a good sign. By the third run you will sound so much better. When you walk out on stage you will enjoy the experience and your audience will connect with you. In the words of Samuel Beckett, a good performance demands that you 'fail, fail again, fail better' in rehearsal. And the magic gadget to support you in all of this? The voice recorder app on your phone. It's your pocket voice coach. I have seen it take speakers from terror to speaking all over the world in the space of a couple of months."**
>
> **Caroline Goyder,** Leading Voice Coach and author of The Gravitas Method (2014)

If you would like to read more about this topic, we recommend you consult the works of Caroline Goyder (www.carolinegoyder.com) and Gary Genard (*How to give a speech*, 2016). You will find their books in the reference list.

CHAPTER 12

12. CONTINUING YOUR SELF-EMPOWERMENT JOURNEY

The journey we undertook for this book has been fascinating and we feel very fortunate that you have allowed us to be your guides. All the people we spoke with have been very open and transparent in their views and their contributions have been invaluable. At the end of each interview we asked the question: 'What advice would you give your younger self, knowing what you know now?' We will share a few of these answers with you here as a final source of inspiration for you on your own journey.

> **"My advice would be not to deny psychological problems, weakness, fear and emotion. Encourage people to let off steam, to be angry, to burst into tears. You can't resolve a conflict unless people ventilate it. I am very comfortable in sending them to counselling."**
>
> **John Brand,** Consultant, Bowmans, South Africa

> **"Do what you love, I strongly believe in that. You have to do the thing that becomes a propeller for your self-confidence. Have the capacity to put things in perspective. Make your world a bit bigger every now and then. That helps you to put things in perspective. And lastly, become aware that you can re-programme yourself. This happened with me when I realised that I am in control of my own destiny. I programme myself, no one else does. At the same time, you don't need to solve all problems you may encounter on your own. Connect with others to solve problems together; you are not alone in life. Keep heart, body, mind and spirit in balance."**
>
> **Jan Zijderveld,** former CEO Avon Inc. and President of Unilever Europe

> **"Stand up more for yourself and reflect on what is the worst thing that can happen to you. Put things in perspective."**
>
> **Pieter Waasdorp,** Director Entrepreneurship, Ministry of Economic Affairs, The Netherlands

> **"Don't take yourself too seriously."**
>
> **Abbe Luersman,** CHRO, EVP and Chief People Officer, Otis Elevator Co

> **"To relax a lot more. I was so stressed about the little things that don't count at all, like you are not invited into a meeting: Oh my gosh, why was I not invited?? All these worries that we have and the mountains we make up, like this leader did not look at me, oh my god, my name was not there on the credit list. Today, I really wonder how I could have worried about that. It is so embarrassing. I am in this job today and you realise half the time you don't know whether you are coming or going. You are not even thinking twice. One day you are feeling fantastic and you are saying a big compliment to this person, and the next day you might be extremely busy and forget to greet another person. At those moments, I am not aware of it, but for others it might be such a big deal. It makes me conscious and I want to appear as still connected, and I want to work hard at it. I would tell my younger self: just relax. It is not these things that count. And another thing: be much more focused around your purpose and journey. This is a journey. I feel much more settled today. I would have pushed a lot more to know my purpose. Speak up a lot more than I did. I did more than the average women on my team and speaking up has been helpful, but I would have encouraged myself to speak up even more and not to be worried about others' perception of me, but to be worried about what is the impact that I am creating. What difference am I making? Whose service am I in? How can I make a bigger difference than I am today? Those are the questions I put far more effort on now."**
>
> **Leena Nair,** former Chief Human Resources Officer (CHRO), Unilever; current CEO of Chanel

> **"Don't take life too hard. Create your own happiness. Do what you love and love what you do."**
>
> **Paul-Peter Feld,** CHRO, Enexis

"Check the facts before jumping to conclusions. Don't allow yourself to worry about things you cannot change. Honestly, worry for the sake of worry does not help."

Michelle Roborg-Sondergaard, Senior HR Executive

"Don't overestimate yourself, but certainly don't underestimate yourself either! And: The Valley is more Fertile than the Summit (Loesje)."

Ron van der Jagt, Senior Executive

"Ground yourself in what you have done well and have a bit more kindness towards yourself."

Joanna Barsh, Senior Partner Emerita, McKinsey & Company

"Don't rush. Sometimes wait a few days before you send things out. Take a pause, because things look different the next day. Don't only focus on leading by example, but also learn how to become a servant leader leading from behind and at a distance. I should have started that sooner; the best lessons I got in my career came from experience and making mistakes; embrace the mistakes you (inevitably) make along the way and focus on what you can learn from them to become better every day."

Andres Cadena, Senior Partner, McKinsey & Company, Bogotá, Colombia

"Learn to put things in perspective. Choose your battles, also when insecure. Lean in, and then learn and make it happen. You will always be happier if you try. If it doesn't work out, you learn and at least you have tried."

Josette Dijkhuizen, Honorary Professor in Entrepreneurship Development and Entrepreneur

> **"To become happy is not about business success. You have to become happy with who you are and your circumstances. If you feel well in your own skin, then you are most effective."**
>
> **Tex Gunning,** CEO, Leaseplan

> **"Put things in perspective. Don't go too fast. Have in mind where you are going and learn your values system well - what is important to you."**
>
> **Beltrán Simó,** Partner, McKinsey & Company, Bogotá, Colombia

> **"Find your confidence from concentrating on the following two things: (1) do what is right, and (2) do it following the right behaviour and intention."**
>
> **Fernando Ferrari,** Senior Partner, McKinsey & Company

> **"Trust people and they will be good to you, that is what I experienced. Treat them greatly and they show themselves great. This is what inner confidence is all about. When people show up in your team, treat them greatly so they will show up greatly next time. Don't belittle them, don't make them feel stupid."**
>
> **Chet Kuchinad,** Chief People Officer, Save the Children International

> **"Enjoy the adventures even more and live in the now as opposed to in the future."**
>
> **Sebastiaan Besems,** Chief Commercial Officer, Burg Group, The Netherlands

> **"The lesson I have learned so far is that there is huge value in spending the time before you embark on something, to evaluate what the value is and what the expectation is and fully understand - what you want to do and if it is something you can do. At the moment, my biggest failing is that people ask me to do something all the time and I just say yes. Then I have got**

potentially 20 people to serve and I did not take the time to think through for myself what I wanted to do."

Senior Executive, anonymous contribution

"Be clear on what you stand for. Think about your strengths and spend more time aligning your actions to your values rather than trying to be someone else. Success is defined in different ways. Whether you are in a role, in transition or traveling, make the most of your experiences as they help define you. The 16 months I spent in Guatemala in a microfinance charity after only working for two years as a young graduate has had a bigger influence on me than any other work experience. Make the most of transitions and connect with as many different people as possible. Your work life experiences define you and make you better at whatever you chose to do!"

Karen Rivoire, Competence Flow Leader, Inter IKEA Group

"Two things. The first one that I have learned from Mark Zuckerberg and Sheryl Sandberg at Facebook is: there are two ways you can fail. One is you fall short of your goals, and the other is that you achieve your goals and you were not aiming high enough. I would say to my younger self, being very risk averse so that, sometimes, I opted for the goals that I knew I had the highest chance achieving and I did not challenge myself enough or stretch myself enough out of my comfort zone. The way I would phrase it is: if these first two don't succeed, you know you are aiming high enough.
Second, related to that, as a goal-oriented person, I was very vulnerable to tunnel vision, and once I got excited about a project or idea, I kind of focused on that; threw myself into it; got totally absorbed, not necessarily being aware of myself that that was going on. As a result, I think I missed an opportunity to learn a wider range of skills earlier in grad school that I would use now if I had done that. But I did not put a lot of time into them because they were like 30 degrees off of what I was trying to accomplish in-the-moment, and I felt like it would be a little bit of a side track or a diversion. And so I would say to my younger self: you need to improve your peripheral vision and part of that is having the confidence to say, "You know what, I don't know how these skills will be useful, but I am

> **interested in learning them and I am going to pursue that even if I can't connect the dots in how they will help me achieve a goal that I am working toward right now. ""**
>
> **Adam Grant,** Professor of Management and Psychology, The Wharton School, University of Pennsylvania

Finally, a few inspirational thoughts to help you on your way:[254]

- Inspiration exists, but it has to find you working. **Pablo Picasso**
- Action expresses priorities ...to believe in something, and not to live it, is dishonest. **Mahatma Gandhi**
- What you do speaks so loudly that I can barely hear what you say. **Ralph Waldo Emerson**
- Do you want to know who you are? Don't ask. Act! Action will delineate and define you. **Thomas Jefferson**
- A real decision is measured by the fact that you've taken a new action. If there's no action, you haven't truly decided. **Tony Robbins**
- There are risks and costs to a program of action. But they are far less than the long-range risks and costs of comfortable inaction. **John F. Kennedy**
- Inaction breeds doubt and fear. Action breeds confidence and courage. If you want to conquer fear, do not sit home and think about it. Go out and get busy. **Dale Carnegie**
- Knowing is not enough; we must apply. Willing is not enough; we must do. **Johann Wolfgang von Goethe**
- Don't think. You already know what you have to do, and you know how to do it. What's stopping you? **Tim Grover**
- If it wasn't hard, everyone would do it. It's the hard that makes it great. **Tom Hanks**
- If you really want to do something, you'll find a way. If you don't, you'll find an excuse. **Jim Rohn**
- Don't think. Act. We can always revise and revisit once we've acted. But we can accomplish nothing until we act. **Steven Pressfield**
- Action may not always bring happiness, but there is no happiness without action. **Benjamin Disraeli**
- There's no difference between a pessimist who says, 'Oh, it's hopeless, so don't bother doing anything,' and an optimist who says, 'Don't bother doing anything, it's going to turn out fine anyway.' Either way, nothing happens. **Yvon Chouinard,** *Founder, Patagonia*

254 With thanks to Brian Pennie https://www.brianpennie.com/

APPS

SELECTED APPS TO SUPPORT MINDFULNESS AND EMOTIONAL FLEXIBILITY

There are many apps out there that can help you to boost your mental resilience. However, it may be hard to decide which ones to choose.[255] Recently, new norms have been developed that can help you in this process.[256] Below we suggest a number of apps and platforms (paid and unpaid) that may be worth exploring, but we strongly recommend that you explore other options as well and see what resonates best with you!

- Headspace: https://www.headspace.com/
- 29K: https://29k.org/ (this free app is based on CBT and ACT)
- Calm: https://www.calm.com/
- Kyan Health: https://www.kyanhealth.com/ (only by invitation code)
- Youper: https://www.youper.ai/
- Mindshift: https://www.anxietycanada.com/resources/mindshift-app
- SAM: http://sam-app.org.uk/
- Super Better: https://www.superbetter.com/
- What's Up: http://www.thewhatsupapp.com/
- Mindful powers (for kids): http://mindfulpowersforkids.com/
- Insight timer: https://insighttimer.com/
- Buddhify: https://buddhify.com/
- Coach me: https://www.coach.me/
- At Ease: https://www.meditationoasis.com/at-ease-anxiety-worry-relief-app/
- ACT companion: http://www.actcompanion.com/

255 https://www.mckinsey.com/industries/life-sciences/our-insights/using-digital-tech-to-support-employees-mental-health-and-resilience

256 See, e.g., www.petrahoogendoorn.com and https://www.iso.org/news/ref2704.html

REFERENCES

REFERENCES

Anderson, C., Brion, S., Moore, D. A., and Kennedy, J. A. (2012). *A status-enhancement account of overconfidence*. Institute for Research on Labor and Employment, UC Berkeley, USA

Ainsworth, B., Bolderston, H., and Garner, H. (2017). *Testing the differential effects of acceptance and attention-based psychological interventions on intrusive thoughts and worry*. Behavior Research and Therapy, 91, pp. 72-77

A-Tjak, J. (2015). *Acceptance & commitment therapy, theorie en praktijk*. Bohn Stafleu & van Loghum, Houten, The Netherlands

Barsh, J., and Lavoie J. (2014). *Centered leadership: leading with purpose, clarity, and impact.* Random House Inc., USA

Brassey, J., De Smet, A. & Kruyt, M. (2022). *Deliberate Calm: how to learn and lead in a volatile world.* Harper Business, New York, USA

Brassey, J., Witteloostuijn, A. V., Huszka, C., Silberzahn, T., & Dam, N. V. (2020). *Emotional flexibility and general self-efficacy: A pilot training intervention study with knowledge workers*. PloS one, 15(10), e0237821

Chen, L. H., and Wu, C-H. (2014). *Gratitude enhances change in athletes' self-esteem: the moderating role of trust in a coach*. Journal of applied sport psychology, 26, pp. 349-362

Clance, P., and Imes, S. (1978). *The imposter phenomenon in high achieving women: dynamics and therapeutic intervention*. Psychotherapy: theory, research & practice, 15(3), pp. 241-247

Coblenzer, H., Muhar, F. (1993-1998). *Atem und Stimme. Anleitung zum guten Sprechen*. G&G BuchsvertriebgesmbH, Wien, Östenreich. (2017 translation in Dutch by: Monika Marlissa-Bork Hoogland. Pearson Benelux, Amsterdam, The Netherlands

David. S. (2016). *Emotional agility: get unstuck, embrace challenge and thrive in work and life*. Penguin Random House, UK

Dewar, C., Keller, S, and Malhotra, V. (2022). *CEO Excellence: Six Mindsets That Distinguish the Best Leaders from the Rest.* Scribner, New York, USA

Dumas, D., and Dunbar, K. (2016). *The creative stereotype effect.* PLoS One, 11(2): e0142567. doi: 10.1371/journal.pone.0142567

Dweck, C. S. (2006). *Mindset: the new psychology of success.* Random House, New York, USA

Dweck, C. S. (2017). *Mindset, changing the way you think to fulfil your potential.* Updated Edition. Little Brown, UK

Emmons, R. A., and McCullough, M. E. (2003). *Counting blessings versus burdens: an experimental investigation of gratitude and subjective well-being in daily life.* Journal of Personality and Social Psychology, 84(2), pp. 377-389

Empson, L. (2018). *If you're so successful, why are you still working 70 hours a Week?* Harvard Business Review, Digital Articles, pp. 2-5

Feldman Barrett, L., (2018). *How Emotions are made.* Electronic edition Pan Books, London

Flaxman, P. E., Bond, F. W., and Livheim, F. (2013). *The mindful and effective employee, and acceptance & commitment therapy training manual for improving well-being and performance.* New Harbinger Publications Inc., Oakland, CA, USA

Foster, R., and Kaplan, S. (2001). *Creative destruction: why companies that are built to last underperform the market, and how to successfully transform them.* Random House Inc., USA

Frank, G. (1999). *Freud's concept of the superego: review and assessment.* Psychoanalytic Psychology, 16(3), pp. 448-463<i>

Frankl, V. E. (2014). *Man's search for meaning.* Beacon Press, Boston, USA

Freud, S. (1927). *The ego and the id.* Authorized translation by J. Riviere. Hogarth Press and Institute of Psychoanalysis 1927. London, UK

Garcia, H., and Miralles, F. (2017). *Ikigai, the Japanese secret to a long and happy life*. Penguin Books, UK

Genard, G. (2007, 2016). *How to give a speech, easy to learn skills for successful presentations, speeches, pitches, lectures and more!* Cedar & Maitland Press, Belmont, Massachusetts, USA

Goyder, C. (2014). *Gravitas, communicate with confidence, influence and authority*. Vermilion, London, UK

Gendlin, E. T. (1981). *Focusing* (rev. ed.). Bantam Books, New York

Grant, A. (2017). *Originals, how non-conformists move the world*. Penguin Books, USA

Gratton, L. (2011). *The Shift. The future of work is already here*. Harper Collins, UK

Gravois, J. (2007). *You're not fooling anyone*. Chronicle of Higher Education, 54(11), pp. A1-A32

Harris, D. (2014). *10% Happier, how I tamed the voice in my head, reduced stress without losing my edge, and found self-help that actually works--A true story*. Harper Collins, New York, USA

Harris, R. (2011). *The Confidence Gap. A guide to overcoming fear and self-doubt*. Robinson Publishing, London, UK

Harzer, C., and Ruch, W. (2012). *When the job is a calling: The role of applying one's signature strengths at work*. Journal of Positive Psychology, 7, pp. 362-371

Hayes, S. C., Strosahl, K.D., and Wilson, K.G. (2012). *Acceptance and commitment therapy, the process and practice of mindful change*. Second Edition. The Guildford Press, New York, London. (E-book edition, Ibooks)

Hill, N., and Stone, C. (1997). *Success through a positive mental attitude. Discover the secret of making your dreams come true*. Harper Collins Publishers, NY, USA

Holbeche, L. (2015). *The agile organization: How to build an innovative, sustainable and resilient business*. Kogan Page, London

Hölzel, B. K., Carmody, J., Vangel, M., Congleton, C., Yerramsetti, S.M., Gard, T., and Lazar, S.W. (2011). *Mindfulness practice leads to increases in regional brain gray matter density*. Psychiatry Res., 191(1), pp. 36-43

Howell, W. S. (1982). *The empathetic communicator*. Wadsworth Publishing Company, University of Minnesota, USA

Huffington, A. (2014). *Thrive: The Third Metric to Redefining Success and Creating a Life of Well-Being, Wisdom, and Wonder*. Harmony, USA

Kay, K., and Shipman, C. (2014). *The confidence code. The science and art of self-assurance - what women should know*. Harper Collins Books, New York, USA

Kegan, R. (1998). *In over our heads: the mental demands of modern life*. Harvard University Press, Cambridge MA, USA

Kegan, R., and Lahey, L.L. (2009). *Immunity to Change.* Harvard Business Press, Boston, USA

Kegan, R., and Lahey, L.L. (2009). *Immunity to change: how to overcome it and unlock potential in yourself and your organization*. Harvard Business School Publishing Corporation, Cambridge, MA, USA. (E-book version, Ibooks)

Kets de Vries, M. (1990). *The impostor syndrome: developmental and societal issues*. Human Relations, 43(7), pp. 667-686

Kets de Vries, M. (2005). *The dangers of feeling like a fake*. Harvard Business Review, 83(9), pp. 108-116

Kets de Vries, M. (2006). *The Leader on the Couch: A clinical approach to changing people & organizations.* John Wiley & Sons, UK

King, L. A. (2001). *The health benefits of writing about life goals*. Personality and Social Psychology Bulletin, 27, pp. 798–807

Kramer, P. (1958). *Note on one of the preoedipal roots of the superego*, Journal of The American Psychoanalytic Association, 6, pp. 38-46

Kruger, J., and Dunning, (2009). *Unskilled and unaware of it: how difficulties in recognizing one's own incompetence lead to inflated self-assessments*. Psychology, 1, pp. 30-46

Lally, P., Van Jaarsveld, C.H.M., Potts, H.W., and Wardle, J. (2010). *How habits are formed: modelling habit formation in the real world.* European journal of social psychology, 40, pp. 998-1009

Larkin, P. (1988, 2003). *Collected Poems*. Faber & Faber, London, UK

Leonard-Curtin A., and Leonard-Curtin T. (2018). *The power of small: making tiny but powerful changes when everything feels too much*. Hachette Books, Ireland

Lin, C-C. (2015). *Self-esteem mediates the relationship between dispositional gratitude and well-being. Personality and individual differences*. 85, pp. 145-148

Mackintosh, M. (1998). *IQ and Human Intelligence*. Oxford University Press, New York, USA

Matthews, G. (1996). *What Makes Life Worth Living? How Japanese and Americans Make Sense of Their Worlds.* University of California Press, Oakland, USA

Masuda, A., Twohig, M. P., Stormo, A. R., Feinstein, A.B., Chou, Y. Y., and Wendell, J. W. (2010). *The effects of cognitive defusion and thought distraction on emotional discomfort and believability of negative self-referential thoughts*. Journal of Behavior Therapy and Experimental Psychiatry, 41, pp. 11-17

Meyer, W. S. (1998). *Therapy of the conscience: technical recommendations for working in the harsh superego of the harsh superego of the patient. Clinical Social Work Journal*, 26(4), pp. 353-368

Mohr, T. (2014). *Playing big: a practical guide for brilliant women like you*. Arrow Books, London, UK

Molinsky, A. (2017). *Reach, a new strategy to help you step outside your comfort zone, rise to the challenge and build confidence*. Penguin Books LLc, USA

Morgesen, J. (2012). *Cognitive recovery and rehabilitation after brain injury: Mechanisms, challenges and support*. Brain Injury: Functional Aspects, Rehabilitation and Prevention, InTech, 2, pp. 121–50

Mruk, C. J. (a) (2013). *Self-esteem and positive psychology: research, theory and practice*. Fourth Edition. Springer Publishing Company, New York, USA

Mruk, C. J. (b) (2013). *Defining self-esteem as a relationship between competence and worthiness: how a two-factor approach integrates the cognitive and affective dimensions of self-esteem*. Polish Psychological Bulletin, 44(2), pp. 157-164

Mruk, C.J. (2019). Feeling good by doing good. A guide to authentic self-esteem and well-being. Digital Edition. Oxford University Press New York, USA

Otto, M. W., and Smits, J. A. J. (2011). *Exercise for mood and anxiety, proven strategies for overcoming depression and enhancing well-being*. Oxford University Press, Oxford, UK

Peters, S. (2012). *The chimp paradox: the mind management programme to help you achieve success, confidence and happiness*. Vermilion, Random House Group, UK

Pennebaker, J. W. (1997). *Writing about emotional experiences as a therapeutic process.* Psychological Science, 8(3), pp. 162-166

Pillay, S. S. (2010). *Life Unlocked. 7 Revolutionary Lessons to Overcome Fear*. Rodale Press Inc., New York, USA

Pillay, S. S. (2011). *Your Brain and Business: The neuroscience of great leaders*. 1st Edition. Pearson FT Press, New Jersey, USA

Pillay, S. S. (2017). *Tinker Dabble Doodle Try: unlock the power of the unfocused mind.* Random House Publishing Group, New York, USA

Pillay, S. S. (2017). *Your brain can only take so much focus*. Harvard Business Review, May 12. Cambridge, MA, USA

Pittman, C. M., and Karle, E.M. (2015). *Rewire your anxious brain. How to use the neuroscience of fear to end anxiety, panic and worry*. New Harbinger Publications, Inc., Oakland, CA, USA

Polk, K.L., Schoendorf, B., Webster, M., and Olaz, F.O. (2016). *The essential guide to the ACT matrix: A step-by-step approach to using the ACT matrix model in clinical practice*. 1st edition. Context Press, Oakland, CA

Porges, S. W. (2011). *The polyvagal theory: Neurophysiological foundations of emotions, attachment, communication, and self-regulation* (Norton series on interpersonal neurobiology). WW Norton & Company

Ratey, J.J., and Hagerman, E. (2008). *Spark! How exercise will improve the performance of your brain*. Quercus, London, UK

Rogala, A., Shoji, K., Luszczynska, Al, Kuna, A., Yeager, C., Benight, C.C., and Cieslak, R. (2016). *From exhaustion to disengagement via self-efficacy change: findings from two longitudinal studies among human services workers*. Frontiers in psychology, 6, pp. 1-12

Rogers, E. & Van Dam, N. (2014). *You! the positive force in change: leveraging insights from neuroscience and positive psychology*. Lulu Publishing, USA

Schaefer, P. S., Williams, C. C., Goodie, A. S., and Campbell, W. K. (2004). *Overconfidence and the big five*. Journal of research in personality 38, 437-480

Schaufeli, W., and Salanova, M. (2007). *Efficacy or inefficacy, that's the question: Burnout and work engagement, and their relationships with efficacy beliefs. Anxiety, Stress, and Coping,* 20(2), pp. 177-196

Schaufeli, W., and De Witte, H. (a) (2017). *Work Engagement in Contrast to Burnout: Real or Redundant?* Burnout Research, 5, pp. 1-2

Schaufeli, W., and De Witte, H. (b) (2017). *Outlook Work Engagement in Contrast to Burnout: Real and Redundant!* Burnout Research, 5, pp. 58-60

Singleton, O., Hölzel, B. K., Vangel, M., Brach, N., Carmody, J., and Lazar, S. (2014). *Change in brainstem gray matter concentration following a mindfulness-based intervention is correlated with improvement in psychological well-being.* Frontiers in Human Neuroscience, 8(33), pp. 1-7

Smits, J. A. J, Berry, A. C, Rosenfield, D., Powers, M. B., Behar, E., and Otto, M. W. (2008). *Reducing anxiety sensitivity with exercise.* Depression and Anxiety, 25, pp. 689-699

Snyder, K., Lambert, J., and Twohig, M. P. (2011). *Defusion: a behavior-analytic strategy for addressing private events*. Behavior Analysis in Practice, 4(2), pp. 4-13

Sone, T., Nakaya, N., Ohmori, K., Shimazu, T, Higashiguchi, M., Kakizaki, M., Kikuchi, N., Kuriyama, S., and Tsuji, I. (2008). *Sense of life worth living (Ikigai) and mortality in Japan: Ohsaki study*. Psychosomatic Medicine, 70, pp. 709-715

Stinckens, N., Lietaer, G., and Leijssen, M. (2002). *The inner critic on the move: analysis of the change process in a case of short-term client-centred/experiential therapy*. Counselling & Psychotherapy Research, 2(1), pp. 40-54

Tabibnia, G., and Radecki, D. (2018). *Resilience training that can change the brain.* Consulting Psychology Journal: Practice and Research, 70(1), pp. 59-88

Van Dam, N. H. M., and Brassey, J. (2017). *Staying relevant in the workplace: develop lifelong learning mindsets.* Bookboon, London, UK

Van Dam, N. (2018). *Elevating learning and development. Insights and practical guidance from the field*. McKinsey & Company, New York, USA

Van Dam, N., and van der Helm, E. (2016). *The organizational cost of insufficient sleep.* McKinsey Quarterly (digital), February

Van Woerkom, M., Oerlemans, W., and Bakker, A. B. (2016). *Strengths use and work engagement: a weekly diary study.* European journal of work and organizational psychology, 25(3), pp. 384-397

Warren, R., Smeets, E., and Neff, K. D. (2016). *Self-criticism and self-compassion: risk and resilience for psychopathology*. Current Psychiatry, 15(12), pp. 18-32

Wegner, D. M., Schneider, D. J., Carter, S. R., and White, T. L. (1987). *Paradoxical effects of thought suppression. Journal of personality and social psychology,* 53(1), pp. 5-13

Webb, C. (2016). *How to have a good day. Think bigger, feel better and transform your working life*. Macmillan, London, UK

Willyerd, K. and Mistick, B. (2016). *Stretch: how to future-proof yourself for tomorrow's workplace.* John Wiley & Sons, Hoboken, NJ, USA

Wolf, E. B., Lee, J. J., Sah, S., and Wood Brooks, A. (2016). *Managing perceptions of distress at work: reframing emotion as passion.* Organizational Behavior and Human Decision Process, 137, pp. 1-12

Wood, A. M., Froh, J. J., and Geraghty, A. W. A. (2010). *Gratitude and well-being: a review and theoretical integration*. Clinical Psychology Review; doi: 10.1016/j.cpr.2010.03.005

ABOUT THE AUTHORS

BIOGRAPHIES OF THE LEAD AUTHORS

Jacqueline Brassey PhD, MAfN

Photo by Danielle Mans-Schouten daniellemansfotografie.com

Jacqueline Brassey (PhD, MAfN) is McKinsey's Chief Scientist and Director of Research Science in the area of People & Organizational Performance and a global leader with the McKinsey Health Institute. Furthermore, she is a researcher at VU Amsterdam, founder and leader of the Lab for Sustainable Human Development and Performance and an Adjunct Professor at IE University in Spain. She serves as a supervisory board member of Save the Children and as an advisory board member of the Master in L&D in Organisations at Maastricht University in The Netherlands.

Jacqui has more than twenty years of experience in business and academia and spent most of her career before joining McKinsey & Company at Unilever. Jacqui holds degrees in both organisation and business sciences, as well as in medical sciences. She has a bachelor's in international business and languages from Avans University of Applied Sciences, a cum laude bachelor's and master's in policy and organisation sciences from Tilburg University, a PhD in economics and business from Groningen University and a joint master's in affective neuroscience from Maastricht University and the University of Florence.

Over the course of her career, she has worked around the world and has been based in The Netherlands, Belgium, UK, Italy and Luxembourg. She has (co-)authored and presented more than fifty articles, books, podcasts and scientific papers in the area of organisational behaviour, learning and leadership development, including *How to demonstrate calm and optimism in a crisis*[257] and

257 https://www.mckinsey.com/business-functions/people-and-organizational-performance/our-insights/how-to-demonstrate-calm-and-optimism-in-a-crisis

Future proof: Solving the 'adaptability paradox' for the long term.[258] Her latest book *Deliberate Calm. How to learn and lead in a volatile world*, co-authored with Aaron De Smet and Michiel Kruyt, will be published in November 2022 by Harper Business.[259]

She loves running, hiking, a good glass of wine and currently lives with her South African/Dutch family in Luxembourg.

linkedin.com/in/jacquibrassey

Prof. Nick H.M. van Dam

Nick van Dam is a human development scientist, an internationally recognised thought leader, adviser, coach, researcher, author and facilitator on learning and leadership development. He is passionate about helping individuals to reach their full potential and is inspired by insights from psychology, psychodynamics, sociology, philosophy and the neurosciences.

Nick has over twenty-five years of business experience as a former Partner, Global Chief Learning Officer, HR Executive and Client Adviser at McKinsey and Deloitte as well as a Business Unit Director at Siemens. As an adviser he has served more than one hundred clients around the world.

He is Chief Learning Officer at IE University (Spain), Director of the IE University Center for Corporate Learning & Talent Management, serves on the University Executive Board and is a professor of Corporate Learning and Leadership Development. Additionally, he is a professor at Nyenrode Business Universiteit (Netherlands) and at the University of Pennsylvania, where he works with candidates in the executive doctoral programme for Chief Learning Officers. He is

258 https://www.mckinsey.com/business-functions/people-and-organizational-performance/our-insights/future-proof-solving-the-adaptability-paradox-for-the-long-term

259 https://www.harpercollins.com/products/deliberate-calm-jacqueline-brasseyaaron-de-smetmichiel-kruyt?variant=40244138344482 and www.HC.com/DeliberateCalm

affiliated with McKinsey & Company as an external senior adviser and faculty member.

During his career, Nick has written articles for various publications and has been quoted by The Financial Times, Wall Street Journal, Fortune Magazine, Harvard Business Review, Business Week, India Times, Information Week, Management Consulting, Chief Learning Officer Magazine and TD Magazine.

Nick has authored and co-authored more than 27 books and numerous articles on learning and leadership development, including *Executive Education After the Pandemic* (2021), *49 Tools for Learning & Development* (2021) *Elevating Learning & Development* (2018), *Leadership at Scale* (2018), *Handbook for Learning and Development in Organisations* (2022, 6th edition – in Dutch), *You! The Positive Force in Change* (2015), *Next Learning Unwrapped* (2012) and *Handbook for Organisation & Management* (9th Edition, 2019). Several of his books have been translated into Mandarin, Portuguese and Dutch.

He is a member of the Consortium for Advancing Adult Learning & Development (CAALD) which includes over thirty leaders, academic researchers and experts and is convened by McKinsey & Company.

Nick received the 2012 Lifetime Learning Leadership Award for his contributions to innovation and learning from The MASIE Center, an internationally recognised think tank focused on workforce education and performance. Under the patronage of the European Parliament Federal Ministry of Education & Research, he received the 2013 Leonardo European Corporate Learning Award for 'Shaping the Future of Organisational Learning and Leadership Development.'

He is the founder of the e-Learning for Kids Foundation, which has provided digital lessons for more than 25 million underprivileged elementary school children.

Nick is a graduate of the Vrije Universiteit in Amsterdam, has a Bachelor's Degree in Education, Economics and Business Economics and holds a Master of Arts Degree in Organisational Sociology from the University of Amsterdam. He earned his PhD in Human Capital Development at Nyenrode Business Universiteit, Breukelen, The Netherlands. He has also completed HR Executive Development programmes at Wharton, IMD and Harvard Business School. As a lifelong learner, he is a candidate at INSEAD's Executive Master in

Change (EMC) programme in Psychodynamics Psychology, Psychoanalyses and System Psychology (estimated completion in 2023).

linkedin.com/in/nickvandam

Prof. Arjen van Witteloostuijn

Currently, Arjen van Witteloostuijn is Professor of Business and Economics at the Vrije Universiteit (VU) Amsterdam and Dean of the VU School of Business and Economics in The Netherlands, as well as Research Professor in Business, Economics and Governance at the University of Antwerp and Antwerp Management School in Belgium. From 1980 to 2019 he was affiliated with the University of Groningen, University Maastricht, Tilburg University and Utrecht University (all four in The Netherlands) and Cardiff University and Durham University (both in the United Kingdom). He has also been a visiting lecturer at New York University (US) and Warwick Business School (UK).

He holds degrees in business, economics and psychology. In 1996-1998 he was Dean of the Maastricht Faculty of Economics and Business Administration. He is a (former) member of the editorial board of the Academische boekengids, Academy Management Journal, Bedrijfskunde: tijdschrift voor modern management, Cross-Cultural and Strategic Management, Economisch statistische be-richten, British Journal of Management, Industrial and Corporate Change, Journal of International Business Studies, M&O: tijdschrift voor organisatiekunde en sociaal beleid, Organisation Studies and Strategic Organisation. Additionally, he was/is a member of the Executive Committee of the European Association for Research in Industrial Economics (EARIE), President of the Dutch-Flemish Academy of Management (NVAM), Chairman of the Board of the Council for Economic, Social and Regional Sciences (ESR) at the Dutch National Science Foundation (NWO), member of the Economic Advisory Council of the Dutch Parliament and a member of the Royal Netherlands Academy of Sciences (KNAW).

Apart from many books and articles in Dutch dailies and journals, he has published widely in several international journals, including the Academy of Management Executive, Academy of Management Journal, Academy of Management Review, Accounting, Organizations & Society, American Journal of Political Science, American Journal of Sociology, American Sociological Review, Economica, Economics of Education Review, European Journal of Political Economy, History of Political Economy, Industrial Relations, International Journal of Industrial Organization, Journal of Business Ethics, Journal of Economic Behavior and Organization, Journal of Economic Psychology, Journal of International Business Studies, Journal of Management, Journal of Management Studies, Journal of Public Administration Research and Theory, Management Science, Metroeconomica, Organization Science, Organization Studies, Party Politics, Personality and Individual Differences, Public Administration Review, Strategic Management Journal and Weltwirtschaftliches Archiv. In 1999 he published a critical analysis of the Dutch 'polder-model': De anorexiastrategie: over de gevolgen van saneren (Amsterdam/Antwerp; De Arbeiderspers) for which he received the Book of the Year 2000 Prize from the Dutch Society of Management Consultants (Ooa) and the Reader Prize 2000 from the Dutch Association of Consultancy Firms (Roa).

He is involved on a regular basis in consultancy and training activities for private and public organisations. His research interests range from international macroeconomics and personality psychology to industrial economics and organisational behaviour.

linkedin.com/in/arjen-van-witteloostuijn-79b766a8

CONTENT EXPERTS WHO CONTRIBUTED TO THIS BOOK

This book has been a wonderful co-creation of great minds. We are immensely grateful for the contributions we received from:

Jacqueline A-Tjak (PhD)
- Clinical Psychologist
- Official ACBS peer reviewed Acceptance and Commitment Trainer and Therapist
- Author of *Acceptance & Commitment Therapy, Theorie en praktijk*

Veronica Azua (PhD)
- Organisational Psychologist and Executive Coach

Anneke Brouwer (BHS)
- Systemic Dialogic Speaker Coach, Executive Voice Expert at The House of Silence
- www.annekebrouwer.com
- linkedin.com/in/anneke-brouwer-4394705

Caroline Goyder (MA)
- Leading voice coach and keynote speaker
- Author of the book *The Gravitas Method*
- https://www.carolinegoyder.com/

Adam Grant (PhD)
- Professor of Management and Psychology, The Wharton School, University of Pennsylvania.
- (Co-)author of *Give & Take*, *Originals* and *Option B*
- http://www.adamgrant.net/

Lynda Gratton (PhD)
- Professor of Management Practice, London Business School, founder of the Hot Spots Movement
- Author of *The Shift* and *The 100-year life*
- http://www.lyndagratton.com/

Russ Harris (MD)
- Director of PsyFlex.
- Author of The Happiness Trap and The Confidence Trap.
- https://www.actmindfully.com.au/

Steven Hayes (PhD)

- Nevada Foundation Professor, Department of Psychology at University of Nevada. Co-founder of Relational Frame Theory and Acceptance and Commitment Therapy.
- Co-author of *Acceptance and Commitment Therapy, Second Edition: The Process and Practice of Mindful Change* and *Get Out of Your Mind and Into Your Life: The New Acceptance and Commitment Therapy*
- https://www.unr.edu/psychology/faculty/steven-hayes

Robert Kegan (PhD)

- Professor of Adult Learning, Harvard University
- Co-author of *An everyone culture* and *Immunity to change*
- https://www.gse.harvard.edu/faculty/robert-kegan

Ingrid Nieuwenhuis (PhD)

- Neuroscientist and specialist in the brain, cognition and behaviour

Srinivasan Pillay (MD)

- Harvard-trained psychiatrist and brain researcher; Chief Medical Officer and Co-Founder of Reulay and CEO of NeuroBusiness Group.
- Author of *Life Unlocked* and *Tinker Dabble Doodle*
- https://drsrinipillay.com/

Brodie Riordan (PhD)

- Industrial/Organisational Psychologist, ICF certified coach
- Co-author of *Using feedback in organizational consulting*

Wilmar Schaufeli (PhD)

- Professor of Work and Organizational Psychology at Leuven University, Partner, Triple I Human Capital, The Netherlands
- Co-author of *The Burnout Companion To Study And Practice: A Critical Analysis*
- https://www.wilmarschaufeli.nl/

Sven Smit (MEng., MBA)

- Senior Partner, McKinsey & Company
- Co-author of *The Granularity of Growth* and *Strategy Beyond the Hockey Stick*

Jan Zijderveld (BMS)

- Former CEO Avon Inc. and President Unilever Europe

SENIOR PROFESSIONALS INTERVIEWED

- Joanna Barsh, Senior Partner emerita, McKinsey & Company
- Sebastiaan Besems, Chief Commercial Officer, Burg Group, The Netherlands
- Conny Braams, Chief Digital and Marketing Officer Unilever
- John Brand (BA, LLB), Consultant, Bowmans, South Africa
- Andres Cadena, Senior Partner, McKinsey & Company, Bogotá, Colombia
- Felipe Child, Partner, McKinsey & Company, Bogotá, Colombia
- Consultant, anonymous contribution
- Josette Dijkhuizen, Professor and Entrepreneur
- Tex Gunning, CEO Leaseplan
- Rick Goings, former CEO and Chairman Emeritus, Tupperware
- Paul-Peter Feld, CHRO, Enexis
- Fernando Ferrari, Senior Partner, McKinsey & Company, Bogota, Colombia
- Rianne Letschert, Rector Magnificus, Maastricht University, The Netherlands
- Abbe Luersman, CHRO, EVP and Chief People Officer, Otis Elevator Co.
- Ron van der Jagt, Senior Executive
- Leena Nair, former Chief Human Resources Officer (CHRO), Unilever; current CEO of Chanel
- Chet Kuchinad, Chief People Officer, Save the Children International
- Ingrid van den Maegdenbergh, Managing Partner The Netherlands, Egon Zehnder
- Lex Meijdam, Professor, Tilburg University, Faculty of Economics
- Karen Rivoire, Competence Flow Leader, Inter IKEA Group
- Michelle Roborg-Sondergaard, VP HR AGC Biologics
- Two Senior Executives, anonymous contributors
- Beltrán Simó, Partner, McKinsey & Company Bogotá, Colombia
- Pieter Waasdorp, Director Entrepreneurship, Ministry of Economic Affairs, The Netherlands
- Jan. J. Wever MD, PhD, Vascular Surgeon, Haga Hospital, The Hague, The Netherlands
- Jan Zijderveld, former CEO Avon Inc. and President Unilever Europe

Other contributors

- Sabine Kal-Hintzen (MSc), creative brain behind the illustrations in this book

- Noor Intisar (MSc), former University Campus Poet, University of Antwerp, contributed the poems for each of the 6 practices
- Tasja van der Veen, Bingo Graphic Design, illustrator who brought the creative ideas and graphic design for the book to life
- Eileen M. Rogers (MA, MPA), editor of the first edition and expert advisor

ACKNOWLEDGEMENTS

The authors would like to thank *everyone* who contributed to the journey of this book. A few people we would like to call out specifically. This second English edition would not exist without the belief and support of *Sandra Britsemmer* and the team at VMN Media. Sandra has become a trusted friend and business partner over the years that we have collaborated with her, and we are very grateful for this! Furthermore, *Danny Guinan*, the English editor of this second edition: thank you for your patience, kindness, outstanding support and the special contribution you made by sharing the lyrics of your song *The Greatest Gift* and the story behind it in this book! Thank you to *Colorscan* who designed the cover and the layout of this book, it truly looks amazing! Special thanks also to *the scientists, experts and leaders* who contributed to this work through interviews and research contributions. Many thanks to the *School of Business and Economics* at the *Vrije Universiteit of Amsterdam* and *IE University* for enabling us to continue our research and work in Sustainable Human Development and Performance. Thanks to *Dr Tobias Silberzahn* who made it possible for us to do our research study in a business setting in Germany, which led to the publication of an academic paper based on the contents of this book. We had the pleasure to work with thousands of students and workshop participants all over the world and are so grateful for the opportunity to help and to develop our work on an ongoing basis as a result. Thank you to all who contributed by helping with content or supporting our work with endorsements! Special thanks to our organisations for enabling us to do this work and bring it to the world. Thank you to the *McKinsey Health Institute (MHI)* and, in particular, *Erica Coe, Kana Enomoto, Martin Dewhurst, Tom Latkovic* and *teams* for embracing this work. The underlying evidence-based approach of this book (Acceptance and Commitment Therapy and Training) aligns strongly with the purpose of *MHI* to help people across the world achieve the best possible brain health. Thank you to *Matthew Smith, Barbara Matthews, Amy Wells, Kristin Brown* and the *Global McKinsey Enduring Priorities Learning Team* and the *Firm Learning Leadership* Team who helped us to bring this content to our colleagues at the Firm. Thank you to Save the Children NL CEO Pim Kraan and colleagues and Patron *H.R.H. Princess Viktória de Bourbon de Parme* for their support from the very beginning. Finally, we owe a huge debt of gratitude to our *families* and *friends* who have inspired and supported us along the way. We are incredibly grateful for all their support and our biggest wish is that our work will continue to contribute to positive global impact!

INDEX

INDEX

A

B

C

D

I

J

L

M

R

S

W

PERSONAL NOTES

Printed in Great Britain
by Amazon

20365195R00224